DATE DUE

DEMCO 38-296

Understanding Ordinary Landscapes

Understanding

Ordinary

Landscapes

Edited by

Paul Groth and Todd W. Bressi

Yale University Press   New Haven and London

Designed by James J. Johnson and set in Caledonia
Roman by The Composing Room of Michigan, Inc.,
Grand Rapids, Michigan.
Printed in the United States of America by Edwards
Brothers, Inc., Ann Arbor, Michigan.

Library of Congress Cataloging-in-Publication Data

Understanding ordinary landscapes / edited by Paul
Groth and Todd W. Bressi.
   p. cm.
  Includes bibliographical references and index.
  ISBN 0-300-06371-7 (cloth : alk. paper). —
ISBN 0-300-07203-1 (pbk. : alk. paper)

  1. Landscape assessment. 2. Human geography.
I. Groth, Paul Erling. II. Bressi, Todd W.
GF90.U53 1997
333.73' 15–dc21   97-5776

A catalogue record for this book is available from the
British Library.

The paper in this book meets the guidelines for permanence and durability of the Committee on Production Guidelines for Book Longevity of the Council on
Library Resources.

10 9 8 7 6 5 4 3 2 1

Contents

Preface

This book explores new directions in cultural landscape studies. Readers who are hoping that it will codify any particular approach to landscape studies, or even narrowly define it, will be disappointed. The authors have been selected to present a broad, interdisciplinary cross-section of questions, subjects, methods, and philosophies for understanding cultural environments. Close agreement was neither solicited nor expected. Instead, contrast and comparison have been encouraged in order to explore the current limits of work being done and to set that work within the context of earlier classic studies. Some of the contributors are critics of cultural landscape studies; others are writers who are at the very core of this endeavor.

The open-ended nature of cultural landscape studies is such that several of the authors in this volume have avoided calling it a "field" or "subject." Indeed, cultural landscape studies is not yet a separate discipline or academic department in the sense that English literature, anthropology, or architecture history are reasonably separate and singular enterprises. Nonetheless, in spite of its open intellectual borders and its wide range of methods, cultural landscape studies is a distinctive collective venture. What all these authors have in common is a love for and fascination with cultural environments and a passion for increasing public understanding of them.

When the authors were invited to join this collaborative effort, the editors asked them, within the context of their recent research, to address one or both of the following issues: first, the reliability and use of visual and spatial information as a source to understand past and present cultures; second, ways to deal with the realities of social and cultural pluralism, and hence plural meanings in the landscape. Underlying such concerns are deeper ones that are at the core of any cultural interpretation: What should our subjects be? What questions should we ask about them? And why do we care?

For readers who are new to landscape studies, the introductory chapter provides a capsule history of the traditions and debates underlying current practice. The next section of the book collects ten examples of research and method under the heading "Landscape Studies." The final six chapters, "Commentary and Future Directions," critique the earlier chapters and cultural landscape studies in general. These authors were encouraged to discuss not only what has been done but also what ought to be done in the near future.

The production of this book was generously assisted by a grant from the Beatrix Farrand Fund of the Department of Landscape Architecture, University of California, Berkeley. In the spring of 1990, the authors represented here were brought together in Berkeley for a public two-day symposium entitled *Vision, Culture, and Landscape*—the first large gathering in the United States of people involved in cultural landscape studies. The symposium and funding of this book were both parts of the celebration of the seventy-fifth anniversary of Berkeley's Department of Landscape Architecture.

Some authors have chosen to update notes or details in their essays; most chapters, however, represent the authors' ideas at the time of the symposium. The collection was in final production at John Brinckerhoff Jackson's death, at age eighty-six, in September 1996. The symposium was not convened to honor Jackson (he had refused to attend if such were the case), nor was this volume planned as a festschrift (in fact, at Jackson's urging the symposium and this collection have included some of his critics). Nonetheless, the editors hope that this book shows both the scope and intensity of interest in the landscape inspired by Jackson's example.

The editors thank Michael Laurie and Randolph Hester, chairs of that department, and Donlyn Lyndon, editor of the journal *Places,* for their support. Paulette Giron, Louise Mozingo, and Stephen Sheppard—who helped to plan the symposium—were also essential to this project, as were the speakers whose papers and commentaries have guided our deliberations but whose work could not be included in a one-volume work. These friends of the project include Frances Butler, Allan B. Jacobs, Peirce Lewis, Burt Litton, Bonnie Loyd, Roger Montgomery, David Stoddart, Marc Treib, and Ervin Zube. In New York, Jennifer Corazzo provided additional photographic research and invaluable assistance coordinating the preparation of the manuscript. In New Haven our editor, Judy Metro, has been both perceptive and patient.

Three of the essays presented at the symposium and revised for inclusion here—Rina Swentzell, "Conflicting Landscape Values: The Santa Clara Pueblo and Day School"; David Chuenyan Lai, "The Visual Character of Chinatowns"; and Wilbur Zelinsky, "Seeing Beyond the Dominant Culture"—appeared in *Places* 7:1 (Fall 1990). Dolores Hayden's chapter, "Urban Landscape History: The Sense of Place and the Politics of Space," originally appeared in her book *The Power of Place: Urban Landscapes as Public History* (Cambridge: MIT Press, 1995). These chapters are reproduced here by permission.

PAUL GROTH

1 Frameworks for Cultural Landscape Study

Americans are like fish that can't see water. Although human life requires the constant support of complex surroundings, most people in the United States do not consciously notice their everyday environments.[1] Universal schooling in science and dozens of television nature programs have begun to sensitize Americans to animals and ecosystems. Yet, even Americans with advanced degrees rarely have concepts for pondering, discussing, or evaluating their cultural environments. These people are in danger of being poor appreciators and managers of their surroundings.

For almost fifty years, several loosely allied groups of writers and scholars have challenged such cultural ignorance in the United States. Most of them have done so under the rubric of cultural landscape studies. This collective enterprise is not a distinct discipline or academic department, but rather a shared enthusiasm for and concern with ordinary, everyday built environments.

For writers in cultural landscape studies, the term *landscape* means more than a pleasing view of scenery. *Landscape* denotes the interaction of people and place: a social group and its spaces, particularly the spaces to which the group belongs and from which its members derive some part of their shared identity and meaning. All human intervention with nature can be considered as cultural landscape: the high-style cathedral or office tower, as well as the Depression-era Hooverville hut, a farmer's barbed-wire fence, or a kitchen garden. Cultural landscape studies focus most on the history of how people have used *everyday* space—buildings, rooms, streets, fields, or yards—to establish their identity, articulate their social relations, and derive cultural meaning. The conviction among cultural landscape

FIG. 1. Main Street in Sauk Center, Minnesota, Sinclair Lewis's home town. The everyday and commonplace setting is densely packed with clues to past and present social relations and meanings. Photo by Paul Groth.

writers is that better knowledge of ordinary environments can foster deeper understanding of American people and American culture and can lessen the environmental dangers caused by people who cannot see and interpret their surroundings.

People in every culture explain and interpret their built environments at some level. Novelists, geographers, journalists, and teachers have all approached the subjects examined in this collection. Yet the organized twentieth-century project of taking the ordinary American cultural environment seriously can reasonably be said to have begun in 1951. In that year, an unknown writer and publisher, John Brinckerhoff Jackson, produced the first issue of *Landscape* magazine.

Jackson was a well-traveled and well-read Harvard history and literature graduate and a former New Mexico rancher living in Santa Fe. Jackson's World War II experience as an army combat intelligence officer had galvanized his conviction that the United States lacked the sort of civilized, intelligent environmental writing that, while in the army, he had found for every small region of Europe. By 1951, Jackson had settled upon the way to begin his campaign to reverse American visual illiteracy: he decided to start *Landscape* magazine to promote the humanistic endeavor that he called cultural landscape studies.[2] Jackson's lively, privately published journal constituted the first interdisciplinary collection of work in America about cultural landscapes and provided a focus for a coherent interest group.

Jackson's free promotional copies of *Landscape* quickly attracted loyal subscribers—an audience of previously scattered geographers, anthropologists, designers, historians, architecture historians, and writers. By his international recruitment of authors, national travels for lectures and conferences, and his overt editorial encouragement of particular subjects, Jackson knit together a group of people who began to think of themselves as sharing a common enterprise. Later university teaching, guest lecturing, and writing intensified Jackson's role as catalyst.[3]

Current Frameworks

In spite of Jackson's centrality, no single paradigm has controlled cultural landscape studies in its first half-century. Two generations of writers and scholars have added their own questions, types of sources, and traditions into cultural landscape study, and the parameters of the enterprise are still open. The following statements enunciate very basic but widely held tenets of cultural landscape studies in the 1990s.

1. *Ordinary, everyday landscapes are important and worthy of study.* At the core of cultural landscape studies is a straightforward question: How can we better understand ordinary environments as crucibles of cultural meaning and environmental experience? A critical word in this formulation is *ordinary*. Everyday experience is essential to the formation of human meaning. When only monuments or high-style designs are taken seriously, the everyday environment is overlooked and undervalued.

The first issue of *Landscape* magazine stated that "there is really no such thing as a dull landscape or farm or town. None is without character, no habitat of man is without the appeal of the existence which originally created it . . . . A rich and beautiful book is always open before us. We have but to learn to read it."[4] In 1951, saying there was "no such thing as a dull landscape" was a courageous act. Americans were forgetting the populism of the New Deal and assumed that the important elements of the environment were marked clearly by fences, admission fees, and large identifying signs showing the way to the entrance.[5] Guidebooks to architecture or city districts pointed out landmark structures but said little or nothing about the spaces between them or the social and economic frameworks in which they existed.

The same situation prevailed among most academic disciplines that looked at the environment. Architects and art historians puzzled over historical or interna-

FIG. 2. Winter view of an agricultural valley near State College, Pennsylvania. Landscape studies have shown that such rural spaces can be seen as areas of innovation, variety, and intellectual interest. Photo by Paul Groth.

tional-style masterpieces. A few geographers looked at generic building types and settlement forms, but by the late 1950s they were being overwhelmed by a wave of more abstract and quantitative work.[6] Anthropologists were losing interest in aboriginal architecture and looked only askance at the landscapes of the dominant American culture. Only a handful of social scientists were using historical studies to understand the present. Social and urban historians had begun to focus on rank-and-file social groups but not their surroundings, forgetting the richly detailed spatial documentation contained in turn-of-the-century social surveys and reports of the 1930s.[7] Moreover, to speak of the importance of the visual record and historical evolution of the *countryside*—and its being equal in interest to the town or city—was highly unusual.

Nonetheless, the voices of *Landscape*'s authors were emphatic and still ring true. Ordinary landscapes are important archives of social experience and cultural meaning. The understanding of landscape by an informed public is urgently needed if citizens are to comprehend the changes in their local communities and countrysides. As the geographer Peirce Lewis put it in 1979, "If we want to understand ourselves, we would do well to take a searching look at landscapes." The human landscape is an appropriate source of self-knowledge, according to Lewis, because it is "our unwitting autobiography, reflecting our tastes, our values, our

FIG. 3. The collision of rural and urban landscapes near Washington, D.C. Because of a lingering pro-rural bias, cultural landscape studies have revealed more about the mid-nineteenth-century farmhouse than about the speculative office towers. Photo by Paul Groth.

aspirations, and even our fears."[8] For such an autobiography to be complete, the selection of cultural landscape subjects must be inclusive.

2. *Present research subjects in landscape studies are likely to be urban as well as rural, focused on production as well as consumption.* Early cultural landscape scholars focused on farmsteads and small towns as records of migration and regional settlement. In such settings, changes could be ascribed to a reasonably consistent group of people who built gradually.[9] A few cultural landscape writers have contended that only rural settings are landscape. For these people the farmhouse, barn, field, and road are truly landscape; the parking lot, suburban neighborhood, and factory are something else, perhaps cityscape.[10] More scholars feel that one term covers all. City, suburb, countryside, and even wilderness are all human constructs, all touched by human management. All are cultural landscape.

Parallel to the urban and rural reach of landscape studies is an interest among its practitioners in production landscapes as well as in landscapes of consumption and leisure. Within the best rural studies, generic farmhouses or barns are not studied as isolated objects; they are seen within the context of the whole farm economy and its relation to city houses and city workplaces. While the farmsteads of land owners have received ample attention, fewer studies have looked at fields, roads, or the housing of farmhands and tenant farmers.[11] To date, urban and industrial production has also attracted less attention. For every forty studies of barns and fields, there has been only one about urban factories, workshops, offices, or corner stores as workplaces.

This book contains more essays dealing with urban subjects than any previous collection of landscape studies, in part to correct the rural-urban imbalance.[12] Three studies in this present volume represent the continuing interest in rural space: David Lowenthal's review of agricultural landscape preservation in Europe, Jay Appleton's appeal for an approach combining both physical and cultural elements, and Reuben Rainey's analysis of the Gettysburg battlefield. Picking up the need to study both consumption and production, Deryck Holdsworth's chapter examines remote logging and fishing camps to study the relationships between masters and workers, capital and labor—an urban, industrial order for distinctly nonurban workers.

Writing about fields, factories, and slums invokes crucial but often divisive discussion of the relationships between political economy and landscape organization. Landscape meanings can be interpreted as noble, nostalgic, or uplifting expressions of choice and group life, and they can also be seen as those of economic exploitation, racism, capitalist accumulation, and a lack of choice. In this collection, James Borchert, Deryck Holdsworth, Richard Walker, and Dell Upton all grapple with ways to reveal the expressions of power within landscape development.

Anthony King's chapter connects landscape research to a Wallerstinian international context of the local and the global. King reminds us that the economic and cultural processes of the United States do not stop at the nation's border. Even in the American colonial period, local landscapes were always inextricably shaped by distant ones. Colonial and nineteenth-century immigration from Africa, Europe, and Asia gave rise to regional differences in the United States, just as twentieth-century war movements did, and transformation of capital continues to do. This multiplicity of possible locational and economic viewpoints is mirrored in the debate over multiple views of a single place.

3. *Contrasts of diversity and uniformity frame essential and continuing debates within cultural landscape interpretation.* A traditional strength of landscape studies has been its speculative interpretation of overarching national or regional identities. Especially in the 1950s and 1960s, just as physicists sought a single, uniform field theory, cultural landscape analysts sought single, unified meanings in the American landscape. Subjects such as the rural grid, the open-lot house, and the front yard have provided clues to ideals that are close to universal.[13] Before 1970, especially, landscape authors seemed to avoid conflict in their choice of subjects.

FIG. 4. House built by a Norwegian-American family in Mayville, North Dakota, 1914. Whether found in a small Great Plains town or in suburban New Jersey, such generic houses are elements in a national landscape, as well as parts of an ethnic landscape. Photo by Paul Groth.

Yet, whatever the location—city or farm, factory or home—landscapes reveal the effects of individuals and local subcultures as well as national, dominant cultural values.[14] The stamp of ethnicity or race on landscape elements, such as German-American barns or African-American shotgun houses, has been a traditional theme in landscape studies; yet they are often studied in isolation, as if no conflict or alternatives have existed around the elements' construction, use, or rebuilding.[15] Since 1970, the reinterpretation of ethnicity and diversity in the United States has brought new types of writers and subjects into cultural landscape study. The new writers are less likely to search for (and hence less likely to find) a single social or cultural value in the cultural environment. They see the landscape not as one book but as multiple, coexisting texts or (in keeping with literary post-modernism) as competing fragmentary expressions. They worry over whose meanings should serve as sources in their research, and they are as likely to focus on cultural or class conflict in the landscape as on cultural unity.

In pathbreaking work, recently published, Dolores Hayden and a team of coworkers organized under the rubric of "The Power of Place" have fought for the idea that the form of a Los Angeles bungalow, firehouse, or street corner may be much less important than its use, occupancy, and the way in which the surviving form can help present-day observers mark minority life.[16] The exploration of ethnic and cultural diversity is also a strong theme in this volume, which includes a chapter adapted from Hayden's book. Rina Swentzell demonstrates a dual set of cultural meanings in Santa Clara Pueblo, New Mexico, as she evocatively compares the authoritarian, barbed-wire compound of her reservation's Bureau of Indian Affairs school to the spaces of the pueblo which, to her, lived and breathed and were an integral part of her existence. David Chuenyan Lai outlines the architectural and retail elements of North American Chinatowns, reinterpreting types of typical commercial buildings as multiple ethnic expressions: Anglo-American in structural shape (and often ownership), infilled with Chinese-American facades and signage. Wilbur Zelinsky, in a commentary chapter, questions Swentzell, Lai, and Hayden. Taking a view long advocated by cultural geographers, he maintains the significance of a national, pervading spatial culture that can still be seen to permeate other realms.

Jackson's chapter in this book is typical of his approach to diversity and uniformity. He begins with the informal arrangements and activities of entertainment in working-class dwellings. He does not indicate race or ethnicity; the inhabitants might be in the rural Southwest or in Harlem. He sees diversity as a given and then searches for underlying similarities in disparate places. Next, Jackson moves to the elaborate and very formal spaces and rules of entertaining guests in middle- and upper-class houses. All this is a prelude to his larger and more abstract discussion of fundamental epochal changes in the American meaning of house, property, and land—emerging notions of access and territoriality that he suggests most Americans may eventually adopt, and many have already.

Neither the search for uniformity (as Zelinsky and Jackson see it) nor the exploration of diversity (as Hayden, Swentzell, or Lai sees it) limits or cancels the importance of the other. When both are well done, they fit together: the local scene, no matter how different from the dominant culture, still has its connections and similarities with the outside. The overarching idea, no matter how powerful, still may have its opposition. Studies of both uniformity and diversity, if they are to be helpful to American environmental consciousness, also call for a range of different publishing modes and venues.

4. *Landscape studies call for popular as well as academic writing, to influence the actions of as many people as possible.* The styles of writing and research in this collection stretch between two poles. On one side are essays in a literary style, aimed at the widest possible audience; on the other side are more traditionally academic articles with extensive footnotes aimed at professional scholarly audiences. The chapters by Rina Swentzell, David Chuenyan Lai, Dell Upton, and

J. B. Jackson epitomize the literary mode; those by Reuben Rainey and Richard Walker, the professional scholarly mode. Several chapters fall somewhere in between.

Landscape magazine has always preferred a literary style. Between 1951 and 1968, Jackson displayed his editorial ideal of articles written for the intelligent lay reader. The journal published virtually no articles with footnotes, even when the authors were academics. Since 1968, the second publisher of the journal, Blair Boyd, has also worked for a literary style and kept a very personal interest in every aspect of the magazine, especially making space for the original and speculative essay on a fresh topic. Also like Jackson, for more than twenty years Boyd generously has donated most of the funds needed to publish the magazine. Boyd has added an editorial board and a full-time editor; articles in the journal are now listed in several citation indexes. There are still no footnotes, although Boyd has allowed a short list of full citations for "further reading" at the end of many essays and *Landscape* continues to welcome both academic and nonacademic writers.

Whether or not they provide footnotes and close attribution of sources, academic writers remain important contributors to the cause of cultural landscape enlightenment. In 1982, landscape architects at the University of Wisconsin began a twice-yearly professional publication, *Landscape Journal,* borrowing

FIG. 5. China Camp State Historic Site, fifteen miles north of San Francisco. This fishing settlement records one variant of Chinese-American workers' lives about 1910, including building types common to other low-income workers. Photo by Paul Groth.

closely on the design format of *Landscape* and aiming partly at a joint professional and public audience. Cultural landscape articles comprise a significant share of the journal's contents. The steady sales and strong impact of two elegantly edited sets of academic articles are also notable. Donald Meinig's collection *The Interpretation of Ordinary Landscapes* (1979) is comprised of nine long essays by senior figures in the field of cultural geography, displaying the work in that discipline up to the mid-1970s.[17] Michael P. Conzen's ambitious collection *The Making of the American Landscape* (1990) gathers the work of eighteen geographers and addresses both regional and local landscape issues of the nineteenth and twentieth centuries. Although it is more academic than literary, it also has a dual academic and popular market.

Whether academic or not, the overarching objective of cultural landscape writing is to inform the public, and the potential applications of landscape studies are political as well as personal. The historical archaeologist James Deetz and several of his graduate students have literally uncovered and interpreted a landscape record of black and white integration in colonial South Africa. This work was begun well before such an outlook was welcomed by authorities in power. Public education projects of the American Association of Geographers and of the National Geographical Society have had strong cultural landscape components. Another venue that straddles public and professional realms is the museum world, where larger numbers of curators are beginning to consider landscape interpretation. Even the U.S. National Park Service is more actively using cultural landscape experts to interpret human history in park environs.[18] In this collection, many of the articles are part of ongoing efforts to support more inclusive historic preservation and local interpretation. David Lowenthal's chapter reviews the challenges created by the rural landscape's ecologically correct, increasingly popular consideration in Europe. He argues for rural preservation concepts that take a national as well as a local approach.

For some of these advocacy roles, academic style is required. For others—especially generating understanding and support among opinion leaders—more popular styles are needed. Most needed are more "amphibious" writers such as Peirce Lewis and Robert Riley who are willing and able to address both professional and lay audiences. Whatever the audience, however, the hardest task for cultural landscape writers is choosing questions and finding appropriate and reliable ways to answer them. For these tasks, an overabundance of choice exists.

5. *The many choices of theory and method in landscape studies stem from the subject's interdisciplinary nature.* To the occasional dismay of neophytes, landscape studies writers have no single approved method or theory. Some practitioners have stayed clear of the discussion of theory, while others have embraced and fought for a number of different intellectual bases.[19] In his chapter in this volume, Jay Appleton describes the collective venture of landscape studies as "a com-

FIG. 6. Cannery workers' houses, Monterey, California. Academic studies of dwellings like these, and more publicly accessible interpretations of them, might have helped museum directors of the Monterey Bay Aquarium (background) include them in their interpretation of Cannery Row. Photo by Paul Groth.

ing together of diverse minds, trained in the thinking habits of different disciplines, many of them traditionally regarded as only remotely connected with each other." Appleton himself argues for an approach that links geological analysis to cultural analysis.

The troublesome but essential concept of *culture* generates many initial complications in what Richard Walker's present chapter calls the "enormous creative tension between cultural and material studies." Apart from a few dissenters, the authors in this volume consider culture a changing set of social relations, rules, and meanings woven through everyday life. For them, culture is not a frozen or superorganic entity that somehow acts upon people and landscapes without their conscious action or knowledge; rather, culture is recreated or changed through individual lives. Thus, the culture of landscape studies is a culture of everyday actions and social structures, a culture that humans mold through conscious and unconscious actions, a culture in which power, class, race, ethnicity, subculture, and opposition are important considerations.[20] Even when practitioners agree upon on a basic definition of culture, applying the concept to the study of human agency, economics, and nature generates divergent alternatives.

The inherent interdisciplinary nature of the built environment further enriches and complicates cultural landscape method and theory. Each discipline and working group has its own rules about making its assumptions implicit or explicit. For scholars in the social sciences, for instance, theory and method must be explicit and rigorous. Novelists and nonfiction writers, however, are often allowed to keep their choices of theory and method completely implicit. Essayists and short story authors can adapt wildly different approaches within a single collection of work. In spite of (or because of) this freedom, some of the most evocative and effective landscape analyses have come from nonfiction writers such as Joan Didion, Wallace Stegner, and George Stewart; novelists such as William Faulkner and Louise Erdrich; and journalists such as Philip Langdon and Susannah Lessard.[21]

At the most basic level of landscape writing, one must distinguish between description (for instance, collections of data or site surveys) and interpretive studies that aim to apply or generate general principles. This dichotomy is also misleading, though, since most landscape work is a combination of description and generalization. Indeed, intelligent description—in the sense of capturing the telling elements of any landscape—is often far superior to, and more analytical than, bad theoretical generalization.

FIG. 7. Business buildings on the riverfront of Louisville, Kentucky. As an expression of private power, the new tower headquarters of the for-profit Humana hospital corporation may have a great deal in common with the nineteenth-century commercial buildings in the foreground, even though its form is very different. Photo by Paul Groth.

The battles between what landscape critics castigate as "merely descriptive studies" and "empty, shallow, theoretical studies" are probably strongest among American cultural geographers. It is also among geographers that landscape studies find their nineteenth-century European roots. Carl Sauer, founder of the "Berkeley school" of cultural geography, began promoting cultural landscape work in the 1920s and stressed field work, exhaustive reading of primary sources, and close attention to questions of migration, diffusion, the development of regional culture areas, and human interaction with the biosphere.[22]

Geographers influenced by the Berkeley school have spread landscape studies to at least seven other North American geography departments.[23] Wilbur Zelinsky, represented in this book, is a Berkeley scion whose interests in the city and the contemporary American scene set him apart from most traditional ruralist Berkeley school scholars. Zelinsky's *Cultural Geography of the United States* is a benchmark text for interest in landscape studies and has recently appeared in a new edition.[24] Another Berkeley geographer, Yi-Fu Tuan, exemplifies interest in "sense of place" as an explication of landscape. Beginning with a strong attention to the methods of phenomenology, Tuan has stressed an individual and psychological approach that is common within the "place" literature.

Within human geography, theoretical views are further split between economic and cultural, Marxist and postmodern, historical and social, and yet other camps.[25] In her chapter in this book, the urban historian Dolores Hayden engages the traditional definitions and uses of place with the French sociologist Henri Lefebvre's concept of the "production of space." This platform allows her to connect overarching dimensions of political economy with details of working landscapes, social group histories, and the development of specific building types.

From Britain and Canada come geographical approaches interrelated with, but also independent from, work in the United States. The masterful historian of the ordinary British landscape W. G. Hoskins has inspired detailed studies of land holdings, rural cottages, and other close documentation of present imprints left from past centuries. Hoskins in Britain plays a role like that of J. B. Jackson in the United States. British archaeologists such as Barbara Bender have gathered increasing interest in landscape as a realm of interpretation.[26] The British Landscape Research Group, formed in about 1970, prides itself in having people who represent "every conceivable point of view." It has held two dozen annual symposia, usually with an announced theme.[27] The cultural historian Raymond Williams did much to infuse social theory and social class consciousness into studies of the landscape, although usually in a more literary mode than one based in detailed trench work; British geographers have extended his approaches and brought them to Canada. In his book *Explorations in the Understanding of Landscape,* the Canadian geographer William Norton elegantly outlines at least four types of cultural landscape study, strongly influenced by the landscape views of the English geographer Peter Jackson.[28] Between the United States and Britain, and between different schools of thought, the definition of the word *landscape* varies. For some British writers (as shown by Jay Appleton and Denis Cosgrove in this book), *landscape* is not so much cultural space but rather a scene or view; Barbara Bender's use is more spatial.

Architects, landscape architects, and design historians also have contributed method and theory to cultural landscape studies. With his first book, *Common Landscape of America,* Harvard University's John Stilgoe extended and made more available the first half of Jackson's famous survey lecture courses in landscape architecture at Berkeley and Harvard.[29] In the 1990s, the largest student audience for landscape studies is found in nine design schools where survey courses have been consistently taught.[30] The Vernacular Architecture Forum, a six-hundred-member organization founded in 1980, has attracted many landscape-oriented writers, researchers, and architecture preservationists to its annual meetings and publications.[31]

Designers and design historians have been less bound than geographers by the necessity for using systematic theory. When drawn to it, they tend to be sympathetic with concurrent theoretical leanings in art history and literary criticism, lately represented by postmodernism. Denis Cosgrove's chapter in this book takes the postmodernist route, addressing landscape through Renaissance paintings and using critical literary theory as a mode of analysis.

In history departments, interest in social or economic theory varies from avid (among social and labor historians) to much less (among most urban and cultural historians). Relatively few historians identify their interests as built space; yet, when their work explains the spatial aspects of human history, historians have been and continue to be significant contributors to cultural landscape studies.[32] The historian James Borchert, for instance, uses classical historical methods and written sources. In this collection, his study of the Lakewood section of Cleveland uses lots, buildings, and continuing neighborhoods as additional primary evidence for Lakewood's development. His close readings of maps, photographs, and other evidence of spatial patterns resemble the methods of geographers. Another contributor to this collection, Reuben Rainey, also crosses methodological lines. Rainey is a landscape architecture historian; therefore, readers might expect a detailed annotation of form. Instead, in this particular work, he uses more textual than visual information to reconstruct the processes that have created and altered our understanding of Gettysburg as a national monument.

By deliberately collecting such varied theoretical possibilities, this volume hopes to make possible at least a bracing immersion in the methodological gene pool. A complete account of the interdisciplinary nature of landscape studies would include contributors in sociology, literature, material culture studies,

FIG. 8. Two workers' houses record neighborhood development in Poughkeepsie, New York. The tiny house on the right, dating from about the 1840s, in size and interior organization contrasts sharply with the house of about 1900 on the left. Both show several phases of investment. Photo by Paul Groth.

American studies, photography, and film—each with its own shifting sets of theory and method.[33] Perhaps there should never be orthodoxy in study with such varied subjects and audiences.

6. *Within cultural landscape methods, the primacy of visual and spatial information is a central theme, even though not all landscape interpretation is based on visual and spatial data.* Much of the immediacy, interest, and emotional appeal of landscape study—for writers as well as for readers—rests on the immediacy of cultural environments: the landscape is directly accessible and makes abstract processes more concrete and knowable. This is true both for visual information (images and scenes as they appear to the viewer's eye) and for the more abstract domain of "spatial information" (representing the underlying organizations and interrelations of space—local, regional, or global—which may be based on visual information but are not strictly visible).

For designers and geographers, the importance of the visual is often axiomatic, and two important articles by geographers cogently review the case: Donald W. Meinig's "Environmental Appreciation: Localities as Humane Art" is both a summary and an appeal for site-based interpretation; Peirce Lewis's "Axioms for Reading the Landscape" sets out closely reasoned guides and principles for landscape study.[34] David Lowenthal has spoken of the rapid increases in the avail-

FIG. 9. Spatial clues to abstract ideas on a factory floor of the Union Iron Works, San Francisco. In this 1885 machine shop, the two white control booths (added about 1910) mark the triumph of central-office efficiency experts over the formerly decentralized fiefdoms of foremen. Photo by Paul Groth.

ability of and interest in images, beginning with the nineteenth-century explosion of lithographs and photographs, and continuing with today's video and computer technologies. Compared to people of earlier times, Americans can now easily retrieve and manipulate their place experiences with a wide range of drawings, photographs, maps, and other images. Lowenthal notes that formerly "fleeting and unverifiable private impressions" have been transformed into a permanent, retrievable, "well-known consensual visual world."[35]

Because the goal of good landscape analysis is both seeing and thinking, the seeming ease of looking and its impressionistic nature have generated concern. Admittedly, visual information at times has been distracting, trivial, or irrelevant in understanding essential human concerns. In much fashionable academic discourse of the twentieth century, the visual has been denigrated.[36] In his essay in this book, Richard Walker reiterates complaints about the Berkeley school's "obsessional interest in culture-as-artifact" and searches for common methodological ground between a spatial approach and other theoretical foundations.[37]

Furthermore, taking visual and spatial information seriously has at times marginalized cultural landscape studies among academics. Cultural landscape's visual impetus contrasts sharply with strictly logocentric work done by other cultural analysts. In the logocentric view, truly intelligent writers work with written texts, not objects; people who put pictures or maps in their books, and who write clearly, are somehow inferior. The critics of visual inspiration, Lowenthal notes, often reject spatial information and instead insist that scholars should "probe deeply hidden structures, seek out the covert agendas of those in power, and engage in historical, economic, and sociological exegesis." He adds that for the critics, genuinely serious inquiry "should be non-visual, hard to read, strictly austere."[38]

Another source of criticism of visual and spatial information is superficial fieldwork. As a method, cultural geographers especially stress the importance of personal fieldwork: going out and looking closely at landscapes to find spatial clues, site-specific interrelationships, and insights to use in sifting through written records. Good (and bad) fieldwork can extend between two extremes: wide-ranging and fairly rapid "windshield surveys" to sense a cross-section of the city, region, or nation; and more painstaking and detailed studies involving on-site sketching to understand the form and composition of landscapes, the measurement and drawing of buildings, gathering of local interviews and written information, and thorough mapping or systematic photography. Unfortunately, hasty or thinly conceived windshield surveys have at times become a shallow basis for cultural analysis. Although such work may be no more frequent than hasty analysis of written sources, it remains more memorable in the minds of critics.

Surely, spatial emphases and fieldwork do not replace the need for rigorous traditional research in print and archival sources.[39] Dell Upton's essay here holds up both the seen and the unseen as important; analyzing one without the other, he says, can lead to seriously incomplete conclusions. In another study in this book, Deryck Holdsworth asks about the reliability of visual information and reminds us that other sources of information may overrule the importance of the visual. He warns that present-day images may not accurately convey past reality, and for that reason he has chosen not to include any illustrations with his chapter. Perhaps his sharpest objections are reserved not for the use of spatial or visual information (which he himself uses) but for the questions and research agendas chosen by previous generations of landscape scholars.

Nonetheless, the primacy of studying the actual landscape, as a method, remains critically important. As Lowenthal puts it, "Seeing is essential, even when it does not entail believing."[40] Spatial and visual information often sparks new and important questions, suggested by oppositions and juxtapositions not apparent in written records. There is nothing particularly easy or automatically facile about intelligently interpreting built space. Rather than being an easy substitute for work with written sources, spatial and visual analysis usually requires additional work. The heavily illustrated article or course lecture often takes twice as much time to prepare as the mere verbal lecture: the ideas of the text must be written, then the ideas of the visual evidence assembled, and then the two parts intertwined. On-site, rigorous preparation and attention are demanded in order to know where to look and how to interpret what is seen. The tasks typically require the collection of expensive and cumbersome site information and photographs. The highest compliment many landscape writers can give to their colleagues is to say that "their eyes are well connected to their brains."

Such visual emphases have also been taken very seriously in the past. In her essay in this volume, Catherine Howett portrays the visual primacy of modernism—and also of some cultural landscape studies—as the last gasps of the authority accorded to vision by the Renaissance elite, whose spuriously objective science gave visual experience a dominance over the other senses, and whose perspective drawing held that single viewing points should be favored.

J. B. Jackson's Work as Guide and Comparison

Taken together, the frameworks of landscape studies—concerning the boundaries of the field, appropriate subjects for study, the search of uniformity versus diversity, questions of audience, deliberations over theory and method, and debates about the importance of spatial information—will continue to include multiple positions. In the work of John Brinckerhoff Jackson we can see one person's decisions within these six frameworks. The most creative and perceptive collections of cultural landscape interpretation in the United States remain the seven books of Jackson's own essays.[41] Indeed, Jackson's work serves not only as an initial point (as with his editing of *Landscape* magazine) but also as a continuing reference point within cultural landscape studies. Whenever the newest writers, including those in this collection, stretch the boundaries of the field, they are usually redrawing frameworks explored and enunciated by Jackson.

As an editor and writer, Jackson eloquently asserted the importance of everyday landscapes: "Over and over again I have said that the commonplace aspects of the contemporary landscape, the streets and houses and fields and places of work, could teach us a great deal not only about American history and American society, but about ourselves and how we relate to the world . . . . The beauty that we see in the vernacular landscape is the image of our common humanity: hard work, stubborn hope, and mutual forbearance striving to be love."[42] At the heart of the field, as Jackson set it, is the exploration and speculation about meaning, especially for present-day inhabitants. Jackson made clear that he was interested in influencing change as well as preservation; he wrote that he worked for "a vision disciplined enough to distinguish what is wrong in the landscape and should be changed from what is worthy of protection."[43]

Jackson did much to spark interest in the importance of ordinary landscape, especially among geographers and environmental designers. On his first visit to Berkeley (in 1956), Jackson sought out Carl Sauer and met the entire geography faculty; he stayed to have a strong influence on the department and the Berkeley school of geography in North America. So, too, a large part of the interest in landscape studies among architects and landscape architects was sparked by Jackson's teaching in the design schools at both Berkeley and Harvard between 1967 and 1978. Jackson's choice of working with designers and planners stemmed in part from his interest in affecting public and private decisions about the landscape.[44]

On the choice of appropriate subjects, Jackson has shown nearly universal curiosity about both rural and urban human environments. In the first issue of *Landscape*, Jackson wrote that the magazine was to be a place to "learn of country things." Nonetheless, for Jackson the height of alienation was not separation from wilder nature but lack of interest in human culture in either the city or the countryside. *Landscape*'s thread of urban topics began with the second issue; by the fourth issue there were more urban topics than rural ones.[45] In the 1950s, as a guest seminar instructor in the Berkeley geography department, Jackson audited not only Carl Sauer's decidedly antiurban seminars but also the seminars where Jean Gottmann was hammering out his ideas for *Megalopolis*.[46]

Jackson also kept in view both production and consumption landscapes. He often wrote about landscapes of economic difficulty and unfairness, of the hardscrabble farmer, propertyless workers in their pickup trucks, and of urban working landscapes—especially in midsized cities—and the need to study them. Typically wary of merely economic explanations, Jackson usually suggested and rarely directly argued causation. He often sought out the social psychology and religious aspects of landscapes.[47]

Addressing the contrasts of uniformity and diversity, Jackson often emphasized the ethnic contrasts of the Southwest, but also looked for abstract ideas and public physical settings (such as the rural grid, the city street, the commercial highway strip) that link disparate human groups rather than separate them. Jackson is also known for associating seemingly unrelated landscape phenomena, such as the changes in highway strips with changes in the American suburban house, and changes in the organization of field lines with changes in the interiors of barns. Recently, when he drew comparisons between uniformity and diversity, he pointed out the opposition between what he called the "vernacular" and "official" worlds, defined in part by income and access to decision-making power.

When he commented on writing style and audience, Jackson despaired at the "totally academic style—dry, without color or detail, stifled by footnotes—written only for a small public of scholars who may (or more likely may not) see the work's landscape potential." He added that "without our being aware of it, here in the U.S. we have developed an attractive, intelligent type of middle-brow informative writing—whether in the *Wall Street Journal,* the *New Republic,* the *Atlantic,* or the *New York Times* magazine section—that ought to indicate to the academy that ideas can be given style, and consequent circulation."[48] In his own writings, Jackson held close to an engaging Emersonian essay style, with a minimal discussion of sources.

Jackson carefully resisted making his methods or use of theory too explicit, although both method and theory were important to him. He worked for analysis, as he put it, as "straightforward and as little systematized as possible," with an "exploratory and speculative point of view."[49] As phrased by Donald W. Meinig, in Jackson's style "all is assertion and argument, . . . much is observed, nothing is measured."[50] Jackson's essay in this collection is typical. He builds from qualitative data—historical research, observations of behavior, photographs, and chance conversations. Although he based his studies on careful reading and observation of the American landscape, Jackson did not typically present readers with detailed case studies of actual farms, towns, or cities. Instead, he constructed evocative generic types.[51]

For someone who was supposedly "not theoretical," Jackson also could be *highly* theoretical. As part of his search for explanation and meaning, he was always an avid reader of academic theory. Directly and obliquely, Jackson constantly suggested regularities, patterns, causes, relationships, and universals. Although he invoked few theoretical systems to support his generalizations, theory was very much present between the lines. When Jackson read a source that was neither spatial nor concerned with material culture at any scale, he creatively gave the work landscape applications. For instance, for his class lectures on recreation spaces, Jackson transformed Roger Caillois's four mostly nonspatial categories of recreation experience into spatial landscape terms; and Michel Foucault's *Order of Things* clearly seems to have influenced Jackson's notion of abstract landscape orders.[52]

In spite of his own avid interest in observing and recording the American landscape, Jackson insisted that, for him, the final object of landscape study was *not* visual form. Nonetheless, the visual is always in his work. Often he carefully chose illustrations or made diagrams and drawings to clarify his thinking and to accompany his essays. He never said that the visual information of the landscape was *un*important; rather, it was not the automatic first priority for discerning meaning. To guard against overemphasis on vision, he consistently emphasized nonvisual sensory inputs. Whenever possible, he avoided travel by automobile and instead traveled by motorcycle, not only for greater mobility but also to engage his other senses, most particularly smell and a kinesthetic sense of road texture and terrain. He collected his students' records of everyday sensory experience.[53] He said that he looked for telling details such as "the sound of snow shovels after a blizzard, the smell of wet bathing suits, the sensation of walking barefoot on the hot pavement." Such fleeting memories as these, he added, "often make a whole landscape, a whole season, vivid and unforgettable." In his desk work of analysis and writing, Jackson stated that he "persist[ed]" in seeing landscape not "as a scenic or ecological entity but as a political or cultural entity, changing in the course of history." For him, landscapes were social constructs, not collected individual designs. The landscape, Jackson wrote, is not a work of art; traditional esthetic criticisms are out of place in landscape studies. "Landscape," he said, "must be regarded first of all in terms of living rather than looking."[54] In this, he exhibited a genuinely radical stance within the enterprise of landscape studies.

Although Jackson was clear and consistent in his personal approach to landscape studies, the editorial directions he set for *Landscape* magazine and his constant and wide-ranging personal reading habits revealed a search for and close regard of other people's approaches. Indeed, when Jackson opened *Landscape* magazine by alluding to the open book of the landscape, he did not write that there was One Best Way to read it. The multiplicity of voices and approaches in cultural landscape studies has brought not incoherence but a flexible, diverse strength. Challenging the cultural ignorance of the American population—helping very different schools of fish to see the water that surrounds and supports them—thus calls for diverse approaches and remains exciting and important.

Landscape Studies

JAMES BORCHERT

2   Visual Landscapes of a Streetcar Suburb

Although the residential landscapes of aging streetcar suburbs like Lakewood, Ohio, have experienced considerable change over the past sixty years, they continue to provide social historians with a cornucopia of visual information on suburban life in the early twentieth century.[1] Lakewood, located on the south shore of Lake Erie immediately west of Cleveland, is a densely packed suburb of 5.6 square miles laid out largely on a grid. Modest single- and double-family houses line narrow north-south avenues, and four wider east-west arteries provide access to downtown Cleveland; two of these, Detroit Street and Madison Avenue, are lined with extensive commercial development.

Although Lakewood appears at first glance to fit the model of a typical middle-class suburb, a closer look at existing landscapes reveals greater diversity.[2] Time has muted the community's sharp differences, but enough visual evidence remains to suggest their presence, if not the extent of their importance. In contrast to the middle-class landscape at Lakewood's core, the edges contain neighborhoods of large mansions or overcrowded tenements, whereas the arteries are lined with extensive apartment developments. Although less populous than the middle-class landscape in Lakewood's core, the edge areas were far from insignificant. Mansions claimed much of the north coast; lakefront estates extended a mile and a half west from the Cleveland boundary. Clifton Park, a planned community in northwest Lakewood, covered more than 140 acres. In 1920, the Village, a tenement district in southeast Lakewood, housed more than 10 percent of the city's residents;[3] apartments elsewhere were home to more than 15 percent of Lakewood's households.[4] The very presence of these minority landscapes in

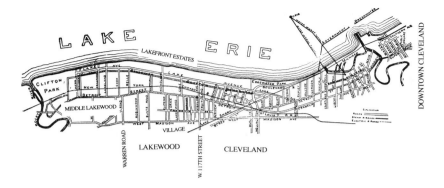

FIG. 10. Lakewood and Cleveland, 1902. This illustration, originally a promotional map advertising a Lakewood subdivision, has been annotated to provide an orientation to Lakewood's site and its various landscapes. Lakewood begins at West 117th Street (Highland Avenue) and runs west to the Rocky River. Cleveland lies to the east of West 117th Street. Streetcar lines ran east-west along Detroit Street, Clifton Boulevard, and Madison Avenue (the latter line did not begin service until 1917). Thomas Arthur Knight, *Beautiful Lakewood: Cleveland's West Side* (T. A. Knight, 1902), 8. Courtesy Cleveland Public Library History and Geography Department.

juxtaposition with a middle-class one demonstrates that different groups with varied resources and lifestyles could shape, within this suburban context, residential environments that fit their needs.

The emergence from 1890 to 1930 of distinct social landscapes in this fairly typical streetcar suburb provides a case study of some of the strengths and limits of visual analysis. Careful study of existing landscapes reveals important insights into earlier patterns of suburban life and culture, but, unsupported by other methods and sources, it can also mislead. On the other hand, traditional historical sources such as census records and newspapers seldom reveal the presence of distinct physical landscapes.[5] Historical visual analysis, drawing on photographs, maps, and other visual records, makes it possible to unravel this seemingly typical middle-class suburb into a series of relatively discrete landscapes. Ultimately, the safest course is to seek multiple confirmation through an approach that combines all three methods.[6]

A Typical Middle-Class Suburb

Lakewood took shape at the turn of the century, as did many streetcar suburbs. Incorporated in 1889 as a hamlet by farmers, resort owners, and wealthy absentee landowners, the community grew rapidly following the extension of three electrified streetcar lines (along Detroit Street, Clifton Boulevard, and Madison Avenue) that radiated westward out of Cleveland. The first line (Detroit) began service to Lakewood in 1893. By 1910, Lakewood village housed more than 15,000 residents and reincorporated as a city the following year; by 1930 Lakewood's population of more than 70,000 inhabitants made it Cleveland's "second city."[7]

Lakewood's demographic profile largely fits that of a typical middle-class suburb. Most residents were native-born whites; household heads held either white-collar or skilled blue-collar jobs. Lakewood also housed a significant foreign-born population, as did Cleveland, a major destination for immigrants. By 1930, foreign-born whites and their children made up 45 percent of the population, with German-, Irish-, and Slovak-Americans constituting the majority.[8] While ethnic differences had important implications for social organizations, their presence in the suburban landscape, save for the Village, remained muted except for the separate churches established by English, German, and Slovak Lutherans and Irish, German, Slovak, and Polish Catholics.

Leading citizens sought to further limit diversity and to exercise greater control over existing populations. This included efforts to push out African-American residents and restrict access to others. By 1930, blacks made up less than 0.2 percent of the population; those who remained held largely personal-service positions.[9] To avoid urban dangers, Lakewood banned alcoholic beverages in 1906 and repeatedly resisted annexation to Cleveland. World War I provided a good opportunity to exert social control even more strongly; public schools dropped German-language courses and students celebrated with a book burning. The city council even debated banning German-language religious services; at the same time city fathers and mothers promoted Americanization efforts and celebrated their unified efforts to defeat the "Huns."[10]

Lakewood's suburban landscape looked much like those emerging on Cleveland's east side or on the outskirts of other midwestern industrial cities. The constraints of the streetcar and developers' concerns for profit produced a very densely settled community. Built largely on a grid with narrow lots, vertical two-and-one-half-story houses, and little land set aside for public uses, the city reached densities even greater than those of Cleveland. By 1930, it housed 12,820 persons per square mile, compared to Cleveland's 12,696;[11] in Cuyahoga County, only East Cleveland, another streetcar suburb, exceeded Lakewood's densities.

Lakewood's diverse landscapes included two different elite neighborhoods, a series of middle-class areas, two apartment landscapes for the well-to-do and less affluent singles and childless couples, and an ethnic, working-class urban village. These distinct environments emerged almost simultaneously as the product of separate forces that acted on both urban and suburban areas.[12]

Lakefront Estates

Elites had been leaving central-city locations throughout the nineteenth century. In both Cleveland and Lakewood, wealthy business leaders began to establish summer homes along Lake Erie as early as the 1880s. Located between Lake
Avenue and the lake, these broad, deep estates began in Cleveland and extended
well into Lakewood.

Businessman/industrialist Robert Rhodes established Lakewood's first summer home in the early 1880s; his large estate marked the western boundary for
the continuous development of this landscape. Although Rhodes eventually
turned his rambling frame house into a permanent home, the building and its
large, informal grounds continued to have the appearance of a summer home;
both understated his position as a capitalist. By 1910, new industrialists, such as
automaker Alexander Winton and cabinetmaker Theodor Kundtz, had established large, formal estates that more fully reflected the emerging landscape. This
borderland showcased the new industrialists' wealth, which was especially important for Winton and Kundtz, whose immigrant status initially limited their access to elite circles.

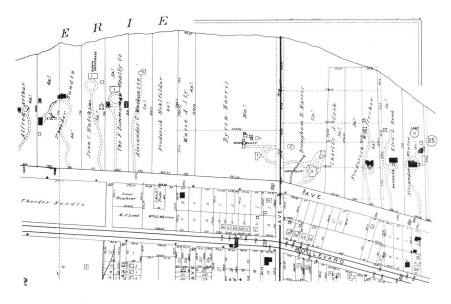

FIG. 11. Lakefront estates. Typical lots were approximately 190 feet wide and run more
than 1,000 feet to Lake Erie. *Plat Book of the City of Cleveland, Ohio, and Suburbs,* vol.
2 (Philadelphia: G. M. Hopkins Co., 1912), pl. 28. Courtesy Cleveland Public Library
Map Collection.

FIG. 12. Theodor Kundtz's "Hungarian Hall" prior to demolition in 1961. Completed in 1903, this was the largest and most elaborate lakefront house in Lakewood. Kundtz used skilled craftsmen from his cabinet-making company to hand-carve interior decorations and furniture; each room was finished in a different wood and hand-painted murals graced the walls. A ballroom, bowling alley, and music room provided space for entertainment. Photo by Byron Filkins. Courtesy The Cleveland Press Collection, Cleveland State University Archives.

The layout of these estates reflected residents' concerns about their lifestyle; with considerable resources, they could well afford to indulge their fantasies. They planned their property independently of neighbors; eclectic house and ground designs reflected this independence. Kundtz's massive stone "Hungarian Hall" castle and Winton's highly formal gardens, which ran from the rear of his house to the lake, represented extreme examples of these developments. Residents entertained in their homes, which had large public rooms (some included third-floor ballrooms). They also enjoyed other diversions, such as those offered by music rooms and built-in bowling alleys. Live-in servants cared for residents, while gardeners and groundskeepers attended to the rest of the estate.[13]

Oriented to the street, lake, and property lines rather than each other, these large estates reflected their owners' detachment from the local community. Low stone or brick walls and gates displaying the names of the estates (for example, "Elmhurst," "Waterside," "Roseneath," and "Lake Cliff") established a barrier along the sidewalk adjacent to Lake Avenue, but they did not distract the view of admiring passersby. With mansions set back from the road, long tear-dropped-shaped driveways gave horse-drawn carriages and automobiles access to large houses. Lake Erie provided a backdrop for broad grassy lawns and gardens in the rears.

This was one of the first suburban landscapes established in Lakewood, and it experienced intrusion by the 1920s. From west of the Rhodes estate to Clifton Park at the northwest corner of Lakewood, developers soon platted streets and smaller lots north to the lake. To the east, the construction of Edgewater Drive bifurcated many estates and led to further subdivision. The Great Depression accelerated such intrusions and ultimately doomed the landscape; only a few of the original estates remain scattered along Edgewater. Nevertheless, high-rise apartment developments from the 1950s to the early 1970s largely maintained estate boundaries and in some cases incorporated their walls and gates into this new landscape. These outcrops demonstrate the presence, if not the extent, of this landscape.

Clifton Park

To the west other elites, including well-established business leaders, industrialists, and professionals, created a more communal environment. The Clifton Park Association had operated a resort at the northwest corner of Lakewood, but the business eventually became untenable. In 1894, the association hired Boston landscape architect Ernest W. Bowditch to plan a residential community of 230 half-acre lots on a curvilinear street pattern.

Bowditch's plan, unlike those for private street developments elsewhere, did not include barriers or even recognizable boundaries.[14] Homes on neighboring streets blend into those of Clifton Park; only the curvilinear roads, larger lots, and larger homes quietly suggested a change in landscape. Individual lot owners determined house and ground design; unlike the owners of lakefront estates, they avoided the use of walls or other barriers. On the other hand, as with lakefront estates, most Park homes lacked the ubiquitous front porches found elsewhere in Lakewood. In both elite areas, neighbors restricted interaction to home or club; the active street life found elsewhere in Lakewood was neither intended nor desired.

Despite the lack of gates at the entrances to Clifton Park, developers intended the neighborhood to be socially exclusive. Promotional literature promised that it would be "restricted . . . to secure to all purchasers alike, immunity from the depreciation of value which would follow the location of business places of any kind,

FIG. 13. Map of Clifton Park by Charles W. Root, circa 1905. Lots that abutted the lake and river experienced development earliest; often, the Park's largest homes were built here. Park residents had streetcar connections to downtown Cleveland on a line down Clifton Boulevard; from 1902 to 1938, they also had access to interurban light rail service along that line. Charles W. Root, from *Clifton Park Land Improvement Company* (Cleveland: Clifton Park Land Improvement Company, n.d.). Courtesy John E. Rupert.

apartment houses, or terraces [row houses] within the limits of the Park." Developers promoted Clifton Park as located "only 32 minutes" from downtown Cleveland and "the finest suburban residence property accessible to Cleveland," with "exceptional advantages of pure air, forest grounds, private parks, [and] bathing beaches."[15]

The Park's social and physical design offered possibilities for a community very different from that of the more individualistic lakefront estates. Several factors reinforced the notion that Clifton Park was a community of equals: the more consistent lot size, a formal community organization, and the dominance of the parklike setting. Self-selection and high land costs produced both a population and a landscape that were relatively homogeneous..

Despite a diversity of structures, new residents kept house design within the community's informal standards. Although these houses were large compared to most in Lakewood, few had ballrooms and bowling alleys. Homes did have large public areas for entertaining, but social life centered on the Clifton Club, which provided "entertainment, recreation, and enjoyment for . . . members, and . . . guests"; it encouraged "cultural and intellectual improvements and social inter-

FIG. 14. The Harry and Mabel Hanna Parsons Home in Clifton Park, prior to demolition in 1965. Built in 1912 by the daughter of the late U.S. Senator and businessman Marcus Hanna, this rambling house was probably the Park's largest with thirty-six rooms, including a bowling alley. Photo by James Thomas. Courtesy Lakewood Historical Society.

course." Opened in 1903, the club contained a large reception room on the first floor, an "elaborately furnished" ballroom on the second, and guest accommodations on the third.[16] A beach, yacht club, and marina added to Clifton Park amenities.

Unlike lakefront estate owners, who were less likely to become involved in community affairs (to fight the development of more apartments, for example), Clifton Park residents took a greater part in Lakewood affairs. The clubhouse hosted occasional meetings of the leading social and cultural organizations, and residents played a key role in the city's decision-making process. This power permitted them in the 1960s to delay but not stop construction of a six-lane arterial highway through Clifton Park. Nevertheless, the neighborhood retains much of its physical character, if not its social elite.

Tenement District: The Village
While elites looked for suburban home sites, manufacturers scanned the urban fringe for large, inexpensive industrial sites along rail lines. In the early 1890s,

the Cleveland-based National Carbon Company purchased a large tract of land on the New York Central rail corridor in the southeast corner of Lakewood and built a factory that produced brushes for electric motors and arc carbons for lamps. Other companies, including Winton Motor and Glidden Varnish, soon built factories nearby.

As an industrial pioneer in this area, National Carbon realized that the site was well beyond the end of the streetcar line and that few unskilled workers could afford to live in the new suburb. In 1894, the same year that Bowditch began to lay out Clifton Park, National Carbon's real estate company platted a residential settlement west of the factory; the grid plan squeezed 424 small lots (typically 40 feet wide by 115 feet deep) along eight cul de sac streets.[17]

In contrast to Clifton Park and the lakefront estates, whose residents largely traced their ancestry to the British Isles, the Village emerged as an Eastern European working-class settlement.[18] Slovak immigrants, who gained a beachhead by obtaining construction jobs building National Carbon's factory, became the

FIG. 15. The Village is sandwiched between National Carbon's factories on the east, Madison Park and a factory on the west, and railroad tracks to the south. From *Plat Books of Cuyahoga County, Ohio,* vol. 6 (Philadelphia: G. M. Hopkins Co., 1927, rev. to 1937?), pl. 4. Courtesy Cleveland Public Library Map Collection.

company's main source of unskilled labor and ultimately came to dominate the neighborhood's population. By 1910, Slovaks made up 70 percent of the Village's residents; Polish, Ukrainian, and Carpatho-Rusyn immigrants constituted most of the rest.[19]

Because of their long work hours and low pay, Villagers faced considerably greater hurdles to home ownership than other Lakewood residents.[20] To assist themselves, Villagers formed a building and loan association and helped each other with home construction. Despite their limited resources, many built large homes to house their families, nuclear or extended, as well as boarders. Others constructed small tenements or front and back houses that could produce rent. This also made housing available for others, particularly single men or small families who could not afford rents elsewhere in Lakewood and who did not want to commute from inner-city immigrant enclaves. Many renters eventually saved enough to establish their own homes.[21]

These conditions produced Lakewood's most closely built neighborhood and a density that rivaled many inner-city areas. At its peak population in 1920, the Village housed more than 4,000 residents, or 78 persons per acre. In that same year Lakewood averaged 14 people per acre, while Clifton Park and adjacent areas contained six; in fact, only two Cleveland census tracts exceeded the Village's density.[22]

The Village landscape effectively hid this density; even today, visual analysis of the building exteriors can produce misleading conclusions. Eastern European builders drew on traditional skills but generally fashioned house facades not unlike those in the surrounding area.[23] Many structures appear to be typical detached two-and-one-half-story single-family homes or traditional Cleveland doubles, while back houses were arranged so they would be largely unseen from the street. Although these forms account for some of the structures, in 1930, 74 percent of Village households resided in multi-family buildings of three or more units.[24]

Village home builders produced structures whose depth exceeded that of typical single- and double-family houses. While the front door gave access only to one apartment, two side entrances opened onto the remaining units. Interior arrangements varied considerably from three to eight units of small, two-room, cold-water flats; the structures were sufficiently malleable to permit rearrangement or different configurations. The origins of this tenement remain unclear. It can be found in limited numbers in immigrant neighborhoods in Cleveland; as with other Village architectural elements, it tends to reflect Slavic folk-housing patterns.[25]

This residential landscape fit the neighborhood's needs well. With many new residents suddenly thrust into the area, integration and social control presented

FIG. 16. This brick tenement in the Village looks like a single-family house. The front entrance provides access only to the downstairs front unit; the entrance to the other six units is on the left side. Photo by James Borchert.

major problems. However, families "adopted" their boarders and tenement builders fashioned interior space so that hallways were accessible to only two or four families. This contrasts sharply with typical tenements, where numerous families used a common entrance and corridor.[26]

While individual home builders decided issues of site, the design of the facade, and the arrangement of interior space, the collective results produced a communal landscape. Working within such constraints as narrow streets and small lots (both determined by the company's subdivision plan), Villagers produced a close, tightly knit physical structure, with street-facing homes separated only by small front yards and streets. While some residents chose to mark off their front yards with fences (a practice uncommon elsewhere in Lakewood, save for lakefront estates), front porches, yards, and especially street corners became common meeting places. Not surprisingly, the Village had Lakewood's most active street life.

Villagers adapted their environment to fit their needs in other ways. To supplement incomes or gain independent employment, many began their own businesses. Even in the Depression year of 1930, city directories listed more than 120 businesses, including 25 grocers and 17 bakers and confectioners.[27] Although the main shopping area was located on Madison Avenue, the entire Village reflected this explosion of entrepreneurial activity. Some Villagers built small rooms in front of their homes to house their businesses, adding to the Village's urban texture.

The neighborhood's eight churches dominated the skyline and ordered its religious, social, and cultural life. Despite low wages and other family demands, Villagers began forming religious congregations at the same time they began building homes; the actual construction of churches and parochial schools followed shortly afterward. Villagers exercised control over both church design and operation to ensure that native design, language, and customs would be preserved. Often located next to houses and stores, these churches furthered the area's urban, mixed-use texture.

Villagers generally found themselves cut off from the life of the larger community. The Village was isolated physically by factories on the east and west, railroad tracks to the south, and a commercial street on the north. Sharply different in ethnicity and class from the rest of Lakewood's residents, Villagers faced scorn from other suburbanites. Most Villagers walked to work at neighboring factories; their other activities took place within the neighborhood or in similar enclaves in Cleveland. Consequently, save for those who did domestic work, most Villagers had limited informal contact with other Lakewood residents.

Today the Village landscape remains largely unchanged, with a few important exceptions. Many owners of the small tenements have reconfigured the buildings into fewer, larger apartments, and most house-front stores have been converted to family rooms.

Middle Lakewood

In Middle Lakewood, the long, broad area between the lakefront estates to the north, Clifton Park to the northwest, and the Village to the southeast, a landscape most often associated with streetcar suburbs emerged. Although the New York, Chicago, and St. Louis Railroad (Nickel Plate) provided commuter service from the 1880s to 1893, the development of Middle Lakewood closely followed the extension of streetcar lines. The Detroit Street line began service in 1893, speeding conversion of that street's elaborate farm landscape. In 1902, the Clifton Boulevard line encouraged development north to Lake Avenue. Madison Avenue streetcar service did not begin until 1917; consequently, South Lakewood developed last.

The sequence of development also depended on landowners, many of whom were successful farmers, to subdivide their farm land into house lots or to sell it

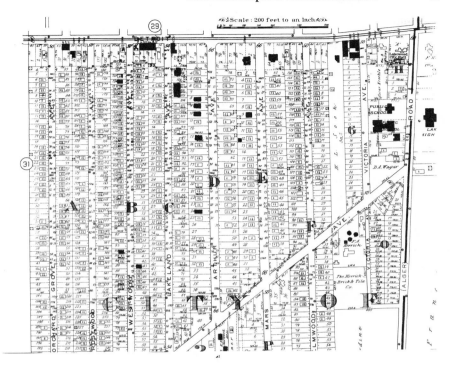

FIG. 17. Middle Lakewood. The north-south residential streets shown here illustrate the varied street width and lot size throughout middle Lakewood. Arthur Avenue, the most prestigious street in this area, is 66 feet wide with house lots 50 by 150 feet; two blocks west, Westwood Avenue, is only 50 feet wide and house lots average 40 by 115 feet. Although the latter are similar to those of the Village, Westwood contains single- and double-family houses rather than tenements. From *Plat Book of the City of Cleveland, Ohio, and Suburbs,* vol. 2 (Philadelphia: G. M. Hopkins Co., 1912), pl. 32. Courtesy Cleveland Public Library Map Collection.

to developers. As they did, an eclectic pattern appeared. Each developer decided the width and depth of lots; since most developments were only several blocks wide, this produced an undulating texture that ebbs and flows every few blocks. Some streets had long, deep lots while others were more shallow. In contrast to Clifton Park's half-acre lots and the Village's 40-by-115-foot lots, Middle Lakewood lots averaged about 45 by 150 feet.[28]

To sell their lots, developers advertised widely and attracted a fairly heterogeneous white, middle-class population. Availability, location, cost, and lot size were the major criteria for a family's site selection; this brought together people from different occupational, religious, and ethnic backgrounds whose main commonality was their pioneer status. Some newcomers purchased lots from developers and either built their own homes, ordered kit houses from Sears, Roebuck, or hired contractors; others rented or purchased lots with homes already built speculatively by developers. Whatever the practice, most builders sited their houses to conform to the setback of neighboring ones.

While few new suburbanites exercised control over the form of this emerging landscape, they established their imprint in the way they used it. Residents moved into a new development at about the same time; with similar lot costs and common problems of new home ownership, they quickly developed strong ties. Most new suburbanites came as young, nuclear, childrearing families. As pioneers on a landscape with few support systems, they quickly learned to rely on each other for help and social life. Neighbors shared child care and shopping, and they entertained each other frequently. Residents also founded block associations; these organizations sponsored community events like Fourth of July celebrations, lobbied at city hall, and took on recalcitrant utility companies. In the absence of communitywide activities, facilities, and consciousness, new suburbanites initially became intensely local in their orientation.[29]

Middle Lakewood's layout supported these activities. The area's slightly raised, detached, single- and double-family houses provided the privacy sought by nuclear middle-class families, while the closely packed residential landscape permitted the interaction necessary for common cause.[30] Limited traffic, narrow streets, and front porches brought neighbors closer; few residents erected front-yard fences to discourage this interaction.

As the population of Middle Lakewood grew, residents who shared similar interests but not proximity began to form a plethora of religious, fraternal, social, recreational, and cultural organizations. While Villagers continued to rely on neighborhood institutions and Park residents focused their attention on the Clifton Club, Middle Lakewood fragmented into a panoply of communities of limited liability. Neighborhood activities continued, but residents increasingly spent evenings with those who shared common interests.[31]

As interest-based, community-wide organizations took hold, newer settlements came to reflect a diminished neighborhood orientation. By the 1920s, new homes featured smaller porches; some had only a stoop, reflecting patterns more typical of postwar automobile suburbs that reoriented the house to the backyard. By the 1970s, many residents retreated to new backyard decks.

Nevertheless, community constraints continued to promote neighborhood interaction. Middle Lakewood, like the Village, was a walking suburb; most men commuted to work by streetcar, passing neighbors' homes on their walks to and from the streetcar stops and sharing trolley rides. With only iceboxes or small re-

FIG. 18. Middle Lakewood double-family houses. With greater setback and more trees, the middle Lakewood landscape appears less dense and lacks the multi-use structures of the Village. The upstairs/downstairs double on the right is a typical Cleveland double with front porches; such houses usually have two to three bedrooms and separate living and dining rooms. The house on the left looks like a single-family home but is a side-by-side double. Photo by James Borchert.

frigerators, housewives shopped nearly every day, insuring that neighbors would interact on a regular basis.

Apartment Landscapes

Both Village and Middle Lakewood residents had great need for accessible shopping. Unlike the Village, Middle Lakewood restricted stores to two arterials, Detroit Street and Madison Avenue, along which builders produced a dense commercial landscape of two- and three-story brick buildings that hugged the sidewalk. Along these two streets residents could find small grocery, produce, meat, and drug stores, as well as bakeries—stores that, along with street vendors, provided the necessities of daily life.

A significant number of apartment dwellers lived above the stores and in units tucked just around the corner on residential streets. Commercial buildings typically included only two upper-level apartments; other buildings, especially the apartments on adjacent residential streets, contained many more units. In either case, units ranged from two rooms with a bath to four- and five-room suites; some offered sun parlors.[32] This part of the apartment landscape offered comfortable, largely utilitarian housing close to the streetcar lines.

In contrast, apartment buildings also were put up along prestigious Clifton Boulevard, Lake Avenue, and Edgewater Boulevard, where they crossed the boundary with Cleveland and on Clifton and Lake in central Lakewood. These buildings stood out from the surrounding area and offered an upscale environment; they also elicited strong reactions from neighbors. Compared to the neighboring large, single-family homes set back from the street, these three-to-four-story brick apartments hugged the sidewalk, producing a sense of density and bulk. Some apartments held as many as 50 units; one ten-story apartment hotel contained nearly 450.

Lakefront, Clifton Park, and Middle Lakewood residents could do little about removing the Village, which was an affront to their sensibilities but which appeared too early for community action; however, they were organized well enough by the late teens to mount a campaign against additional apartment structures. Concerned about the possibility of declining property values and a deluge of city riffraff, residents formed the Lakewood Home Owners' Protective Association to block further apartment construction. By 1918, they convinced the city council to pass an ordinance "to prevent the ruin of certain beautiful residence sections of the city by the erection of unsightly, cheaply built, congestion-breeding apartment houses."[33]

Despite these concerns, this apartment landscape often provided better amenities and rents equal to or greater than those for many Middle Lakewood single- or two-family homes. Four-to-seven-room "modern suites" with steam heat, elevators, and indoor parking and occasional views of downtown provided residents with the benefits of suburban living without the burdens of home maintenance. The apartment hotel, "the first of its kind on the west side," promised elevators, an indoor garage, dining room, ballroom, beach, and a small boat harbor.[34]

While the apartment developers attracted much antipathy, their tenants remained largely invisible to the larger community. Since most were white and native-born, they easily blended into the suburban population. Families could use their apartments as a steppingstone to home rental or purchase. Others, whose lifestyles diverged from the suburban norm, could remain anonymous. In either case, apartment dwellers benefited from the suburban location, which offered good shopping and convenient access to downtown Cleveland; the impact of

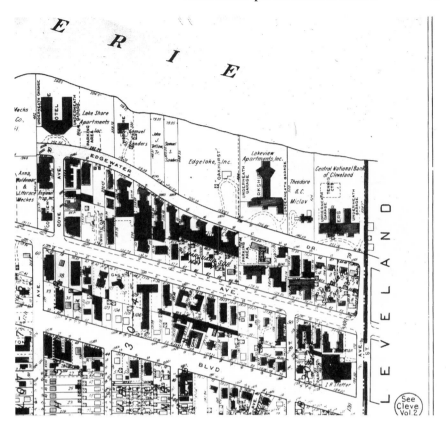

FIG. 19. Apartment landscape. The intrusion of apartments along Clifton Boulevard, Lake Avenue, and Edgewater Drive from West 117th Street to Cove Avenue is clear in this plat map. Construction of the ten-story Lake Shore Apartments (hotel) in 1928 set the stage for the disappearance of many lakefront estates; the emergence of the "Gold Coast"—twelve high-rise luxury apartments and condominiums—completed the process in the 1950s and 1960s. *Plat Books of Cuyahoga County*, vol. 5 (Philadelphia: G. M. Hopkins Co., 1956, rev. to 1958), pl. 1. Courtesy Cleveland Public Library Map Collection.

these residents on and their use of the environment is much more difficult to trace, however.

Unlike the rest of Lakewood, the apartment landscape has grown dramatically since 1950. While the existing structures remained unchanged, new construction produced a high-rise "gold coast" on the eastern site of lakefront estates; new apartment developments also appeared across much of Middle Lakewood.

FIG. 20. Edgewater Cove Apartments, circa 1954. Built in 1917, this attractive English Tudor building offered thirty spacious units of one to three bedrooms; the latter had two baths. Although the building lacked an elevator, it did have a garage and views of downtown Cleveland and the adjacent lake. Close to the streetcar line on Clifton Boulevard, it offered residents quick transportation to downtown Cleveland. The Cleveland Press Collection, Cleveland State University Archives.

Visual analysis provides important insights into the living patterns of Lakewood's new suburbanites at the turn of the century and since. While the forces of change have altered the landscapes in which they lived, much visual evidence remains, providing data that can be tested against the historical record. Many traditional historical records, valuable as supporting evidence in this study of Lakewood, would not reveal the presence of so many different landscapes. On the other hand, historical visual analysis helps to reveal the full diversity of classes and lifestyles.

There are dangers in relying too heavily on visual analysis of the existing landscape. So many of the lakefront estates are gone that only historical records can suggest the extent of their presence.[35] Reading the existing landscape requires care in other ways. Bisected by a six-lane highway and lacking walls and gates, Clifton Park today appears to be a continuation of neighboring homes along Lake

Avenue. Even more misleading are the facades of Village tenements that look like single or double homes.

Visual analysis, nevertheless, can be a powerful tool for social historians interested in how ordinary people have lived and ordered their lives. In Lakewood, as in many other communities, perhaps, visual analysis can reveal the efforts of different groups of people to construct and maintain distinct environments that contrast sharply with those adjacent to them. Each landscape reflected the resources and needs of its residents.

Finally, viewing both the physical environment and the way space is used provides a double-check on our understanding of a culture. But visual analysis, like other research approaches, is not foolproof. One must push further to grasp how space is organized and used and to determine its meanings.

DERYCK W. HOLDSWORTH

3 Landscape and Archives as Texts

Visual information (and thus the landscape) can be a useful catalyst for both research and, especially, teaching. But it can rarely stand alone in providing convincing explanations about questions of human geography.[1] In this chapter, I not only examine work that draws upon both visual cues and archival evidence, but also seek to locate what is called "the landscape tradition" within evolving research frameworks in human geography.

My own training in historical research methods leads me to see the landscape largely as a repository of relics, a mere fraction of the stuff of the past that contributes to the current scene. Examination of the landscape reveals only partial evidence of the social and economic forces at work in the world. Thus for anyone concerned with understanding long-term transformations, traditional landscape analysis inevitably offers only a limited scope of inquiry. To get behind and beyond the landscape, the archives (or, more broadly, the historical record) provide firmer evidence and encourage a richer analysis of social and economic change.

Explaining What We See

All vision is subjective, and in the end all interpretation is personal. How can we explain what we see? The Swedish geographer Torsten Hägerstrand recently reflected on why the landscape tradition had rarely satisfied generations of social geographers: "A major difficulty with the landscape concept as it is normally understood is this limitation on the visual surface of things. I believe this limitation explains why Carl Sauer with his deep interest in the consequences of human agency through time soon moved beyond his initial formulations. So have most other scholars as soon as they have attempted to explain what they have observed."[2]

When I completed my doctoral dissertation, I realized how strongly I had been pulled beyond the landscape tradition. I had spent several years trying to accumulate evidence that let me understand why builders built and consumers owned or rented a distinctive range of housing types on the west coast of North America at the beginning of this century.[3] Yet for all I thought I now knew about Queen Anne houses, California bungalows, Tudor cottages, and dozens of other housing types from walking or driving the streets of Vancouver, I was reading a landscape that was often more than a half-century detached and had been continually altered by current living. I was encountering an ensemble of house, garden, and neighborhood that had been revalorized for people considerably different from those who participated in its earlier development.

All the textures that my eye could see, such as the nuances of a certain builder's use of trim or a certain architect's plan preferences, were simply design variants within specific strategies of land and property development. The more interesting questions were associated with the forces that lay behind those pattern books—the scale of enterprise for the carpenter/contractors, the strategies of real estate firms as they subdivided particular parcels of land, and, more abstractly, the operation of the mortgage market and the land market as they empowered the labor force with a range of purchasing possibilities. What social processes were shaping the physical form?

Census and assessment records barely exist for Vancouver's early years, and building permits only give the cost of houses and the names of owners, builders, and (if any) architects. Consequently, some characteristics of the surviving built environment—for example, street and lot patterns, house sizes, setbacks, and the (later) visual appearance of the structures—could reveal some useful morphological evidence.[4] But the more I examined that evidence, the more it seemed profitable to probe data on the standard of living, wage rates, land costs, and the organizational shifts in the construction industry (ultimately the costs of housing, land, and labor) if I really were interested in working-class housing.[5] The surface could provide a partial reading, but the substructure remained invisible.

For me, a key strand of the answers to my original questions revolved around home ownership. Vancouver was an industrial city where most employment was associated with sawmills, canneries, docks, or railroads. For such an industrial city, the working class seemed to do surprisingly well. I could document extremely high rates of home ownership compared to English industrial cities or eastern North American cities, such as Toronto or Buffalo. Yet the emergent Marxist social geography was telling me that this high level of home ownership was a dupe—

that home ownership, or, more accurately, mortgage indebtedness, merely guaranteed a docile, stable labor force.[6] I concluded that further work on the social meaning of working-class housing would have to move beyond what style and appearance could reveal; my hundreds of landscape slides were no longer data to be analyzed, but instead devices to help me come full circle, to give readers (or students in classes) some concrete images to latch onto while an argument was developed from other data. In addition, as I moved away from the familiar detail of Vancouver to work and teach elsewhere on the continent, and as I realized more and more that my reading of that West Coast landscape revealed as much about my class and ethnic background,[7] the subjectivity of the landscape approach began to trouble me.

Yet I was loathe to abandon totally the sense that a house *as seen* revealed something about the circumstances of a person. The house as symbol of self[8] was important, and the existential meaning of ownership was valuable, even if it meant it was a "Faustian bargain" from a capital/labor perspective. If this side of the fence was worth pursuing, could it be pursued with a landscape perspective? The link between house and culture, between artifact and individual, has always been much easier to define in preindustrial, folk communities than in a consumer-oriented industrial society. And that is why so much of the tradition established by Fred Kniffen and Estyn Evans has had a persistent following in cultural geography.[9]

However, it is difficult to apply the notion of common housing to the settlement landscapes of the industrial era, as has been clearly shown in work that John Jakle, Robert Bastian, and Douglas Meyer present on "the common house" in twenty small towns in states from the Atlantic seaboard to the Mississippi River.[10] They go on a tour of surviving landscape evidence in small-town America, an intriguing journey that unfortunately leads them to few conclusions. Perhaps understandably, the unspoken conclusions point to the limits of culture-region studies, and to the firmer need to examine the political economy of the housing market and housing industry.

Individuals do express themselves through their housing, of course. Paint color, lawn decoration, and other surface embellishments of forms that people bought rather than built signify individual sovereignty and, often, collectively reveal interesting patterns. It is fascinating, for example, to note the ways in which some recent Portuguese immigrants in Toronto have modified existing housing with their choice of exterior paint color, their additions of religious artwork, or their alteration of porches and rooflines. But for any number of reasons, other immigrants from the same islands in the Azores did not represent themselves in such an iconographic manner, and their ethnic or class landscape signatures are indecipherable.

Ethnicity and class are revealed in the landscape only in partial and often ambiguous ways. When I moved to Pennsylvania, my repeated visits to industrial towns in coal-mining and steel-producing areas gradually shaped a research curiosity about the meaning of a strange amalgam of house/garage/stable in the rear alleys of some working-class (and, by implication, from the adjacent eye-catching church spires) ethnic neighborhoods. Although useful as a catalyst, the landscape evidence too often, and too quickly, proved irrelevant; an examination of historic Sanborn fire insurance atlases revealed that the alley structures that survive today are a mere fraction of the total number that had been built. When those Sanborn maps were cross-referenced with manuscript census returns, tax assessment lists, and mortgage records, it was possible to construct a fascinating picture of the role of alley houses as just-in-time production by property capital and some fractions of labor to provide rental accommodation for recent immigrants in a transforming industrial economy.[11]

Had I pursued my curiosity solely through analysis of the visual evidence, the published essay and evidence would have been entirely different. They would have focused on the distinctiveness or similarity of alley forms and materials compared with the houses at the fronts of lots. But, to be honest, such an approach would have been fueled by the romantic notion that these alley houses were organic, while the front houses were mass-produced—that here was folk building in the midst of industrial production—but there would have been precious little evidence with which to convince anyone. Relying on landscape evidence alone for work on such informal housing would be like using the silhouettes of church spires in these towns to read ethnicity, thus closing off lines of analysis that probe a range of occupational, class, and family characteristics and open up the category of ethnic to wider scrutiny. The palimpsest of settlement forms provides ephemeral evidence to be read by the landscape tourist, but it is work on issues like land and property markets and political resistance to regulations like zoning that provides a firmer arena for understanding relic landscapes within the context of historically specific urban social spaces.[12]

The further we reach back in time, the less landscape evidence there is of bottom-end, cheap, impermanent, and organic stock. Michael Steinitz, for example, has convincingly demonstrated that a very skewed subset of the housing past of Massachusetts survives today. Field observations suggest an eighteenth-century landscape dominated by large, two-story houses but, Steinitz writes, "more recent historical research clearly points to serious methodological problems with the cultural geographer's traditional reliance on field reconnaissance of a small number of surviving buildings to reconstruct historic patterns."[13] Steinitz shows the country mansions and the huts and hovels defined ends of a spectrum in which the overwhelming center was "the landscape of the middling farmer . . . composed of modest, one-story houses of two or three rooms."[14] The currency of visual clues as the sole route to the construction of cultural hearths and culture regions, for those who like to draw arrows of diffusion westward, is devalued by attention to the historical record.[15]

The distinction between knowledge derived from the landscape and knowledge derived from the archives is equally evident if we consider the way that some view the urban landscape, especially the skyscraper, as a clearly readable text.[16] Many cultural geographers (and architectural historians) are preoccupied with height and style of buildings, and who project some phallocratic importance to height alone. They do not try to go beyond the skyline and behind the facade to probe the forces that produced the need and the demand for office space at certain sites at certain times.[17] In his essay "Reading the Skylines of American Cities," for example, Larry R. Ford gives far too much attention to landmark structures of different eras and implies that the corporations associated with those named skyscrapers are the sole tenant. He asserts that "it is of some importance that the visual outline be read for the economic, planning, social, and aesthetic meanings."[18] Only slightly problematic, it seems, is the fact that multitudes of speculative office buildings clutter that skyline: "today it is sometimes difficult to read the skyline and know if much of the space is actually being used."[19] Notwithstanding the fact that looking at the tenant list in the foyers of these towers would enable a different reading, an understanding of the "economic, planning, social, and aesthetic meanings" of the historic landmark structures that are his focus requires attention to corporate histories, real estate records, and the like.

Ford's treatment of some classic New York skyscrapers is revealing. He regards the Metropolitan Life Building, completed in 1909 and seven hundred feet tall, as a stand-alone building visible on all four sides, with no apparent sense that the tower component was the eighth phase of a building program that had begun at Madison Avenue in 1893. The overall program had transformed most of one city block, and part of a second, with a set of office buildings between ten and sixteen stories tall before the firm added what was largely speculative office space in the tower.[20] Similarly, the Singer Building, completed in 1908, had a landmark, 612-foot tower that was, at the time, the tallest in the world. But this, too, was part of a building project that had begun a decade earlier with ten- and fourteen-story buildings (in which the Singer Sewing Machine Company ran its operation) and cumulated with this slim tower, which had inefficient office space.[21] The Woolworth Building may have been 792 feet tall, but it is perhaps of more interest that when the building opened in 1914, F. W. Woolworth and Co. occupied only the twenty-fourth and part of the twenty-third floors, and that much of the tower portion was slower to rent than lower floors.

None of these three buildings can be simply read as head office buildings; they are just as much part of the speculative stock as the non-name generic buildings around. While the Singer, Metropolitan Life, and Woolworth towers certainly attract the eye, dozens of other new skyscrapers being built nearby offered many times more office space. If the landmarks on the skyline are the bold headlines, this broader volume of real estate—researched through commercial directories and corporate histories—provides the fine print; examined carefully, this is still readable, and it offers a fuller tableau.[22] Which text is to be read, and how deeply?[23]

It is interesting to note that Ford uses the concept of diffusion in order to examine why the skyscraper only moved slowly beyond New York before the 1920s. Again, the concept of diffusion too easily comes along with the landscape approach as an effort to impose a process, and thus imply an explanation, whereby skyscrapers appear at certain sites at certain times. The landscape tableau on which this diffusion supposedly takes place is almost entirely devoid of any sense of economic forces and of all sense of cities as control points for the management of economic systems.[24] Seattle might have been one of only eleven cities with a skyscraper more than five hundred feet high by 1930, but Philadelphia, not in that list, had many times more office space than Seattle. The transformation of downtown vertical silhouettes can be linked to changes in regional and national economic systems, but the text that tells us this can be found far more often in corporate records.[25]

From this brief inspection of work that reads housing and skyscrapers, I conclude that the limitations of the cultural landscape approach are that it has been rooted in a rural, premodern, noncorporate world. It is largely ahistorical, it is very often individualistic and populist (thus in tension with any sort of class perspective), and it rarely gets at collective processes. What possibilities, then, are there for retaining the nuances of landscape approaches while developing research frameworks that focus more explicitly on social and economic process?

The Shifts to Theory

To assert that one must go beyond the cultural landscape approach to undertake effective research in human geography is not to sweep aside the power of either the landscape or vision as a catalytic device, curiosity tweaker, and, one hopes, a confirmation of other research. Instead, it is a comment influenced by currents within human geography today. What is the context of such a stance? Why is there now a broad dissatisfaction with the landscape approach?

The 1970s was a good decade for those in geography who supported the landscape perspective. Humanistic geography began to find a niche as the field of geography readjusted itself in response to the excesses of spatial science that had influenced the field during the 1960s and the 1970s. Humanistic geography's proponents drew large crowds at meetings, and its programmatic statements were widely read.[26] There was an energetic focus on ordinary people, ordinary places, and people as real, living beings rather than some abstracted point in a system. Within that broad umbrella of humanistic geography, there was room for something called "the landscape perspective." David Lowenthal had been instrumental in developing this new way of thinking about landscape in the 1960s.[27] More people became aware of the magazine *Landscape*, edited and published by John Brinckerhoff Jackson. Perhaps the flagship statement of this subgroup was a collection of nine essays published in 1979 and edited by Donald Meinig, *The Interpretation of Ordinary Landscapes* (with the subtitle "Geographical Essays");[28] especially influential were the pieces by Meinig ("The Beholding Eye: Ten Versions of the Same Scene") and Peirce Lewis ("Axioms for Reading the Landscape").

Ordinary landscapes, ordinary people, and everyday life were everywhere. See them and the truth awaits. For example, Meinig captioned one illustration, an "ordinary" street of Victorian houses photographed in winter, and surrounded by bare trees, gray snow banks and parked cars, as follows: "In its focus on the vernacular, cultural landscape study is a companion of that form of social history which seeks to understand the lives of ordinary people."[29] And Lewis wrote: "Our human landscape is our unwitting autobiography, and all our cultural warts and blemishes, our ordinary day-to-day qualities, are there for anybody who knows how to look for them."[30]

During the 1980s the shine went off the landscape group's attractiveness to a broader audience, in large part because human geography shifted. A more theoretically driven social geography (perhaps represented best by the journal *Society and Space*) and a more politically driven analysis, both in contemporary and historical geography, emerged and began to occupy more mainstream positions within human geography. Ordinary people and ordinary places were still there, but seen as elements in social, economic, and political changes ("transformation" and "restructuring" were the new words) that were played out at a range of scales from local to global. For contemporary social geographers, "ordinary" people were more likely seen for their gender, class, or ethnic characteristics in both the wage-labor and domestic spheres, and ordinary places were communities or localities being contested by different interest groups.[31] As such, the traditional, and essentially landscape, approach was rarely an appropriate framework for understanding complex social geographies.

The route to ordinary people now led through a more careful consideration of gender, class, ethnicity, and race. There is an almost total absence of women scholars in the landscape tradition in human geography.[32] Its output rarely connected with feminist themes. Janice Monk, for example, wrote about the "male orientation in landscape scholarship"[33] that has overlooked sources such as weaving, pottery, and quilting.[34] The public historian Heather Huyck categorized most of the bibliographic sources on the cultural landscape as biased "towards male interaction with landscapes, leaving much to be studied and written."[35] For many feminists, this landscape tradition offers a totalizing view that does not consider, and often not even respect, the position and participation of women in places. Gillian Rose devoted an entire chapter in her book on feminism and human geography to the problems of the masculine gaze, and thus the uncomfortable power implications of the landscape perspective.[36]

The new analysis also considered issues of class. Stephen Daniels examined the landscape commissions of painter Humphrey Repton[37] to "explicate the conflict and tensions in rural landscapes that seem on the face of it to have none," and used the novels of Raymond Williams to explore the duplicity of landscape.[38] Donald M. Mitchell, looking at a different San Joaquin Valley than the one described by cultural geographer James Parsons of the University of California, uses historical commissions on migrant labor as the central text through which to see the ways in which capital has worked to make as invisible as possible the built environments of labor that are essential for the successful agribusiness in that valley.[39] And Paul Knox took a decidedly political perspective in seeking out the taste makers and property interests that lay behind the restless urban landscape of the Washington, D.C. area.[40]

Ethnicity and race have been central foci in cultural studies in the United States, Canada, and Britain.[41] Kay Anderson's examination of Vancouver's Chinatown is more concerned with the construction of racial category than with delineating built environment signatures,[42] and Peter Jackson, in a study of Bradford's woolen mills, has demonstrated that racial as well as gender-based categories of labor are constructed and redefined.[43] Sarah Deutsch, under the heading "landscape of enclaves," but with no reliance on visual landscape, offers an effective analysis of the language, gender, and economic systems that wove a pattern of race relations which "made the West a messy place."[44] An interesting readjustment from work that saw "ethnic" as synonymous with "folk," and pioneer buildings as folk continuities from old world to new, is revisionist work by Thomas Carter. He now argues that Scandinavian houses in Utah are not folk houses but simply attempts by the victims of enclosure to mimic the bourgeois, consciously designed housing constructed in the old country by farmers who benefited from enclosure.[45]

So, paralleling the broad interest in locality that redefined the field of regional geography of the 1980s, power, conflict, class, gender, and ethnicity were among the dominant ways of broadening the horizons of human geographers to investigate how and why people and places were being marginalized or restructured. In that context, to focus solely on "the landscape" or "the individual" was too ingenuous, since these labels mask important defining aspects of everyday life. Sidestepping in one's research categories such as class, race, or gender was seen more overtly as being implicitly supportive of the status quo.

The contrast in approaches is nicely revealed in a thoughtful essay by Peirce Lewis, "Facing up to Ambiguity," in which he suggests that "the Brooklyn Bridge is no less magnificent because we know that Boss Tweed corrupted its financing. Its geometry is no less marvelous because its cables were woven by sweated workers, or because the bridge helped convert the green hills of Long Island into a dingy suburb of New York."[46]

Landscapes, like freeway interchanges, oil refineries at night, Manhattan-type skylines, or plains agribusinesses, are interesting to look at despite their corporate pedigree, and Lewis encourages us to marvel at their complexity "if only because it reflects the wonderful variety and complexity of humankind itself."[47] The approach stands in clear contrast to the work of scholars like David Harvey, Richard Walker, or Neil Smith on the ways that capital has shaped built environments and groups of people, or that of John Fraser Hart on the ways that rural America has been transformed as farming practice and farm economics have altered.[48] For these and other scholars, a concern for social process requires additional approaches to that of encountering the landscape.[49]

This new working interest in culture, power, and theory pointed toward a new cultural geography. Landmarks early in this transition include a powerful analysis by David Harvey of the building of the Basilica of Sacre Coeur in Paris,[50] pointing to the way in which landscape per se reinforces clichés and myths; realities have to be excavated from other sources. In the same year, Barbara Rubin laid out an analysis of the origins of the commercial strip, seeing in it a tension between rational and informal systems, a blending of petty proprietorship and corporate franchising, and she castigated those who simply rant about the chaotic appearance of the strip today.[51] Both these essays, published the same year as Meinig's *Interpretation of Ordinary Landscapes*, drew on historical evidence to shed light on elements of the current landscape, and to discuss ideology and power.

Neither of those pieces intended to carve out a new niche or subdiscipline. Those in the new cultural geography of the mid- to late 1980s did intend a reconstruction by stressing ideology, power, and symbolism. The works of Denis Cosgrove and Peter Jackson are especially important,[52] as well as arguments presented by Jim Duncan, Derek Gregory, and David Ley.[53] For some, this is a Commonwealth-tinged debate, since for many of these practitioners the meaning of culture has been influenced by the writing of the English cultural historian Raymond Williams.[54] As Paul Duncum has summarized recently:

The neo-Marxism which informs much of Cultural Studies in England offers more analytical muscle than the liberal pluralism which pervades American Popular Culture Studies. The merits of Marxist cultural analysis are twofold. They involve social position and method. In opposing the status quo Marxist analyses possess a keener eye to the operations of cultural practice than a position which is more or less part of the status quo. Second, in hypothesizing a dominant ideology and in stressing its centrality to cultural comprehension, Marxist analysis establishes a base on which all cultural products and practices can be both described and evaluated in an openly contestable way.[55]

In his recent attempt to recast cultural geography through a dialogue with social geography and cultural theory, Peter Jackson asserts at the outset that he employs a more expansive definition of culture than is commonly used by cultural geographers. At the heart of his project is the view that culture "is a domain, no less than the political and the economic, in which social relations of dominance and subordination are negotiated and resisted, where meanings are not just imposed, but contested."[56]

For many scholars who have taken up this new cultural/social geography, the social processes they seek to unravel must be seen historically. For Allen Pred, language was central to his uncovering the impact of industrialization on everyday life in nineteenth-century Stockholm;[57] and for Michael Watts the "grammar of place" is uncovered through the "micro-physics of power, the strategies and the interpretive struggles, [the] recouplings and reclassifications that accompany them."[58] Structuration theory was clearly useful for Barney Warf's teasing out the forces that established, structured, and remade the Pacific Northwest lumber economy,[59] as indeed it informed Derek Gregory's historical research on the Yorkshire woolen industry.[60]

The Marxist critique has sharpened the scholarly agenda for work on the built environment. Jon Goss, seeking to link built environment and social theory, comments:

> Distinctive forms of building are undoubtedly significant in reconstructing spatial patterns of past cultures. However few geographical studies of architecture as a cultural artifact succeed in moving beyond this simple correlation to explain why and whereby architecture becomes cultural artifact, how cultural and architectural institutions might be related, and why some forms were reproduced while other forms remain only as relics. Without such theory architectural geography is merely a component of the geography of artifacts on a par with say plowshare geography or the geography of kitchen utensils. In fact cultural geographers in general failed to interpret culture as a unitary complex of social relations, abstract

beliefs and material or symbolic forms in the sense advocated by cultural anthropologists. Geographic description has been decidedly thin.[61]

The individual dwelling and the vernacular, core elements of landscape study for John Brinckerhoff Jackson,[62] and the "stuff" of cultural geographers in general, falls short for researchers interested in broader issues of social, cultural, and economic change.

Reconciling Vision, Theory, and Historical Evidence

Unlike many aspects of the quantitative revolution in geography, the shift to more theoretically informed work on locality or social space has not been associated with rigid dogma. Early chapter-and-verse importation of Marxist thought into geography, as with more recent debates about structuration, deconstruction, and postmodernity in human geography, have been folded into a plurality of perspectives. Many recognize the importance of the built environment as a shaper as well as a reflector of social relations and few would wish to reject the catalytic value of visual evidence.[63] The shift toward theory has influenced many scholars interested in the built environment, a traditional research focus for those who privilege landscape analysis.

A landmark example of how to approach artifacts from a theoretically informed perspective is offered by Anthony D. King, whose analysis of the shelter type called "bungalow" moved beyond taxonomy and regional history in India, England, Europe, and other continents to consideration of capitalism, imperialism, urbanization, and the land market, thereby framing the investigation of the production of a global culture.[64] A second cluster of examples of work that convey an effective understanding of everyday life and the deeper structural changes in economy and society, that fuse locality and landscape, includes the research by Mike Davis on Los Angeles, Richard Walker on the San Francisco Bay Area, Sharon Zukin on New York, and Paul Knox on Washington, D.C.[65] Third, such theorizing is not necessarily economic, as indicated in the review by Cole Harris of the potential contributions of Foucault, Habermas, Mann, and Giddens for informing his work in historical geography.[66] A fourth variant emphasizes the importance of iconography and symbolism, so well developed by Denis Cosgrove in his work on the Venetian landscape.[67] Last, the geographer Ted Relph, long interested in landscapes of placelessness, has sought to ground his understanding in philosophy, and, more recently, in the historical record to calibrate the evolution of, and reasons for, a standardized modern landscape.[68] The bottom line, in this new constellation of interests, is the need to be explicit in recognizing the methodological dilemma of determining "the links between a particular landscape artifact, its socioeconomic and aesthetic contexts, and the actors who directly produced and/or created that artifact."[69] We do not simply read.

By stressing my personal preference for the historical record, I should stress that I am not trying to privilege some subdisciplinary hierarchy in which historical geography has exalted status. It is all too easy to be trapped by the availability of data, and, as Jeanne Kay and Stephen Hornsby have recently debated, too many documents were written by men and described men's worlds at the expense of understanding of the role of women.[70] Moreover, from Richard Dennis's British perspective, a great deal of American historical geography is still very concerned with past landscapes and is not tuned into the gender and locality debates that have reinvigorated discussions in Britain.[71]

In my own work, I have used corporate archives, fire insurance plans, assessment records, property transfer records, mortgage records, and the manuscript census to try to make visible, to bring out of concealment, what is not visible in today's landscape. Such a historical record provides a useful additional lens for viewing what does remain and what does survive, illuminating earlier phases of place making and of economic and social restructuring. Obviously, viewing today's landscape in a mood of open naiveté has merit, too, and it often yields hunches that lead toward research and understanding. But I worry when the results of research are presented through visual media that imply for beginning researchers that vision is the quickest and most reliable route into inquiry. Ultimately, where one looks and how one looks often depend on which disciplinary context one is choosing to work.

RINA SWENTZELL

4

Conflicting Landscape Values: The Santa Clara Pueblo and Day School

Two very different relationships to the land are repre-
sented by the Santa Clara Pueblo, in New Mexico, and the Bureau of Indian Affairs (BIA) day school established next to it. These relationships reflect the divergent world views of two cultures, as well as their differing methods and content
of education.

Pueblo people believe that the primary and most important relationship for
humans is with the land, the natural environment, and the cosmos, which in the
pueblo world are synonymous. Humans exist within the cosmos and are an integral part of the functioning of the earth community.

The mystical nature of the land, the earth, is recognized and honored. Direct
contact and interaction with the land, the natural environment, is sought. In the
pueblo, there are no manipulated outdoor areas that serve to distinguish humans
from nature. There are no outdoor areas that attest to human control over nature,
no areas where nature is domesticated.

Santa Clara, where I was born, is a typical Tewa pueblo with myths that connect it to the nearby prehistoric sites and that also inextricably weave the human
place into a union with the land whence the people emerged. The people dwell
at the center, around the *nansipu,* the "emergence place" or "breathing place."
The breath flows through the center as it does through other breathing places in
the low hills and far mountains. These symbolic places remind the people of the
vital, breathing earth and their specific locations are where the people can feel
the strongest connection to the flow of energy, or the creation of the universe. The
plants, rocks, land, and people are part of an entity that is sacred because it
breathes the creative energy of the universe.

FIG. 21. Santa Clara Pueblo, 1879. Photo by J. K. Hillers. Courtesy Smithsonian Institution, National Anthropological Archives.

The physical location of Santa Clara Pueblo is of great importance—the Rio Grande snakes along the east of the pueblo; the mysterious Black Mesa, where the mask whippers emerge, is to the south; the surrounding low hills contain shrines and special ceremonial areas; and the far mountains define the valley where humans live.

This world, for me as a child, was very comfortable and secure because it gave a sense of containment. We roamed in the fields and nearby hills. At an early age we learned an intimacy with the natural environment and other living creatures. We learned of their connectedness to rocks, plants, and other animals through physical interaction and verbal communication. We gained tremendous confidence and an unquestioning sense of belonging within the natural ordering of the cosmos. Learning happened easily. It was about living. In fact, the word for learning in Tewa is *haa-pu-weh*, which translates as "to have breath." To breathe or to be alive is to learn.

Within the pueblo, outdoor, and indoor spaces flowed freely and were hardly distinguishable. One moved in bare feet from interior dirt floors enclosed by mud walls to the well-packed dirt smoothness of the pueblo plaza. In this movement, all senses were utilized. Each of the various dirt surfaces (interior walls, outdoor walls, plaza floor) was touched, smelled, and tasted. Special rocks were carried in the mouth so that their energy would flow into us. Everything was touchable, knowable, and accessible.

FIG. 22. Kiva at Santa Clara Pueblo, 1930. Photo by Fayette W. Van Zile. Courtesy Smithsonian Institution, National Anthropological Archives.

There was consistency in that world because the colors, textures, and movements of the natural landscape were reflected everywhere in the human-made landscape. Reflection on the cosmos was encouraged. Separation of natural and human-made spaces was minimal, so conscious beautification of either outdoor or indoor spaces was not necessary. Landscaping—bringing in trees, shrubs, and grass for aesthetic reasons—was thought to be totally unnecessary. The mobility of humans and animals was accepted, but the mobility of plants rooted in their earth places was inconceivable.

The pueblo plaza was almost always full. People cooked outdoors, husked corn, dried food, and sat in the sun. The scale of the pueblo plaza was such that I never felt lost in it even when I was the only person there.

The form and organization of the pueblo house reinforced the sense of security and importance of place. One sat on and played on the center of the world (the *nansipu*) and thereby derived a sense of significance. Houses were climbed on, jumped on, slept on, and cooked on. They were not material symbols of wealth but were rather, in Thoreau's terminology, a most direct and elegantly simple expression of meeting the human need for shelter.

Construction methods and materials were uncomplicated. The most direct methods were combined with the most accessible materials. Everyone participated, without exception—children, men, women, and elders. Anybody could build a house or any necessary structure. Designers and architects were unnecessary since there was no conscious aesthetic striving or stylistic interest.

Crucial elements of the house interiors were the low ceilings; rounded and hand-plastered walls; small, dark areas; tiny, sparse windows, and doors; and multiple-use rooms. All interior spaces were shared by everybody, as were the exterior spaces. The need for individual privacy was not important enough to affect the plan of pueblo houses. Privacy was viewed in a different way; it was carried around within the individual and walls and physical space were not needed to defend it. Sharing was crucial.

Within the house, as without, spirits moved freely. Members of families were sometimes buried in the dirt floor and their spirits became a part of the house environment. Besides those spirits there were others who had special connections with the house structure because they assisted in its construction or because they were born or died in it. Since houses survived many generations, the spirits were many. Houses were blessed with a special ceremony similar to the ritual performed for a baby at birth. There was also an easy acceptance of the deterioration of a house. Houses, like people's bodies, came from and went back into the earth.

Ideas that characterize the pueblo human-made and natural environments, then, are that humans and nature are inseparable, that human environments emulate and reflect the cosmos, that creative energy flows through the natural envi-

FIG. 23. Santa Clara Pueblo: view from roof of Pueblo Church, 1899. Photo by Vromen. Courtesy Smithsonian Institution, National Anthropological Archives.

FIG. 24. Santa Clara Pueblo: view from roof of Pueblo Church, 1899. Photo by Vromen. Courtesy Smithsonian Institution, National Anthropological Archives.

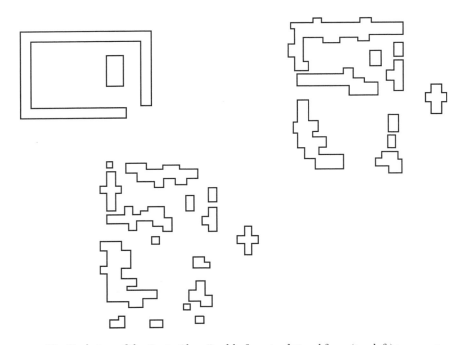

FIG. 25. Evolution of the Santa Clara Pueblo from traditional form (top left) to recent years (bottom). Drawings by Rina Swentzell.

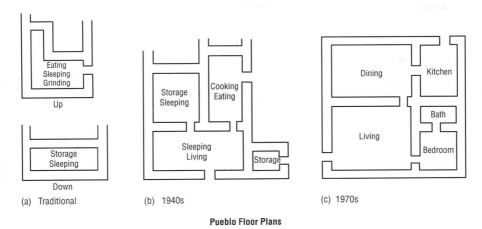

Pueblo Floor Plans

FIG. 26. Typical pueblo interior room arrangements: (a) traditional, (b) 1940s,
(c) 1970s. Drawings by Rina Swentzell.

ronment (of which every aspect, including rocks, trees, clouds, and people, is alive), and that aesthetics and the cosmos are synonymous.

How Western Education Shaped the BIA Day School Landscape

"The goal, from the beginning of attempts at formal education of the American Indian, has been not so much to educate him as to change him."[1]

Santa Clara Day School was introduced to such a world in the early 1890s during the BIA's golden age of constructing schools for Native Americans. In the very early years of European settlement in America, various religious groups attempted to civilize and Christianize Native Americans. In 1832, that responsibility was assumed by the Commissioner of Indian Affairs and the focus narrowed to civilizing Native Americans.

From 1890 to 1928, the goal was to assimilate Native Americans; the tactics were dissolving their social structure through Western education and destroying their land base. After 1928, when an influential government study asked for "a change in point of view" in how Native Americans should be educated, programs in bilingual education, adult basic education, training of Native American teachers, Native American culture, and in-service teacher training were initiated across the country. But these programs were halted almost as quickly, and certainly before the ideas reached Santa Clara Day School.

The years after 1944 saw a new determination to terminate Native American

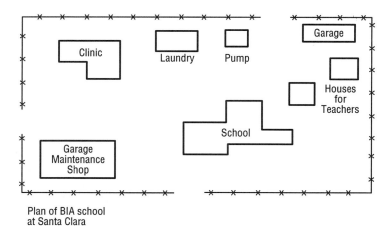

Plan of BIA school
at Santa Clara

FIG. 27. Santa Clara Bureau of Indian Affairs school grounds: plan. Drawing by Rina
Swentzell.

reservations and abolish the special relationships between Native Americans and
the federal government, relationships that had been guaranteed by centuries of
law and treaties.[2] It was during this time, from 1945 to 1951, that I attended Santa
Clara Pueblo Day School.

The government school grounds and buildings, built during the 1920s, not
only reflected that attitude of changing and civilizing Native Americans but also
characterized the general Western European attitude of human control that
seems to stem from the Renaissance glorification of human capabilities. Everything had to be changed to make it accord with the Western way of thinking and
being. The BIA school compounds reflected a foreign world view that opposed
the pueblo world and its physical organization.

At Santa Clara, the BIA school complex was located a quarter of a mile from
the center of the pueblo and had a barbed-wire fence around its periphery. That
fence defined the complex and effectively kept the two worlds separate. The cattle guards and the double-stiled ladders built over the fence provided the only
openings into the compound. They kept out both animals and old people. All large
rocks and natural trees had been removed a long time before I was a student and
there were but a few foreign elm trees in the barren, isolated landscape.

The loss of trust that occurred when people moved from the pueblo to the
school setting was most striking. Within the pueblo, preschool-aged children
were allowed enormous freedom of activity and choice; to a great extent they were
trusted as capable of being in charge of themselves. This liberal assumption cre-

ated its own self-fulfilling prophecy. Since pueblo children were expected to care for themselves in an adequate, responsible way, they generally did.

But within the BIA school, there was a different attitude: The overall atmosphere was one of skepticism. The fence was an expression of the lack of respect and trust in others. Although the formal reason given for the fence was that it kept out animals, everyone in the pueblo knew its purpose was also to keep people out. It was unsettling to know that other people had to protect themselves physically from community.

As the school grounds were separate from the life and environment around them, so were the various structures located within the compound separate from each other. There were separate laundry and shower buildings—as part of the civilizing effort, everybody, including adults, was supposed to take showers. Also included in the compound were a health clinic, a maintenance shop, the main school building, and small separate houses for the teachers. All of them were scattered seemingly randomly in the approximately five-acre compound.

Within the school building, children were grouped into rooms according to grade level. Inside the various classrooms, the divisions continued. Those who could read well were separated from those who could not. Individual desks and mats were assigned. Individual achievement was praised. Concentration on the individual, or the parts, which has become the hallmark of modern American society, was strongly emphasized. This was in contrast to the holistic concepts of the pueblo, which emphasized togetherness and cooperation and which were expressed in connected and multiple-function structures.

The floor plan of the school was efficient and designed to create an aspiration of moving up—the good old American attitude of upward mobility—from one room and grade level to the next. The move, however, was always disappointing because there were expectations that something special would happen in the next

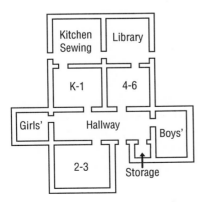

FIG. 28. Santa Clara Pueblo Day School: plan. Drawing by Rina Swentzell.

room, but it never did. The whole system had a way of making people unhappy with the present situation. Again, this was totally foreign to pueblo thinking, which worked toward a settling into the earth and, consequently, into being more satisfied with the moment and the present.

Inside the schoolhouse the ceilings were very high. The proportions of the rooms were discomforting—the walls were very tall relative to the small floor space. The Catholic church in the pueblo also had high ceilings, for Spanish priests sought to maximize both interior and exterior height in the missions they built. But in the church there was no sense of overhead, top-heavy space. It had heavy, soft walls at eye level to balance its height, as well as dark interiors that made the height less obvious.

Although there were plenty of buildings on the school grounds, it seemed that there were never enough people to make the spaces within the grounds feel comfortable. Everything seemed at a distance. The message was, Don't touch, don't interact. The exterior formality of the structures, as well as the materials used, discouraged climbing on them, scratching them, tasting them, or otherwise affecting them. There was no way to be a part of the place, the buildings, or the lives of teachers who lived there.

The creation of artificial play areas on the school grounds within the pueblo context and community was ironic. The total environment (natural as well as human-created) was included in the pueblo world of play. Play and work were barely distinguishable. Every activity was something to be done and done as well as possible; the relaxation or joy that play gives was to be found in submerging oneself in the activity at hand.

Play and work were distinguished from one another in the BIA school, and specific time was assigned for both. There were recesses from work, yet play was constantly supervised so that the children could not discover the world for themselves. Every possible danger was guarded against. Lack of trust was evident in the playground as opposed to the pueblo setting, where we roamed the fields and hills.

It was apparent that the Anglo teachers preferred indoor and human-made spaces over the outdoors, and they tried to instill this preference in us. In the pueblo, the outdoors was unquestionably preferred.

The saddest aspect of the entire school complex was the ground. There was no centering, no thought, no respect given to the ground. The native plants and rocks had been disturbed a long time ago and the land had lost all the variety one finds in small places created by bushes, rocks or rises, and falls of the ground. The ground had been scraped and leveled, and metal play equipment was set upon it. It was also a gray color, which was puzzling because the ground in the pueblo plaza, only a quarter of a mile away, was a warm brown.

FIG. 29. Buildings at the BIA school were constructed with pitched roofs, which were foreign to the Pueblo residents. Photo by Rina Swentzell.

The sensation of being in the pueblo was very different from that of being on the school grounds. The pueblo plaza had soulfulness. It was endowed with spirit. The emergence place of the people from the underground was located within the plaza and the breath of the cosmos flowed in and out of it. The land, the ground, breathed there; it was alive. The school grounds were imbued with sadness because the spirit of the place, the land, was not recognized. Nothing flowed naturally. The vitality of the school came from faraway worlds, from lands described in books. Appreciation of the immediate landscape was impossible.

The Legacy of Conflicting Landscape Values

The pueblo and the school grounds were imbued with different cultural values, attitudes, and perceptions, and the students who moved from one setting to the other were deeply affected by those differences.

The school was part of a world that was whole unto itself and its orientation toward the future, time assignments, specialized buildings, artificial playgrounds, and overall concern with segmentation were elements of a conscious world view that was not concerned with harmony and acceptance of spirituality in the landscape.

The government did not come to Santa Clara Pueblo out of inner kindness or benevolence. Rather, the government was dealing with Native Americans in what it considered to be the most efficient manner. This efficiency, which was so apparent in the structures, took away human interaction and dignity. We had to give ourselves totally to this order.

BIA authoritarianism assured the absence of any human-to-human or human-to-nature interaction. The monumental structures and sterile outdoor spaces in no manner stimulated the community to enter and exchange communications at any time or at any level of equality. In that people-proof environment, the natural curiosity that children have about their world was dulled and respect for teachers far exceeded respect for the larger forces in the world.

Santa Clara Day School was a typical American school of its era—isolated and authoritatively emphatic. Its visual landscape read accordingly with the surrounding fence, the barren land, and the tall, pitched-roof structures scattered within the compound.

But the longest-lasting impact may not be visual. The two physical settings taught different types of behavior to pueblo children. Consequently, lack of confidence and feelings of inadequacy have become characteristic traits of children who lived in the pueblo and went to the BIA school.

REUBEN M. RAINEY

5

Hallowed Grounds and Rituals of Remembrance: Union Regimental Monuments at Gettysburg

Preserved Civil War battlefields are remarkable works of alchemy. Agricultural landscapes scarred and littered with the ephemeral debris of battle have been transformed into sacred precincts composed of immaculately tended lawns and forest edges marked with row upon row of stelae, obelisks, triumphal arches, megaliths, allegorical buildings, cannon, and sculptured figures. In these sacred precincts human deeds and natural process are frozen in time to evoke reflection on fundamental values. Decisive historical moments are fixed forever by granite and bronze soldiers repulsing an attacking enemy. Nature's process of succession, which would have erased the battle's open fields of corn and wheat and redrawn them with thick forest, has been halted as much as possible by careful management. At Gettysburg it is July 1–3, 1863, forever; at Antietam it is always September 17, 1862.

The time and expense required to create and maintain these landscapes were immense and focused on a single goal: establishing memorial landscapes that would evoke reflection on the essential meaning of the Civil War to those who fought in it and to those who continued to live in the society it transformed. Preserved battlefields and other types of memorial landscapes are apt illustrations of David Lowenthal's insight that landscape "is memory's most serviceable reminder."[1] The psychodynamics of this may elude us, but the reality of our experience attests to it. A visit to Dachau brands our consciousness with the staggering horror of the Holocaust in a way no written text or photograph can. There is something about the experience of the physical reality of the place, of being there, of walking over the grounds, that admits of no substitute. Of course, one brings

67

to the site knowledge and historical memory, which have been shaped by photographs, written texts, and numerous other sources. One's immediate sensation of the landscape fuses with these prior associations to produce deeper understanding. As William Hubbard aptly reminds us, such memorials cause us to "reknow something in a new, perhaps more profound way."[2]

Gettysburg was the first Civil War battlefield to be preserved, setting a precedent for all others. A brief analysis of that effort between the years 1863 and 1913 will reveal how the battlefield was understood as a memorial landscape by those who survived the battle, those who visited as tourists, and those who managed its preservation. Crucial to this effort was the dedication of Union regimental monuments, which comprise 93 percent of all monuments on the field. The making of these monuments and the rituals of their dedication are essential to our understanding of what the Gettysburg landscape meant to nineteenth-century Americans.[3] What it means to us today is obviously a separate issue and will not be addressed in this essay. However, understanding its significance to nineteenth-century Americans can enrich the associations we bring to it today, as we strive to reknow it in a much altered world of thermonuclear weapons and dizzying political change.

Between 1863 and 1913, efforts to preserve Gettysburg developed in three interrelated phases. The first lasted from July 1863 to April 1864. Two major accomplishments marked this period. Seventeen acres of the battlefield were set aside and designed as the Soldiers' National Cemetery to contain the remains of 3,512 Union dead. The Commonwealth of Pennsylvania initiated this effort, and the cemetery itself was designed by landscape architect William Saunders. A second, independent effort complemented the first. In April 1864, David McConaughy, a Gettysburg attorney, formed a private corporation of local citizens, the Gettysburg Battlefield Memorial Association. Its mission was to preserve the major portion of the Union battle line outside the precinct of the cemetery as a memorial to the "valor and sacrifice" of the Union soldiers who had fought in the battle. The creation of such a vast landscape as a monument was unprecedented in American history.[4]

President Abraham Lincoln's famous address on November 17, 1863, at the dedication of the Soldiers' National Cemetery gave classic expression to the philosophy that governed the efforts of all who were engaged in the preservation of the battlefield throughout the nineteenth century. Gettysburg, Lincoln said, was "hallowed ground" sanctified by the blood of the Union dead and wounded who had sacrificed themselves to preserve the nation's unity. To preserve it was to commemorate a great victory. But the battlefield also stood as a reminder to present and future generations of their obligation to take whatever action necessary to preserve the Union and the freedom of all its people. Both that portion of the field set aside as a cemetery and the rest of the battle's terrain were viewed as what John Brinckerhoff Jackson called a "traditional monument," which not only instructs us about the great historical events of our culture but also reminds us of present and future social and political obligations. Such a monument is a guide to the future as well as a celebration of the past.[5]

Lincoln's address was quoted time and time again in the next fifty years by those involved in the preservation of the battlefield, and a portion of it was chiseled on the shaft of the mammoth Soldiers' National Monument erected in the cemetery in 1869. In the following years, Gettysburg was most often referred to as "hallowed" or "sacred" ground, but it was also frequently called "a place of national pilgrimage," "our national shrine," "our Mecca," "our nation's Westminster Abbey," "paradise of heroes," and "a vision place of souls."[6]

The second phase lasted from 1864 to 1895. During this period the private corporation in charge of the battlefield gradually transformed it from cultivated cropland and forest into a vast outdoor gallery of state and regimental monuments commemorating the bravery and sacrifice of the various units of the Union Army. This is what gives the present-day battlefield the appearance of a vast sculpture garden. The corporation constructed roads to link the various portions of the field and purchased more land. At the end of this period the memorial landscape comprised some 522 acres.

The third phase began in 1895, when the stewardship of the battlefield passed into the hands of the federal government's War Department by an act of Congress. The department continued to encourage the erection of monuments, constructed seventeen miles of well-engineered roads, and purchased more land, including some that had been the location of Confederate troop positions. By 1913 the vast memorial landscape had grown to about eight hundred acres. The War Department had an additional agenda—to use the field as an outdoor classroom to teach military tactics to its officers. To expedite this, it erected large observation towers and placed all over the field cast iron tablets whose austere military prose succinctly recorded the major events of the battle "without praise or without blame."

This phase ended on July 1–3, 1913, the fiftieth anniversary of the battle, with an elaborate celebration that saw approximately fifty-five thousand Union and Confederate veterans camped on the field in an enormous tent city laid out and funded by the army. The press proclaimed it a triumph of American planning and sanitation engineering. During the elaborate three days of ceremony, the veterans engaged in various rituals of reconciliation and national unity. They shook hands at famous landmarks of the battlefield, such as the wall that had figured so prominently in Pickett's famous charge; they dined together and swapped war stories. No subsequent celebration equaled the scale or the intensity of this great reunion.[7]

All three phases are significant, but phase two, which primarily involved the design, construction, and dedication of almost two hundred regimental monuments, is especially revealing as to how the battlefield was understood by large portions of the American people in the nineteenth century. Veterans returned to the field to dedicate these monuments. Their inscriptions and statues edified and instructed tourists. Guidebooks featured them like venerable family members in a photo album. Veterans serving as battlefield guides used them to conjure up vivid images of heroic deeds in the minds of their listeners.

Yet if one is to understand the central role of these monuments in transforming the field into a memorial landscape, one must do more than describe their forms and materials, label them stylistically, and decode their rather obvious military iconography. One must complement visual analysis with documentary research and explore such matters as who designed them, who constructed them, who funded them, what legal constraints affected their forms, and how they were the focus of elaborate and expensive rituals of dedication. Only then can one begin to grasp in any depth their meaning and significance.

The monuments in question were all erected by Union veterans. With one exception, no Confederate monuments were placed on the field until much later, in the early twentieth century. Almost all monuments dedicated during the period 1863–1895 were those of individual regiments, the basic building block of the Union Army. Ninety percent of the regiments were composed of civilian volunteers from the various states. A regiment numbered between four hundred and eight hundred troops and was commanded by a colonel. It was officially designated by a number followed by the name of the state from which its members came—for example, the "Sixth Pennsylvania Volunteer Infantry." But regiments also liked to give themselves nicknames of fierce creatures, such as "Tigers" and "Wildcats," which symbolized pride in their fighting prowess. One group with apparently a more horticultural bent named itself "Orange Blossom Regiment."

The first regimental monument erected at Gettysburg was placed in the Soldiers' National Cemetery in 1867 by the First Minnesota Infantry, which had suffered 82 percent casualties in the battle. The monument, a simple marble urn on a pedestal, a familiar Greek Revival cemetery monument of the time, was dedicated to the regiment's dead. However, in 1879 regiments began to erect monuments on portions of the field outside the cemetery honoring survivors as well as the dead.

The Gettysburg Battlefield Memorial Association actively promoted the erection of such regimental monuments, which were also used as markers for troop positions. Their number accelerated rapidly after members of the Grand Army of the Republic, the chief national organization of Union veterans, gained control of the Gettysburg Battlefield Memorial Association in 1880. By 1895 some 200 monuments been erected. The peak year was 1888, which saw the dedication of 150 monuments on the eve of the twenty-fifth anniversary of the battle.

At first regimental associations funded their own monuments privately through subscription drives and other fundraising activities. However, they soon teamed up with the politically powerful Grand Army of the Republic and successfully lobbied their state legislatures for financial support.[8] The states had a keen sense of pride in their veterans and often competed with one another to provide the most generous funding,[9] contributing anywhere from $500 to $1,500 per regimental monument. The states also covered expenses of all regimental members to travel to the elaborate dedication ceremonies, and these costs often exceeded those of the monuments themselves.

State monument commissions, composed of six or eight veterans serving without pay, approved monument design, administered the state funds, helped mark regimental positions on the battlefield, often supervised monument construction, and planned dedication ceremonies. Even with the dedication of the monuments, their work was not finished. They compiled accounts of the dedication ceremonies and photographs of the monuments and had them printed in handsomely bound, multivolume sets that were distributed free of charge to all veterans, elected state officials, and all the state's public schools. Additional copies were sold to interested buyers. Clearly, the veterans were not satisfied simply to erect objects on the field to commemorate their deeds. They wanted to preserve the meaning of these statues, obelisks, and stelae for present and future generations though written sources.[10]

The state monument commissions also worked with the Gettysburg Battlefield Memorial Association to make sure all of its regulations concerning monuments were followed. These regulations were rather minimal, dealing almost exclusively with inscriptions, location, materials, and foundations. The association was most concerned with the historical accuracy of the inscriptions and insisted that all accounts of the battle and casualty counts conform exactly to the official battle records of the Department of War. Indeed, their zeal for historical accuracy was equal to that of the most obsessive nineteenth-century German historian. Gettysburg was to be a precinct of exact historical memory, not of myth.[11]

Inscriptions on the monuments were required and were to include the name of the regiment in clear letters no less than four inches tall, a brief account of its action, its casualties, and its place and date of organization. If a regiment wished, it could list other battles in which it had participated. It was extremely important that the monument be placed on the exact spot on the field where its regiment had gone into action, a requirement that gave rise to some heated disputes among regiments, but the state memorial commissions and the association usually worked things out. In some cases, the disputes had to be settled in court.

Monuments were required to be made of bronze or granite, or a combination of the two, insuring low maintenance and durability; nothing else was allowed. Foundations had to be deep and solid, and the base of the monument was to be surrounded by turf to present a "neat" and "pleasing effect." This latter requirement did much to transform the battlefield's appearance from that of agricultural land to that of an English park.

These were the only regulations.[12] There were no rules whatsoever regarding the form of the monuments themselves beyond the minimal lettering requirement. Rather, the association encouraged diversity of formal expression, lest the display of monuments become monotonous and rigid rules stifle the regiments' right to individual expression.[13]

The monuments were almost always designed by the veterans themselves. Perhaps they should be labeled "veterans' vernacular." A regiment usually formed a monument committee that worked with the state commission and the association, which, of course, had to approve the design. Often the design was kept a secret from the other members of the regiment, and its unveiling at the dedication ceremony was the climax of the proceedings. The regimental committees worked with various monument companies which helped them to refine their designs and keep within the budget. (One could purchase just so much bronze and granite for $1,500, an allowance that would obviously not cover elaborate sculpture or intricate structures.) In some cases, regimental committees supplemented the state allowance with additional funds raised through subscription drives. A few of the larger, more expensive monuments were funded by private donations from wealthy benefactors.

Most of the monuments were built by a few major monument companies in the Northeast, such as Smith Granite Company, New England Monument Company, and Van Amringe Monument Company. Most of these companies had their own staff of sculptors and carvers and owned their own quarries.[14] Often the regimental monument committee sketched out a design and invited various companies to bid for the commission. Usually there was some give and take between the regimental monument committee and the monument company staff, who often refined the original design. However, the records make it clear the veterans were always actively involved in the design process and held very definite ideas about what designs they thought appropriate. If a bronze sculpture was called for, the monument company usually would subcontract it to a foundry such as Bureau Brothers in Philadelphia or the National Fine Arts Foundry in New York. Bronze tablets and official state seals were also subcontracted. On occasion, if the money was available, the veterans would commission an independent sculptor to produce a statue, but this was rare for regimental monuments.

What sort of design ideas governed the veterans in creating their regimental monuments? Their dedication speeches reveal their preferences.[15] They wanted a "dignified," "imposing" structure built of durable materials. They preferred rough "quarry finished" bases, which symbolized for them their own durability and ruggedness as soldiers. They liked to contrast polished surfaces with rusticated ones for variety. They frequently mentioned the need for "symmetry" and "good proportion" (although the latter was never defined). They certainly wanted their monument to be a unique work, unlike that of any other regiment. In fact, they found great meaning in the profuse variety of individual regimental monuments on the field: they understood these monuments to be a celebration of the common citizen soldier who was the bulwark of American democracy. Nondemocratic countries honored only their highest military officers, but a democratic society celebrated its state regiments of volunteers. The variety of monuments also attested to the pluralism of the Union Army and the indispensable role of each of its regimental units acting in concert. To view them in place on the battlefield and to read their inscriptions was to understand how victory was won through such cooperation.[16] High-art critics were not so sympathetic to the veterans' love of variety and do-it-yourself design. In 1895, the *Century* magazine bemoaned the profusion of "tombstones" at Gettysburg and called for fewer monuments on the nation's battlefields, and for these to be designed by sculptors and architects of distinction.[17] The veterans paid no attention to such critics.

Freestanding figurative sculpture was popular but expensive, so few regiments could afford it. When it was commissioned, the veterans almost always wanted it to depict a decisive moment in the action of the regiment. They usually preferred an ideal soldier figure who would represent them all, but sometimes actual individuals, particularly heroic color bearers, were depicted. The facial expression of the figure also received much attention. It was required to be "resolute," "dignified," and "brave." There are a few allegorical figures, but the overwhelming preference was for realism. The details of the uniform had to be accurate.[18] It was also important that a statue's pedestal be well crafted and different from the pedestals of other statues on the field.

Regimental monuments tend to be one of four general types: the shaft, which can be a column, obelisk, or rectangular block on a base; freestanding human figures on a pedestal; symbolic objects, such as fortified towers or, in one case, an open book; and natural elements, such as granite boulders or the carved likeness of a tree. At Gettysburg, the shaft is by far the most frequent form (comprising 87 percent of all monuments), followed by human figures on a pedestal (10 percent), symbolic objects (two percent), and natural objects (one percent). The domi-

FIG. 30. Monument to the
Fourteenth Connecticut Infantry.
Photo by Reuben M. Rainey.

nance of the shaft has to do with finances, of course. It was about all you could afford unless you raised additional funds.

The monument dedicated in 1884 by the Fourteenth Connecticut Infantry is
a typical shaft. It is about seven feet high and is constructed entirely of granite. Its
symmetrical form was seen to be "dignified" and "imposing." Its tripartite division into base, die, and cap is quite typical. Atop the cap is the clover-leaf symbol
of the Union Army's Second Corps, to which the regiment belonged. The bronze
plaque on the die relates the events and casualties of the battle. This unit had
helped repel Pickett's charge on the climactic third day of the battle.

The monument commemorating the Sixth Pennsylvania Volunteers is a more
elaborate shaft. Additional private funds were raised to construct an imposing
nineteen-foot-tall obelisk of alternating blocks of pink and gray Rhode Island
granite. The symbolism of this monument is very rich, as indicated in the regiment's dedication service program:

> The style is that of the most ancient forms of memorials and is sym-
> bolic of the enduring nature of the regiment's service. The rough-quarry

faced stone symbolizes the rugged, substantial, everyday veteran character of that service, the foundation stones, one might say, upon which success was built. The clear cut margins, washes and faces would point to the effective, complete nature of the record made by the regiment. The polished panels upon which the name and assignments of the command are inscribed are typical of the shining example held up to future generations of what their manhood had enlisted for, fought for, then surrounded with a halo of glory. As a whole the memorial points as a finger to heaven reminding all of the heroes that fell that we might stand erect.[19]

The monument erected in 1890 by the First Pennsylvania Cavalry is a typical example of a freestanding human figure on a pedestal. The bronze figure was cast by the Bureau Brothers Foundry and was sculpted by H. J. Ellicott. The rusticated granite pedestal symbolizes the ruggedness of the unit. The seven-foot-tall statue depicts an actual episode of the battle. The First Pennsylvania had been ordered to back up the Union infantry against Pickett's charge on the third day of the battle. The figure crouching on one knee gazes intently at the advancing Confederates, ready to fill any breach in the line of defense at a moment's notice. All

FIG. 31. Monument to the Sixth Pennsylvania Volunteers. Photo by Reuben M. Rainey.

FIG. 32. Monument to the First
Pennsylvania Cavalry. Photo by
Reuben M. Rainey.

details of uniform and equipment are meticulously accurate, a matter of great importance to the regimental committee. The statue is on the very spot where the unit formed its battle line and depicts an action they all performed. It faces the exact direction from which the Confederate infantry charged. The ideal countenance of the figure, embodying "bravery" and "resolution," represented the entire regiment. The emphasis on the site-specific nature of the sculpture, this freezing of an actual episode on the exact spot where it occurred, and the photorealistic details are quite typical of this type of regimental monument. Many realistic battle scenes are depicted in less-expensive bas relief on various shaft-type monuments.[20]

Symbolic objects are quite rare. An interesting example is the monument erected by the 150th New York Infantry on Culp's Hill, where the unit had held fast against the fierce Confederate offensive of the second day. It is an imposing twenty-three-foot, eight-inch-high granite tower with a ten-foot by ten-foot base. Its total cost was $4,400, about three times the New York state allotment. Certain elaborate details on the bronze plaque, such as the regimental flag, were carved by sculptor George Bissell. The names of the killed and wounded are engraved on its bronze tablet. This personalizing of the monument is exceptional—most simply listed the number of casualties. The symbolism of this monument is also rich, as discussed in its dedication program:

> It is composed of thirteen massive stones, emblems of national birth, unity and stability.
>
> Here we stood 600 strong, shoulder to shoulder, riveted to these rocks by loyal love to the Union and the government of our fathers.
>
> So the massive stones of this monument, reared one above the other, are significantly appropriate, each holding the other in place, representing a tower of invincible strength.
>
> They also fitly typify the unity, love and mutual respect which characterized officers and men of this regiment.
>
> May this monument endure forever . . . inspiring courage, loyalty and true manhood, which are the life-blood of the Republic . . . .[21]

Examples of the final category, monuments depicting natural elements, are very rare. One of the most interesting is the one erected by the Ninetieth Pennsylvania Infantry. Sculpted in granite, it represents a massive oak tree whose top

FIG. 33. Monument to the 150th New York Infantry. Photo by Reuben M. Rainey.

FIG. 34. Monument to the
Ninetieth Pennsylvania Infantry.
Photo by Reuben M. Rainey.

has been blasted away by a cannonball still lodged in the top of the trunk. In the
shattered treetop a bird is tending its nest. Attached to the trunk are bronze repli-
cas of various kinds of military equipment (including a rifle and knapsack),
sculpted with great accuracy. This tableau represents an actual occurrence in the
battle. A nest of baby birds was shot out of the tree, and a member of the regiment
risked his life to replace the unharmed birds. The bird, a dove, was also referred
to in the dedication ceremony as a symbol of "the era of peace and good will" following the end of the war. Again, the emphasis is on commemorating a precise
event of the battle and on almost photo-realistic representation of military equipment.[22]

One notes a similarity between many of these battlefield monuments and Victorian cemetery monuments. The typical shaft, with its tripartite base, die, and
cap, looks very much like an enlarged version of a typical mid-to-late nineteenth-
century tombstone decked out with corps symbols, military equipment, and
bronze plaques. The obelisk was a popular funereal monument during the early
and mid-nineteenth century. Veterans, in designing their monuments, may have
been influenced by these precedents. Also, while the battlefield monuments do
not mark actual grave sites, they have a didactic and hortatory purpose, very simi-

lar to the monuments in nineteenth-century American rural cemeteries such as Mount Auburn, Greenwood, and Spring Grove. Many of these monuments were, of course, derived from ancient Greek and Roman precedents. A row of regimental monuments along Gettysburg's Cemetery Ridge recalls the similarly aligned marble monuments of Kerameikos, ancient Athens's renowned burial ground for its distinguished citizens. Iconographic linkages of Athenian "democracy" and/or Roman republican values with the new American republic were commonplace in nineteenth-century America.

The dedication ceremony of a monument was an elaborate affair and often cost more than the monument itself. Frequently the governor of the state, members of the state monument commission, and other dignitaries were in attendance. Such festivities were in keeping with nineteenth-century Americans' love of lengthy public spectacles imbued with theatrical qualities. An average crowd was about one thousand people and included, of course, the surviving veterans of the regiment, as well as their friends and extended families. A typical ceremony opened with a prayer by the regiment's chaplain as the crowd gathered around the flag-draped monument. This was followed by stirring band music and the reading of poems composed by members of the regiment commemorating its valor and suffering. Then commenced several orations by former officers and enlisted men, each of which could last well over an hour.[23] The climax came with the unveiling of the monument amid great applause and cheering. The monument was then officially conveyed to the ownership of the Gettysburg Battlefield Memorial Association for care and maintenance. The service usually ended with a prayer or with the assembled crowd singing "America." The veterans then gathered around the monument for a group photograph, which often was reproduced in the state's publications about regimental monuments.

The orations were often quite eloquent. For many veterans, speaking at these ceremonies was the high point of their lives.[24] The orations dealt in the most minute detail with the history of the regiment and its particular deeds of bravery in the battle. There was much discussion of the issues of the war, the preservation of the union, and slavery. Some orators went into lengthy histories of slavery in the New World or the making of the Constitution. Some recalled the great pain and suffering of the war, as if the ceremony provided a catharsis for long-repressed memories. But the tone of the speeches was mostly positive and celebratory. They reminded their audience of their present and future obligations to the nation. Often they called for reconciliation with their former Confederate adversaries, some of whom might be in the crowd. A few of the speeches were a bit cantankerous, protesting errors on the monument's bronze plaque or the improper placement of the monument on the field. One of the more colorful episodes occurred when the Wildcat Regiment, the 105th Pennsylvania Infantry, unveiled its monument. The shaft appropriately featured a wildcat's head in bronze, but the veterans were chagrined to find that the wildcat looked more like a tame house cat. They demanded a more ferocious image, which was put in place a year later.[25]

Many speakers also referred to the healing power of nature, which had restored the battlefield and its surroundings to a pastoral beauty, symbolic of the healing of the nation itself. In so doing, they were employing the nature imagery of renewal and transformation frequently used in nineteenth-century funeral orations, especially those held in such rural cemeteries as Mount Auburn in Cambridge, Mass.[26] Frederick Law Olmsted and Calvert Vaux had also called upon the therapeutic power of the pastoral in their designs for Central Park and Prospect Park.

These dedication speeches reveal much about nineteenth-century American culture. Behind the calls for national unity one senses a nation threatened by internal problems of urban poverty and labor unrest. The long-felt need to prove to other nations that America, too, had a long and glorious history is also apparent. Some speakers claimed that Gettysburg had surpassed Marathon and Waterloo in its significance for world history. Some offered nationalistic bravado over the recent victory in the Spanish-American War, in which Union and Confederate veterans had fought together. In dedication ceremonies held closer to the end of the century, when Jim Crow laws were proliferating, fewer and fewer speakers mentioned slavery.

The memories evoked were highly select. Mostly the war was recalled as a war of brave charges, of homeland defended, of noble enemies worthy of one's steel, of chivalric deeds and compassion for one's enemies. Little was said of the prisons of Andersonville, and nothing about the atrocities committed against black troops at Petersburg and other battles. There were no recollections of the brutality of total war, which destroyed civilian crops and farms, or of the senseless slaughter of troops through tactics based on little understanding of the killing power of modern weaponry. The war was remembered as having been fought for principle, not territory. The veterans were absolutely certain of the righteousness of their cause, and their victory was God's seal upon their endeavors. The prosperity of the new unified nation was also a sign of God's blessing.[27]

Now we can begin to understand why these aging veterans engaged in such a flurry of monument making on the hallowed ground of the preserved battlefield. Obviously, they wanted to be appreciated and remembered by future generations for their sacrifices and deeds of valor. It was no doubt a great joy to reunite with their former comrades for what would be, for many, one last reunion on this field of glory. They may have indulged in nostalgic hyperbole and the making of myths, but they understood something of great importance. No society can continue to flourish without perpetuating its fundamental values through rituals of remembrance and the making of monuments. They have left us a valuable legacy.

DAVID CHUENYAN LAI

6

The Visual Character of Chinatowns

"Chinatown" means different things to different people at different times and in different cities. Chinatown can be conceived of as a social community, an inner-city neighborhood, a suburban shopping plaza, a skid row district, a historic district, a tourist attraction, a place of mysterious evil, or a cultural hearth. Although our perception of Chinatown may be shaped by our knowledge of it as a social entity, our perception is also influenced by the act of seeing.

It is the facades of the buildings in Chinatown that constitute the most striking visual component of place character. Western architects or contractors built most of the old Chinatown buildings, but they tried to create "chinoiserie" or exotica by modifying or manipulating standard Western architectural forms. In the Chinatowns of Victoria and Vancouver in British Columbia, for example, buildings exhibit both Chinese decorative details and Western facades constructed in the prevailing commercial Italianate and Queen Anne fashions of the day.[1] Other Chinatowns, such as those in San Francisco, Seattle, Vancouver, and Montreal, still have cohesive groupings of similar nineteenth-century buildings. These blend features of both Chinese and Western architectural styles.

Although a homogenous style of Chinatown architecture has never developed, Chinatown structures usually contain several architectural features rarely found on other downtown buildings. The most common elements are recessed or projecting balconies, upturned eaves and roof corners, extended eaves covering the main balconies, sloping tiled roofs, smooth or carved columns topped with cantilevered clusters of beams, flagpoles, and parapet walls bearing Chinese inscriptions.[2]

FIG. 35. Decorative features such as green or yellow tiled roofs, moon-shaped entrances, and Chinese inscriptions transform these three buildings in Chicago into typical Chinatown structures. Photo by David Chuenyan Lai.

Recessed balconies dominate the upper stories of many Chinatown buildings. This element may be a duplication of practices in Hong Kong, Macao, Canton, and other cities in south China, where the facade of a building is set back at each level and the facade plane is met by a wrought iron balcony. Recessed balconies are common in south China because they help keep building interiors cool in the summer and warm in the winter. On rainy days, residents dry their clothes on bamboo poles hung in the recessed balcony.

A recessed balcony also provides an open space for children to play and for households to worship the heavens during the Chinese New Year and other festivals. In Chinatowns, most Chinese association buildings have recessed balconies, which are useful when the interior assembly hall is too crowded during a festival celebration or when there is a street parade.

I have not come across any building with a recessed balcony outside Chinatown except one in Portland: The Waldo Block, a three-story building at the corner of Washington Street and S.W. Second Avenue, has a recessed balcony, but it is four city blocks south of Portland's Chinatown. Even so, a search of the history of the block reveals that it was owned by the Gee How Oak Tin (Zhi Xiao Du Qin) Association during the late 1880s, when Chinatown included that block.[3]

The facades of Chinatown buildings are usually covered with Chinese decorative details.[4] The major decorative elements include schemes of gold, red, green, yellow, and other brilliant colors; animal motifs, including dragons, phoenixes, or lions; plant motifs, including pine, bamboo, plum, and chrysanthemum; other motifs, including pagodas, lanterns, bowls, and chopsticks; inscriptions of stylish Chinese characters such as *fu* (happiness or blessings) and *shou* (longevity); signboards inscribed in Chinese characters; hanging lanterns; doors, windows, or archways that are circular, moon-shaped, and overlaid with ornate lattice work; and decorative balustrades adorned with frets.

In traditional Chinese architecture, the colors and animal motifs are believed to influence the fortune and destiny of a building's occupants. Red signifies happiness, gold is linked with prosperity, yellow is the imperial color, blue is associated with peace, and green is associated with fertility. Certain mystic animals such as dragons and phoenixes are believed to be auspicious and are commonly carved or painted on walls, columns, and shop signs.

Chinatown also is visibly different from other city neighborhoods because of structures such as the Chinese pavilion in Seattle, the Chinese pagoda in Mon-

FIG. 36. The On Leong Chinese Merchants Association Building in Washington, D.C., is a good example of a Chinatown building with many decorative and structural components. Photo by David Chuenyan Lai.

treal, and the Chinese gardens in Vancouver and Winnipeg. There are also Chinese decorative features, such as telephone booths and bilingual street signs in Chinese characters and English letters. Chinese fittings such as pagodas and lanterns are used as decorative features on many restaurants and gift shops in Chinatown.

Lavishly decorated Chinese arches or gateways are prominent landmarks of many Chinatowns across North America.[5] For example, Chinese arches serve as a symbolic entrance to Chinatowns in Boston, Chicago, Edmonton, and Winnipeg. Two Chinese arches in Los Angeles function as entrances to a shopping plaza. A Chinese arch is a symbolic entrance to the Chinese Cultural Center in Vancouver. In Victoria, the Gate of Harmonious Interest was built to commemorate cooperation of the Chinese and non-Chinese citizens of the city in the rehabilitation of Chinatown, as well as the harmony of the city's multicultural society.

The way our serial views of Chinatown are linked may cause our minds to mold the chaotic images of Chinatown into a perceived coherent precinct. In Victoria, for example, intricate networks of picturesque arcades, narrow alleys, and enclosed courtyards are still found behind the commercial facades of the old buildings. The architectural components relate harmoniously to the scale of people passing through the street: We see a large, impressive gateway, then details of its design, then facades of the three-story buildings, then the street, sidewalks, people, and vehicles, and finally the alleys and courtyards. The scales of the various parts of Chinatown integrate hierarchically, giving us a sense of complexity, coherence, and satisfaction.

We are keenly conscious of objects and the intervals between them—signboards, merchandise, telephone booths, sidewalk benches, and street lamps. Closely spaced, they make us visually aware of the densely populated and overcrowded streetscape—and community—of Chinatown.

CATHERINE M. HOWETT

7

Where the One-Eyed Man Is King: The Tyranny of Visual and Formalist Values in Evaluating Landscapes

Survival is not possible if one approaches the environment, the social drama, with a fixed, unchangeable point of view—the witless repetitive response to the unperceived.
MARSHALL MCLUHAN and QUENTIN FIORE

The impact of television and other communication technologies in contributing to the dynamics of social and political upheaval in China, Eastern Europe, and the former Soviet Union during recent years ought to inspire a rereading of the work of Marshall McLuhan, who in his lifetime liked to play the dual roles of canny jester and oracle. More than a quarter-century has passed since McLuhan heralded the imminent transformation of the world into a "global village" liberated by new forms of "electric media" from the long history of the West's cultural dependence upon reason and visual experience as the organizing principles of life and institutions.

For McLuhan, television was not a visual medium comparable to printed texts or photographs, which present data arranged in ways that presume the existence of logical and sequential connections between things and concepts. Television, he argued, is a "cool" medium—an extension of the sense of touch rather than of sight—that is indifferent to the narrative structure and informational bias of print technology; it is more akin to the unstructured, patternless "mosaic" effect of certain primitive art and oral traditions based on inherited myths.[1] Whatever the value of McLuhan's analysis of contemporary media, his critique of the common cultural inheritance that predisposes Western societies toward certain ways of viewing the world—both in a literal, physical sense and metaphorically—is shared increasingly by a body of scholarship within the disciplines of philosophy, environmental psychology, art history, literary criticism, and cultural geography.

The Kantian notion that human consciousness actively and essentially determines our perceptions and interpretations of reality is now accepted as a truism, as is the corollary precept that an individual's consciousness is profoundly shaped by the cultural community to which one belongs. Yet, despite this awareness that every judgment made about some part of the world "out there" is inescapably subjective and value-laden, aesthetic predispositions, preferences, and prejudices often remain unexamined. While it is certainly not possible for individuals or social groups within a given culture to inventory and analyze with scientific objectivity the whole range of values that inform their evaluations of a variety of experiences, the task of exploring the origins, history, and evolution of shared values is indispensable to understanding ourselves. With respect to the physical environment specifically, an understanding of why we are inclined to make a specific set of values the basis of environmental assessment and decision making may liberate us from the false conviction that our judgments and actions are based on rigorously objective and inviolate standards.

This essay explores the origins of the high priority that Western Europeans and Americans place upon the way places look, based on our expectation that to be considered "beautiful" or "well designed," a readable and traditional formal ordering of visual elements should be present. While it would be absurd to suggest that we can or should ignore the dominant role that seeing plays in most human encounters with the environment, the translation of visual sensory dominance into specific aesthetic values is a consequence of culture, not of nature. Moreover, if an almost exclusive investment of value in visual and compositional values blinds us to other potential attributes of the landscapes we experience, we are left poorer for our failure to discover and exploit additional—and in some cases alternative—sources of aesthetic satisfaction. Obviously, too, design and policy decisions based on a culturally conditioned aesthetic canon whose premises remain largely unexamined simply perpetuate environmental biases that may actually subvert ecological and/or social goods.

McLuhan traced the historic roots of our preoccupation with visual values and highly structured spatial compositions to a revolution in the representation of images and of space that occurred in the Renaissance. He believed that the fifteenth-century invention of movable type was conceptually linked to the invention or rediscovery of the optical science of perspective by Renaissance artists and architects. Both of these devices involved a linear, uniform, and continuously replicable process that defined the world in visual terms and emphasized a fixed point of view and a detached observer/reader. Renaissance perspective figured forth a visual paradigm of spatial order derived from formal units of measurement, dominated by vertical and horizontal axes, and characterized by symmetry and harmonious balance of parts within a unified whole.

McLuhan's playful comment on the hierarchical structuring of this simulacrum ("A piazza for everything and everything in its piazza"[2]) is, however, well

FIG. 37. Illustration from Hans Vredeman de Vries, *Perspective Das ist Die Weit beruemhte Kunst . . .* (The illustrious art of perspective) (Leiden, 1604). IDC bv Microform Publishers.

supported by John White's painstaking analysis of the intentions and effects of Renaissance illusionistic perspective in *The Birth and Rebirth of Pictorial Space*. White makes the point that the achievement of verisimilitude made possible by the new techniques for counterfeiting the appearance of real three-dimensional space on a planar surface was not more revolutionary than the achievement of a new kind of pictorial *organization:* "The subordination of all objects to a single set of rules is far more than a mere device for closer imitation of the natural world. The measured relationship between each element of the pictorial world is a potent factor in increasing the unity of the composition, as well as its realism."[3]

What began in Renaissance painting as an extraordinary artistic transfiguration of the everyday world of experience inevitably came to condition the ordinary expectations of what the observing I/eye—that fixed point determining the lines along which forms were dispersed in perspective space—should perceive in the real environment outside the frame of the picture. The idealized formal order in a painted landscape or urban scene suggested a model for the design of actual spaces, for buildings and streets and gardens, even for large rural estates and entire cities. First came the conceptual framework of the plan, imposing an abstract geometrical order on the apparent disorder or chaos of the original environment; then came, in the great age of Baroque architecture and urban design, increasing delight in the manipulation of perspectival vistas, in the landscape as spectacle and as theater. John Brinckerhoff Jackson's 1979 essay "Landscape as Theater" suggested the connections between the metaphor of "theater" applied to physical places (the Theater of Geography, the Theater of Cities), the emergence of theatrical drama as a dominant art form, and the design of gardens and urban landscapes meant to ravish the eye by means of heroic scale, dazzling displays of water and light, and well-defined, intricately modulated spatial sequences intended to serve as appropriate settings for exalted human action and social intercourse.[4]

The scientific revolution that spanned the period from Copernicus's assault on medieval cosmology in the mid-sixteenth century until Newton's publication of his *Principia* at the end of the seventeenth century provided philosophical reinforcement for the visual and formalist emphasis of renaissance and baroque design. Galileo attributed to science the standard of an objective knowledge of nature, based on its mathematical, predictable, and measurable reality, as opposed to purely mental, and therefore subjective, human responses to nature. Descartes

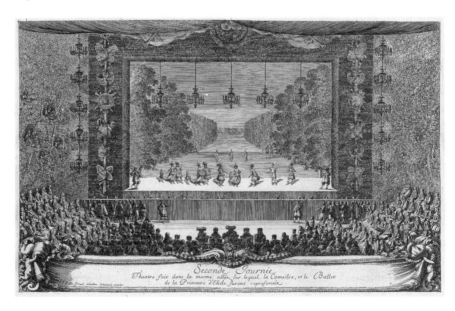

FIG. 38. Israel Silvestre, *Les plaisirs de l'isle enchantée* (Paris, 1664). King Louis XIV, seated at center, with audience in the gardens of Versailles. Actual trees and hedges were used to frame the stage for a ballet performance within the garden. The Metropolitan Museum of Art, The Elisha Whittlesey Fund, 1930.

pressed still further the fundamental distinction between man and a nature conceived metaphorically as a vast machine composed of objects moving in space. Only the thinking self stood outside this universe of matter extended in space. The inescapable conviction of his own existence that his mental activity produced in Descartes led him to conclude that he was "a substance whose whole nature or essence consists in thinking, and whose existence depends neither on its location in space nor on any material thing."[5]

Cartesian dualism thus posited a fundamental metaphysical separation between the subjective, rational person and objective, material, mechanical nature. Newton, in his turn, set out to demonstrate that all natural phenomena could be explained in terms of indivisible atoms moving in an infinite universe of space under the influence of measurable physical forces and according to universal laws. The Cartesian-Newtonian paradigm established both the description of the material universe and the methodological parameters within which valid knowledge of the universe might be acquired. This paradigm dominated scientific thought in the West until the advent of the "new physics" early in the twentieth century.[6]

It is not surprising, therefore, that when aesthetics emerged as a distinct philosophical discipline in the eighteenth century, its claim to credibility, to having the potential to discover and articulate meaningful truths about art or nature, rested on its identification with objective scientific investigation; indeed, one eighteenth-century philosopher defined aesthetics as "the science of sensory knowledge."[7] Moreover, the space of the physicists—the Newtonian space described as an objective and universal abstraction independent of the atomic matter moving within it—lent itself to consideration of the familiar world as an agglomeration of objects that impinged themselves upon human experience and hence might be observed, analyzed, and classified by a methodical but scrupulously disinterested process of human inquiry. This insistence upon the separation of the observer from the object of study invested visual perception with a privileged function among the senses contributing to the aesthetic experience of an art object: "When the study of art finally achieved its emancipation and identity late in the Enlightenment, this intellectualist visual model . . . became . . . the governing metaphor for the explanation of aesthetic experience, which emerged as a contemplative attitude for appreciating an art object for its sake alone."[8]

The same insistence upon distanced and disinterested observation as the basis for aesthetic judgment was easily transferred to the landscape inasmuch as it was considered as an object for contemplation. Landscape paintings had, in fact, composed an artistic genre singularly suited to the notion that a landscape was best appreciated when contemplated at a distance by an observer outside of the actual scene being depicted: "The desideratum seems to be to regard the painting as a totality, visually objective and complete. Division, distance, separation, and isolation are equally the order of the art and the order of the experience, for the features of the painting shape the character of our perception."[9]

The influence of the painted landscapes of Claude Lorrain, Gaspard Poussin, Nicolas Poussin, and Salvator Rosa on the development of the English landscape gardening school in the eighteenth century has been well documented.[10] Advocates of the new style celebrated its fidelity to nature, in comparison with the deliberate display of artifice and human control in the classical tradition of renaissance and baroque landscape design. Yet the landscape designs of the eighteenth-century "improvers" were dedicated to the creation of a very specific set of images of nature, pastoral or picturesque in character, that were valued for their presumed capacity to excite an aesthetic response in the mind of the human observer of the scene. Edmund Burke's *A Philosophical Inquiry into the Origins of Our Ideas of the Sublime and the Beautiful* (1757) had proposed a descriptive typology for landscapes based on a specific set of physical attributes, just as a scientist might classify biotic types according to their physical characteristics. Beauty, for example, inhered only in scenes or objects that exhibited "Smallness, Smoothness, Gradual Variation, and Delicacy of Form." Burke deemed smoothness so essential to beauty that he could think of nothing beautiful that was not smooth: "In trees and flowers, smooth leaves are beautiful; smooth slopes of earth in gardens; smooth trees in the landscape."[11]

Because the aesthetic experience was chiefly centered in the mind's response to visual stimuli arranged in patterns that transformed a landscape into an object of contemplation, landscape designers of the English school continued to conceive of their art in a way that is analogous to theatrical scenographic composition, just as designers within the earlier classical tradition had done. They relied principally on the manipulation of visual devices to accomplish their ends, borrowing certain techniques, such as the treatment of near and far distances using *repoussoir* (or heightening light and shadow), directly from the landscape painters. But perhaps nothing illustrates better the preoccupation with the careful contrivance of prospects than the frequent employment of such architectural follies as William Kent's "eyecatcher," intended to enliven the distant horizon on the hill across the river from Rousham, or the ruined castle at Wimpole, which joins a gothic tower, two projecting walls, and a screen of trees to convey the false impression of a ruined but actual building.

Similarly, the Reverend Joseph Spence, friend of the poet Alexander Pope and self-styled designer of gardens, listed among his sixteen "general rules" for landscape composition the requirement to "conceal any disagreeable object" and "open a view to whatever is agreeable," as well as to "conceal the bounds of your grounds everywhere." Obviously, the design of landscape scenery required the elimination of whatever features of the real world failed to please the eye and suit

FIG. 39. Drawing, ca. 1740, by William Kent of the mill with attached gothic folly and arched "eyecatcher" sited on a hilltop beyond the garden at Rousham. Country Life Picture Library.

the purposes of the pictorial composition; screening was as essential a device as enframement or focusing. Spence's rules also illuminate the priority given to perspectival devices that control the way the human eye will register the spatial form of the landscape: He urged designers to "make objects that are near seem farther off by showing more of the intermediate ground, increasingly narrowing the view toward them," and to "draw distant objects nearer by planting what will fall in and unite, to the eye, with distant objects."[12]

This application of the renaissance device of false perspective to the practice of the informal or natural style of the English landscape gardening school makes clear the essential continuity underlying the two stylistic traditions, now commonly classified as classical and romantic. The revolutionary aspect of the English eighteenth-century school had to do with a dramatic change in the pictorial content of the designed landscape, and the new formal vocabulary that had to be developed to express that content; it did not challenge the theoretical and philosophical foundations of the renaissance idea that the artist's or designer's task was to produce a work manifesting an abstract but comprehensible visual order and a harmony and balance of parts within the unified whole. To pursue the analogy with the theatrical arts, one might say that the script, the dramatic text, was new, requiring new sets and a new cast of characters, but that the play was performed in the same old theater, with the audience seated silently, as always, outside the proscenium.

The new script, of course, focused chiefly on the man-nature relationship, nature appearing to the eighteenth-century sensibility as the most perfect image of the divine order permeating the complex invisible clockwork of the universe. Raymond Williams has observed a peculiar irony in what he believes to be one consequence of the new attitude toward nature promulgated by the landscape gardening school's "improvers." Williams suggests that when nature became the actual subject matter of the new landscape style, it was thereby absorbed into the same process of objectification that the renaissance legacy of separation between the human observer and the world "out there" had set in motion. Once understood as an objective reality essentially separate from humankind (in spite of our mental and affective responses to it), nature itself could be used, transformed, exploited as a resource or commodity: "As the exploitation of nature continued, on a vast scale, and especially in the new extractive and industrial processes, the people who drew most profit from it went back . . . to an unspoilt nature, to the purchased estates and the country retreats. . . . There is more similarity than we usually recognize between the industrial entrepreneur and the landscape gardener, each altering nature to a consumable form."[13]

Williams further implies that the emergence in the next century of the conservation movement—which might be understood, in his terms, as the effort to set aside reserves of the "nature" commodity—has not always been free of any association with this ambiguous, somewhat compromised defense of nature.[14]

The history of American environmental attitudes, as they developed from the seventeenth century to the present, may be seen as largely continuous with the European paradigm. The astonishing reality of the New World's discovery stimulated a series of metaphorical explanations of how its physical landscape was to be understood—from the rediscovered Eden awaiting the generation of a new Adam, cleansed of the Old World's corruption, to Puritan William Bradford's "hidious and desolate wilderness, full of wild beasts and willd men,"[15] waiting to be redeemed by the unremitting labors of the children of light. Both of these interpretations presumed that a civilizing agrarian order had to be imposed on the raw landscape of America. It was not until the nineteenth century, when the painters of the Hudson River School composed landscape scenes on canvas that framed the American pastoral or picturesque within the pictorial conventions of Claudean tradition, that Americans began to see—literally, to see—their native landscape as an object of aesthetic value. The dawning of that new awareness helped to produce an audience, at mid-century and later, for the burgeoning literature aimed at educating the taste of Americans in art, architecture, and landscape design.

The popular writings of the landscape gardener Andrew Jackson Downing, for example, provided something like a correspondence-school course in aesthetics for middle-class Americans unused to thinking about their domestic properties as a venue for artistic expression, and uncertain about how to proceed with the task of improvement. Landscape gardening differed from ordinary gardening, Downing explained in his *Treatise* of 1841, in that its purpose was "to embody our ideal of a rural home": "It is, in short, the Beautiful, embodied in a homescene. And we attain it by removal or concealment of everything uncouth or discordant, and by the introduction of forms pleasing in their expression, their outlines, and their fitness for the abode of man."[16] Downing thus frankly acknowledged the artifice, abstraction, and manipulation his art demanded; the natural scenes that were to be designed as a proper ambiance for rural villas are not meant to provide an experience of "real" nature. They were, rather, to be idealized landscapes in the tradition either of the Claudean Beautiful or Rosa's Picturesque, as Downing restated these two stylistic canons in his analysis of the "modern" school of English landscape gardening that he offered to Americans as a model. He made it clear that it was the visual and pictorial effect of the whole scene, a harmonious

FIG. 40. Thomas Cole, *River in the Catskills*, 1843. Oil on Canvas, 28 ¼ × 41 ¼ in. (71.1 × 104.7 cm). Note the contemplative figure in the foreground. Gift of Mrs. Maxim Karolik for the Karolik Collection of American Paintings, 1815–1865. Courtesy Museum of Fine Arts, Boston.

composition of house and grounds together, that would convey to the world at large proof of the owner's refined taste and moral respectability.

The values that Downing translated for Americans into a simplified typology of landscape styles have exerted a more tenacious hold on the national psyche than the styles themselves, which are perpetually subject to changes in fashion. These values derive from the long tradition according absolute primacy to visual qualities in designed landscapes of any kind—high-style or vernacular, in cities, towns, suburbs, or strips—and by extension in the natural landscape as well. An appearance of readable order—of harmonious organization according to one or another possible compositional system, however simplified or reduced to a minimal "tidiness"—is seen as an essential attribute of any landscape having aesthetic value, which has therefore come to be thought of as synonymous with visual or scenic quality.

Thus R. Burton Litton, Jr., in describing the goals and methodology of visual inventory and analysis of natural landscapes, insists first of all on the need for a rigorous objectivity and suppression of "personal bias" in the researcher,[17] and then recommends unity, variety, and vividness as the aesthetic criteria by which the visual inventory may be evaluated: "Unity is the quality of all parts being joined

FIG. 41. "Mrs. Camac's Residence," from A. J. Downing, *Treatise on the Theory and Practice of Landscape Gardening, Adapted to North America* . . . (New York, 1841). Hargrett Rare Book and Manuscript Library, University of Georgia Libraries.

FIG. 42. Photo by R. Burton Litton of stratified wilderness, Shoshone National Forest, Wyoming, used to illustrate a "feature landscape" in which dominating landforms create a striking silhouette. R. Burton Litton. From "Visual Assessment of Natural Landscapes," in Barry Sadler and Allen Carlson, eds., *Environmental Aesthetics: Essays in Interpretation* (Victoria, B.C.: Department of Geography, University of Victoria, 1982), 107.

together into a single and harmonious whole. Unity is also expressed by landscape compositional types, one of which is a feature dominated landscape. An example is that of an isolated mountain peak, large in scale and of an unusual skyline contour, dominating a set of smaller scale peaks and ridges along with their forest cover, their lakes and streams."[18]

To understand, in their broad outlines, the artistic and scientific developments that from the time of the Renaissance to the present have determined the cultural predisposition of Western societies to experience the world in particular ways, and with particular expectations, is to come closer to an understanding of ourselves, caught in the vortex of social, intellectual, and even physical processes that challenge, erode, or completely overturn these traditional assumptions, these ingrained and largely unexamined habits of mind—and eye. Twentieth-century theoretical physics has replaced the three-centuries-old Newtonian world view of ordered systems, which were immutable laws of matter operative in the universe beneath the apparent confusion of our perceptual experience, with a description of the world as chaos beneath the illusion of order. It has challenged, across many disciplinary lines, the Cartesian dichotomy between the perceiving self and a measurable, knowable, predictable world outside the self: "In modern physics, the universe is experienced as a dynamic, inseparable whole which always includes the observer in an essential way. . . . Traditional concepts of space and time, of isolated objects, and of cause and effect, lose their meaning."[19]

Within the sciences, an ecological paradigm is being proposed as a useful substitute for mechanistic dualism—with the understanding that ecology in this sense embraces not only biological systems but also nonliving elementary physical systems.[20] In philosophy, in the social sciences, in literature, and in art, new critical languages reflect the struggle to think about the world and the nature and meaning of human activity within it in ways that accommodate the physicists' new vision of the universe. The artist Robert Irwin, who moved from painting to environmental installations that he describes as "phenomenal" and "conditional," has posed the question: "What can we expect to know when we insist on predetermining what is possible by positioning as fundamental the proposition of a simplistic and absolute dichotomy between 'the perceiver' and 'the thing perceived.' . . . What our perception presents us with (at every moment) is an infinitely complex, dynamic, whole envelope of the world and our being in it."[21]

Within the discipline of cultural geography, the same process of revision has led to proposals for alternative aesthetic paradigms, rejecting the conceptualization of the world around us as an agglomeration of distinct objects, in favor of a view of the environment as "total setting," a field of action in which the human observer participates, in which there is continual reciprocal exchange between person and world. Aesthetic values, in this model, would be inseparable from judgments of ecological soundness or well-being.[22] In architecture and landscape design, on the other hand, the principal legacy of modernism has been the central importance attached to formalist values rooted in consideration of the work as an autonomous three-dimensional composition whose aesthetic quality derives largely from the abstract geometry of its structural and spatial relationships and the transparency of its technological solutions. The early twentieth century's failed utopian dream of an architecture that would serve as an instrument of social reform—James Wines speaks of Le Corbusier's "ecstatic vision of elysian communities living in Cartesian towers set in sylvan parks"[23]—became an easy target for critics after World War II. By that time, the proliferation of "super objects," as Manfredo Tafuri labeled the monolithic towers of the International Style,[24] came to be seen as inimical to genuine urbanistic values. Alison and Peter Smithson's *Team 10 Primer* of 1967 summarized a dialogue among a new generation of architects demanding greater emphasis on the needs of communities and more flexible, responsive, and evolutionary design rather than "static monuments."[25] Robert Venturi's *Complexity and Contradiction in Architecture* of 1966 had similarly challenged modernism's purist reductionism, although Venturi's manifesto shifted the argument to a comparative critique of historic styles. His celebration of the deliberate sensuosity and flamboyance both of baroque tradition and of "the everyday landscape, vulgar, and disdained"[26] opened the floodgates to postmodernism's tidal surge of historicism, contextualism, and ornamentalism—often merging fragments from classical sources with familiar elements of the vernacular landscape. Yet, as Martin Filler has observed, postmodernism, "which began . . . as a populist rejection of rigid and repetitive late modernism, has turned out to be just as formalist and schematic as the style it intended to supplant."[27]

By contrast, a significant body of recent architectural criticism draws upon the literature of phenomenology, particularly Martin Heidegger's reflections on an experience of building and of dwelling that becomes one with the experience of being itself and hence is totally alien to the phenomenon of placelessness that increasingly characterizes modern settlements. In an essay proposing an "architecture of resistance" directed toward overcoming the "universalization" that destroys indigenous cultural traditions and regional diversity, Kenneth Frampton uses Heidegger to argue for "a more directly dialectical relation with nature than the more abstract, formal traditions of modern avant-garde architecture will allow." Frampton also wants to encourage architectural strategies to replace the inordinate emphasis on visual perception with an appreciation for the way "a whole range of complementary sensory perceptions . . . are registered by a labile body: the intensity of light, darkness, heat and cold; the feeling of humidity; the aroma of material; the almost palpable presence of masonry as the body senses its own confinement; the momentum of the induced gait and the relative inertia of the body as it traverses the floor; the echoing resonance of our own footfall." Such realities, Frampton maintains, "can only be decoded in terms of experience itself; [they] cannot be reduced to mere information, to representation or to the simple evocation of a simulacrum substituting for absent presences."[28] In making the heightened awareness of a person physically and psychologically responding to a building or a place a critical aspect of its realization as architecture or landscape, Frampton stands against the dominant cultural tradition that gives primacy to pictorial and scenographic values.

Reflection upon the historical evolution within our cultural tradition that has predisposed us, whether we are aware of it or not, to apply certain aesthetic criteria in evaluating the landscapes with which we engage ought to have the effect of stimulating an exploration of alternative values as grounds for judgment. Without such an effort, we will continue to live and move blindly within environments that we fail to see or to know intimately or profoundly, simply because we are conditioned to view them with an appraising eye, to see how they measure up against subliminal standards of visual organization and landscape meaning that we have been taught to value exclusively, indifferent to the wealth of knowing, feeling, and caring for places that begins with our earliest childhood experiences of engaging the world. Indifferent, too, as Raymond Williams suggested, to the processes at work in environments that meet or fail to meet arbitrary standards of visual acceptability or beauty. McLuhan said that it was long past time to put aside the "aloof and dissociated role of the literate Westerner. . . . The partial and specialized character of the viewpoint, however noble, will not serve at all in the electric age. . . . The aspiration of our time [is] for wholeness, empathy, and depth of awareness."[29]

DENIS COSGROVE

8

Spectacle and Society:
Landscape as Theater in
Premodern and
Postmodern Cities

One of the most pervasive features of contemporary land-
scapes is the conscious creation and manipulation of meaning through place images. The architectural references in both new "greenfield" landscapes like West
Edmonton Mall and Eurodisney and in the recycled heritage landscapes of cities
like Baltimore and Glasgow are a key element in the success of spaces designed
for consumption. As the critic David Harvey puts it, selling these landscapes rests
upon "the projection of a definite image of place blessed with certain qualities,
the organization of spectacle and theatricality [which has] been achieved through
an eclectic mixture of styles, historical quotation, ornamentation and diversification of surfaces."[1]

The commercial success of such landscapes depends on the way consumers
interpret them and is prompted by sophisticated representation that is often directly provided through promotional literature, museum techniques, written
identification, simple and repeated graphic motifs, and organized performance
and pageantry.[2] For example, in Glasgow—European city of culture in 1990—
more than a thousand events and spectacles were scheduled into a program of
public celebration of place through a re-presented landscape.

Making sense of these postmodern landscapes has challenged critical and progressive commentators. Theorists have regarded the superficial, fragmented,
capricious, and spectacular aspects of these landscapes and their emphasis on the
play of images as a deceptive mask that hides deeper, less attractive realities. One
of the most sustained and serious critics has been David Harvey, who reads the
postmodern landscape with its "architecture of spectacle, . . . its sense of surface

99

glitter and transitory pleasure, or display and ephemerality" as a logical response to the most recent phase of space-time compression in capitalist development and its concomitant cycle of "creative destruction." Harvey persistently distrusts images as depthless and superficial, aligning them with aesthetics, while he privileges the capacity of text and narrative to represent a true and thus ethical history: "Aesthetics has triumphed over ethics as a prime focus of social and intellectual concern, images dominate narratives, ephemerality and fragmentation take precedence over eternal truths and unified politics, and explanations have shifted from the realm of material and political-economic groundings towards a consideration of autonomous cultural and political practices."[3]

Elsewhere, Harvey reads the contrast between image and text as one between being and becoming, the former reactionary, the latter progressive. He regards the visual image as somehow less truthful, less real, than the word and the text; the argument of the eye less trustworthy than that of the mind.

The tension between visual and textual truth that Harvey resolves so decisively in favor of the latter is the subject of this chapter. But rather than present the relation between image and text as one of opposition, I shall present it as a dialectic between representational modes, or metaphors, historically in a constant and intense struggle over meaning. In Western culture it is in theater that visual and textual modes of representation have been most fully integrated, and since the Renaissance the history of theater has been intimately related to the development of landscape.[4] I shall explore the use of spectacle and theater as spatial metaphors in the Renaissance to throw light of the struggle between visual and textual truth in contemporary landscape criticism.

To exemplify the argument I shall concentrate on sixteenth-century Venice. I shall examine two painted images of Venetian landscape, relating them to the changes in both textual strategies in historical writing and modes of theatrical representation that were taking place in Venice, the greatest commercial city of medieval Europe, struggling to adjust to the economic, geopolitical, technical, and cultural changes that were ushering in the modern world.[5] The role played by landscape and its representation in the commercial and cultural life of Venice at that time bears similarities to that played in postmodern consumption spaces.

Spectacle and Theater as Metaphors in the Renaissance

Distrust of images is deep-seated in Western thinking, following a long conservative tradition of respect for the stable and substantive authority of text—biblical, scholastic, philosophical—and distrust of the mutability, versatility, and disguise associated with visual representation. Iconoclasm has been strongly aligned with moral zeal for Holy Writ, both sacred and secular: in the regular destruction of images in the Byzantine church and in the iconic depredations of Calvinist and Stalinist regimes. European culture simultaneously has given primacy to sight as a pathway to true knowledge while deeply suspecting it.[6] Western thinkers have frequently sought to probe beneath the world's appearances to reach a deeper, more authentic truth which can only be fixed in text: in the written word or mathematical symbol.

For those concerned with landscape, however, it seems impossible not to take the visual image seriously. In Europe, the word *landscape* was used to refer to a painted image long before it was applied to actual environments. The compositional language of designed landscape has been derived so strongly from the visual arts that restricting landscape analysis to a textual metaphor, which is strongly advocated by some contemporary commentators, seems historically and empirically perverse.[7] On the other hand, offering a theory of landscape does require translating landscape into words and text. Thus, landscape critics and scholars are inevitably drawn back, to a degree, to texts.

Sixteenth-century Europe witnessed both the emergence of landscape as a new way of representing human relations with the physical environment and, in the humanist search for truth through analogy and correspondence, a brief period of close linkage between visual and textual truth.[8] We can observe this in the metaphorical complexity of visual terms at this time. The word *spectacle,* for example, could mean simple display or it could mean something to wonder at, something mysterious and magical. It could also take on the sense of a mirror through which truths that could not be stated directly could be seen reflected and perhaps distorted. Finally, it could mean an aid to more accurate vision, as in corrective eye lenses.[9]

Spectacle was a consistent ingredient in theater, although renaissance humanists were beginning to distinguish more clearly than their medieval forebears between pageant and scripted drama in the classical sense.[10] Theater itself not only had the architectural meaning, derived from the ancients, of a playhouse and the performances staged there, but also meant a conspectus: a place, region, or text in which phenomena are unified for public understanding. Not surprisingly, this sense of theater was particularly appropriate for representing scientific knowledge, notably of the greater world of the cosmos or the globe (the name of Shakespeare's own theater) and the lesser world of the human body. Abraham Ortelius's great world atlas of 1570 was titled *Teatrum Urbis Terrarum* and published within a decade or so of Giulio Camillo's famous "memory theater" in Venice, constructed as a mnemonic for all human knowledge.[11] The painter Pieter Brueghel, an intimate of Ortelius, represented the world's landscape as a stage upon which human life was acted out.[12] Descriptions or chorographies of local areas were conceived in terms of theatrical observation, combining written historical and geographical narrative with graphic illustrations that seem today as much landscape paintings as maps. John Speed's work *The Theatre of the Empire of Great Britaine* (1611) is an example. Such works were also given the title *speculum,* picking up the sense of visual truth. Thus theater, understood as a glass or mirror to the greater world, was a common metaphor for revealing order in the macrocosm through an interplay of image and text.

Correspondingly, in the case of the microcosm, the human body was examined and displayed as a public spectacle in the anatomy theater. The sixteenth century saw the construction of the first such structures, in Padua and Bologna. Their rising circles of concentric seating, from which one looked down on the lesser world of the corpse displayed on the dissection table, were analogous to the structure of the greater world. Anatomy theaters had by law to be open to the public, who came masqued for dissections, which were officially scheduled at Carnival season and regarded as one of its spectacles.[13]

Spectacle in Venice

The concept of carnival is frequently employed in discussions of representation and promotion in postmodern consumption spaces. In the renaissance city one can observe a parallel significance of carnival as a significant element in both civic and commercial life. It was the most temporally extended and socially inclusive of the many public events that regularly punctuated the annual calendar of the premodern city and which deployed architecture and landscape to generate civic solidarity.

Renaissance Venice was the paradigmatic city of such spectacular civic ritual,[14] and its urban landscape has consistently been read and represented as theater. In renaissance Venice on at least ninety days normal work was suspended for what historians until recently have regarded as noneconomic activities, including thirty *andante,* scheduled excursions by the doge for ritual visits to specified points within the city and lagoon.[15] Such moments of highly choreographed public display demanded the widest possible participation, incorporating both citizens and visitors through a series of overlapping allegiances. Regular procession and spectacle bound together the entire community, the body politic, in rehearsing the political and moral order of the city. They celebrated and reproduced the Venetian sense of place, of Venice as a complete and perfect world, which was architecturally inscribed above all at the political heart of the city: the great stage setting of the Piazza di San Marco and the Piazzetta.[16]

In light of developments in the postmodern consumption economy, we are coming to recognize that these events also had considerable economic significance: "rather than reducing the working year, public festivities may have extended it, for they offered opportunities for advertisement and sale of luxury goods, stimulated the growth of the service sector and generated casual employment."[17] On a great festival, such as Ascension Day, when the doge ritually married Venice to the sea, the city was crowded with merchants and pilgrims awaiting the opening of the sailing season; the display took on something of the character of a trade fair. While "some festivals make the government appear the pupils of Macchiavelli, from another angle they look like a tourist board."[18]

The focus of Venetian ritual was, of course, the Piazza di San Marco and its surrounding buildings. Often described as a stage set, this celebrated apotheosis of urban landscape design is, in fact, an eclectic assemblage of architectural styles. Its focal element, the Basilica di San Marco, is a pastiche of Santa Sophia in Byzantium decorated by the random spoils of Venetian pillage in the East: bronze horses, porphyry columns, and marble panels. San Marco's buildings and spaces were continuously altered and elaborated, most comprehensively in the middle years of the sixteenth century.[19] It provided a vast setting in which more than a third of the city's population could gather to participate in celebrations of the *genius urbis* (spirit of the city). It would not be inaccurate to describe this space in terms now regularly employed for postmodern landscape: "an architecture of spectacle, with its sense of surface glitter and transitory pleasure, of display and ephemerality, or jouissance."[20] In the piazza every genre of public spectacle could and did take place, from ecclesiastical ritual and the display of treasured relics gathered in the basilica to state processions organized around the person of the doge, to the burlesque of carnival and the antics of popular circus performers.

We can discover much of Venetian ritual from the texts of diarists and other written archival sources, but the most vivid record exists in graphic images, on the great canvases that decorated the walls of the *alberghi* (boardrooms-cum-shrines) of the Venetian *scuole* (corporate bodies that played a central role in the social and ceremonial life of Venice). Although open to the nobility, they were governed by non-nobles and their constitutions and privileges mirrored those of the state, allowing an outlet for the political and status aspirations of groups that were otherwise disenfranchised by Venice's impenetrable oligarchy. Scuole participation in state ritual emphasized this function and their members would compete for privileged places in the tightly ordered and highly stratified processions, in which ceremonially robed scuole members displayed their own precious relics and icons, simultaneously revealing their craft skills: "The mast of the brig furnished by the *specchieri* [mirror makers and glaziers] was decorated with mirrors which flashed in the sun, hurting the eyes of the spectators. They were outshone, however, by the goldsmiths who decorated their boat with a 'lantern made completely from cups and chalices of gold and silver, and from every angle the boat shone, thanks to the great quantities of gold and silver on display all over it.'"[21]

Competition was also practiced in commissions for decorating the meeting rooms of the scuola. The standard form was to commission a cycle of paintings celebrating miraculous events connected with the scuola's patron, or members or sacred relics. Almost invariably, these events were shown to take place either at recognizable locations within the city of Venice or in invisible cities—imaged and imagined places constituted by fanciful reassembly of Venetian buildings. Thus the most significant events of the scuole were integrated with the public meaning of the republic; painting acted as a spectacular mirror in which the meaning of Venice was reflected and enhanced. Normally, the cycle of paintings corresponded to a written chronicle held, and at times updated, by the confraternity itself—a text that legitimized the scuole's myth, but, as we shall see, a text that was itself subordinate to the visual image.

We shall consider two such images whose differences reveal something of the ways that the relationship between image and text was being reconstituted in Renaissance Venice. The first is Gentile Bellini's *Procession in the Piazza di San Marco,* painted as part of a cycle of nine images for the Scuola Grande di San Giovanni Evangelista in the opening years of the sixteenth century. The second is Jacopo Tintoretto's *Translation of St. Mark's Body* from a cycle produced in the 1550s for the Scuola Grande di San Marco. Both illustrate a dramatic and miraculous event and locate it recognizably in the heart of Venice, in the Piazza di San Marco in Bellini's case and in the courtyard of the Doge's Palace in Tintoretto's. Both also display the body of Venice, but place the corporeal metaphor differently.

Procession in the Piazza di San Marco

Bellini's *Procession in the Piazza di San Marco* is a perfect example of what has been called the "eyewitness" style of Venetian narrative painting. This style originally developed in the decorative mosaic cycles of the Basilica di San Marco and reached its peak at the turn of the sixteenth century in the painted scuole cycles by the Bellini family, Vittore Carpaccio, Giovanni Mansueti, and Lazzaro Bastiani. In these painters' works a sacred event recorded by chroniclers is presented in recognizable landscape and authenticated by the presence of large numbers of ordinary people.

In the Bellini *Procession* the specific miraculous event is implied rather than demonstrated and it would pass unnoticed by an uninitiated observer, as it does to most of the scores of people shown on the canvas. In the group of men who watch the white-robed brothers of the scuole display their most precious relic— a fragment of the true cross—in the doge's procession, one single figure kneels. He is Jacopo de Salis, a merchant whose son is at this moment dying in Brescia

FIG. 43. Gentile Bellini, *Procession in the Piazza di San Marco.* Accademia, Venice. Courtesy of Osvaldo Bohm.

from a fractured skull. The father's act of piety will result in the miracle of his son's complete recovery.

Gentile's image is a sophisticated and highly dramatic landscape representation. Clever manipulation of perspective opens to our eyes the full width of the piazza while simultaneously enhancing the elevation of the Basilica di San Marco, the iconographic heart of the republic. The event occurs during a key ritual in the Venetian calendar, the doge's procession on the Feast of St. Mark, which wound around the piazza en route from the palace to mass in the basilica.

The composition allows Gentile to give prominence to the commissioning scuola while showing its members soberly participating in the broader civic ritual, even to the point of displaying the crests of other scuole along the fringe of the canopy that protects and enhances their own icon. Thus the corporate body of Venice, both in its political expression of doge, Senate, and Great Council, and in its more demotic form of the scuole, is displayed on the ordered stage of the gridded piazza.

In the same space a recognizable cross-section of Venice's cosmopolitan population—*popolari* (the largest class of Venetians, neither nobles nor citizens), Germans, Greeks, Turks, indigents, and a dwarf—emphasize universal participation in the normality of the event. Flattened like a backdrop, but dominating the scene at the perspective point of the painting, is the basilica, whose portal mosaics (rendered by Gentile with astonishing accuracy) record another miraculous cycle, the ninth-century translation of St. Mark's body to Venice and its burial in the basilica, which is the legitimizing story of the Venetian myth.

Although the specific miracle is not seen, Jacopo's act is witnessed by the entire body of Venice and by us, just as the procession itself is witnessed by and gives witness to the place of rest for the evangelist's body. Gentile's emphasis on the basilica as the miraculous heart of the holy city and the ritual procession in honor of Venice's patron render the specific miracle of healing more natural—it occurs in a sacred place, while the numbers of witnesses and the arbitrary point that the procession has reached make it singular.

Spectators are a crucial element in these "eyewitness" paintings. The narrative techniques of the works correspond to the chronicle mode of historical writing still favored in early renaissance Venice, one in which the authenticity of the text depended upon maximizing both local detail and numbers of testimonials. Indeed, pictures themselves, like Gentile's, would be called upon by later chroniclers, who would authenticate the truth of their written histories by offering verbal descriptions of events as they had been depicted in paint: "A painting was . . . more than an evocation of the past, or a vehicle for inciting religious devotion through the representation of a miraculous event. It was, in fact, a piece of testimony with a status equivalent to a public document or written history: an instrument of proof that such an event had actually happened."[22]

The huge cast of individuals in these paintings acts like the chorus in Greek drama; its presence mediates between audience and event, establishing the credibility of the latter to the former. In this sense the "eyewitness" paintings are doubly theatrical, but in the sense of theater as spectacle or pageant, one that privileges image over text, presenting a static image of being rather than a narrative or change and becoming.

Translation of St. Mark's Body

Renaissance humanists distrusted the "eyewitness" painters' appeals to vision alone as a guarantor of truth, and, indeed, the entire mode of chronicle history writing. They placed their trust, rather, in the authority of authenticated text. Among the critical humanist contributions to historical scholarship were emphasizing the accuracy of the text—identifying original documents and securing their authenticity through philological techniques; the contextual placing of the text to establish a single, correct meaning; the challenging of historical myths through ascertainable facts: names, dates, words, and documents (that is, textually); the establishment of a secular history freed from eschatology and appeals to divine intervention; and the use of new disciplines like archeology, numismatics, and topography as aids to historical verification.

In writing their narratives, however, humanist historians did more than merely record the sources upon which they drew. Their histories were to be *in-*

FIG. 44. Jacopo Tintoretto, *Translation of St. Mark's Body.* Accademia, Venice. Courtesy of Osvaldo Bohm.

venzioni, personal syntheses, based upon true sources but composed in such a way as to expose the causal structures behind the events they described and to elicit the underlying order in the world of appearances. In other words, they revealed truth through their own texts. A key technique for achieving this was rhetoric, the contrived use of elegant language and grammar to gain maximum moral and emotional force in the narration. In every way, then, humanism elevated text over image: *ut pictura poesis.* The most elevated genre of painting was *istoria,* which depicted the "great deeds of great men" and was composed according to a clear spatial and narrative hierarchy. Istoria provided a parallel in painting to the changes in historical narrative, conjoining both image and text while subordinating the former to the latter. History painting indicates another feature of renaissance humanist culture: the celebration of the individual, including the stature and dignity of the individual human body. These ideas influenced the mainstream of Venetian culture from the turn of the sixteenth century.

They are exemplified in the historical writings of Marchese Vincenzo Giustiniani, Sabellico, and Navagero, and in the paintings of Titian, Paolo Veronese, and Tintoretto.[23]

When we turn to Tintoretto's painting, we see the full impact of humanism's resolution to the discourse of text and image. It depicts the moment in A.D. 828 when two Venetian merchants, having removed the body of St. Mark from its sarcophagus, carry it through the streets of Alexandria to begin the return voyage to Venice. The presence of the uncorrupted body allows the merchants miraculous passage through the hostile Alexandrian streets, terrifying those who would prevent the body's removal.[24]

Tintoretto's composition is dominated by the merchants and, above all, by the muscular, foreshortened body of the saint. St. Mark's body, whose physical presence in Venice legitimated the mythical meaning of Venetian landscape, is re-presented to us in anatomical detail, much as actual bodies were publicly displayed in the anatomy theater. It is placed to the right of the central perspective axis defined by the architectural setting and the gridded markings of the piazza. That axis is deceptive, leading past the center of the drama to an indistinct white building in the depth of the painting. The drama of the event is increased by a complex set of diagonals: a fallen camel driver attempting to restrain his frightened beast, another man on the ground clutching a violently flapping curtain, and the sepulchral figures rushing panic-stricken into a building on the left which is modeled on the interior courtyard of the Palazzo Ducale at Venice. The sky is thunderous, the illumination eerie, and the atmosphere ghostly.

The composition is highly theatrical, not to say melodramatic. Indeed, "theater" in the architectural and narrative sense seems a more appropriate term here than "spectacle" or "pageant," terms that apply to Bellini's *Procession in the Piazza di San Marco*. The architectural setting resembles contemporary indoor stage designs for the tragic scene and the sharp perspectives of Palladio's contemporary Olympic Theater at Vicenza. The central characters tumble precipitously toward us, locked together in tense physical interaction and caught at a moment snatched from a continuing drama, rather than parading in separate, static pageant before us. The event is authenticated rhetorically rather than through factual detail and observation, a textual as much as a visual strategy.

The reasons for this shift in the relative authority of the narrative and pictorial modes in Venetian culture are complex. Some result from developments in humanist discourse and changing influences and fashions in painting, notably the influence of exiled Roman painters in mid-sixteenth-century Venice. They also reflect an altered political and ideological climate. Tintoretto's Venice, the only remaining free republic in an Italy otherwise dominated by Spain and France, was no longer the secure and serene city-state of Gentile's time. It was severely threatened by Turkish power, its maritime hegemony was under strain from the emerging Atlantic economies, and it was struggling for religious autonomy against the Counter-Reformation papacy. Its own internal ideological structures were tightening and the modes of public participation in civic spectacle and theater were being recast by an increasingly aristocratic patriciate.

The Venetian noble Daniele Barbaro's discussion of *scenografia* (scenography) at midcentury applies a patrician humanist concept of rank and hierarchy to theater. Not only does he accept the Aristotelian hierarchy of tragedy, comedy, and satire (with its social, spatial, corporeal, and gender correlates), but he suggests a threefold ranking of public drama into *theater* properly so called—an enclosed structure for the performance of scripted plays and musical recitals— *amphitheater* for athletics and feats of physical prowess, and *circus* for the performance of gladiators and animals. Each should have its own appropriate building and location in the city, and each consciously appeals to a different social rank.[25] Quite clearly, the scripted performance, based on a text, is here elevated over the purely visual spectacle, and the raising of tragedy over all other dramatic forms tends to tarnish lesser genres of theater with moral disapproval. The text-based form of theater is the preserve of those in power, those with authority through their exercise of reason. This form of theater takes place increasingly in the closed playhouse, away from vulgar gaze. More purely visual, spectacular forms of theater are for the masses—they appeal to sense rather than intellect. By the same token, Tintoretto represents the body of Venice no longer as public and corporate, but as mystical and individual: the sacred, uncorrupted corpse of St. Mark.

If we raise our vision from the local and contingent changes in society and culture in Venice over the years that elapsed between Gentile's and Tintoretto's works, we may read these two images in the broader context of the emerging modernism that Harvey is concerned to document. Venice was the paradigm merchant capitalist city of the premodern age. Its landscape—through architecture, ritual, and painting—both expressed and legitimated its economic life, social cohesion, and political order. The processes that would result in Venice's decline as an economic and political power and the congealing of its social order were increasingly in evidence by the later sixteenth century, when Tintoretto was painting. The rise of the Atlantic economies as the organizing core of a world system, the European struggles over reformed and individualist Christianity, the scientific and technological revolution, and the adoption of new conceptions of space and time were intensely felt in Venice and debated among its intellectual and patrician class.[26] While it is inaccurate to see renaissance humanists as simple forefathers of the Enlightenment, they stand at the juncture of the premodern and modern worlds, anticipating many of the latter's key intellectual features: "All Enlightenment projects had in common a relatively unified common-sense of what space and time were about and why their rational ordering was important. This common basis in part depended on the popular availability of watches and clocks, and on the capacity to diffuse cartographic knowledge by cheaper and more efficient techniques. But it also rested upon the link between Renaissance perspectivism and a conception of the individual as the ultimate source and container of social power."[27]

These are all aspects of modernism that Harvey regards as presently under challenge from postmodernism. Venice's landscape thus gives us an insight into struggles over representation in the period of transition to the modern period, struggles that suggest parallels with those surrounding its presumed closure today. There are highly suggestive similarities between Bellini's representational strategy and the ways that landscapes are deployed in the production and promotion of place images today. In Bellini's static image, the aesthetics of display seek to express the moral solidarity of the entire Venetian commonwealth as an achieved and perfect state. In Tintoretto we anticipate the modern in the ethical elevation of text over image, individual over collective, and becoming over being.

It would be wrong to freight our two landscape images of Venice with the entire burden of the change from premodern to modern modes of spatial apprehension and representation, although I have indicated how aspects of that change may be read into them. However, in their very distinct and different approaches to image and text, surface and depth, spectacle and dramatic narrative, they serve to remind us that Harvey's critique of the depthless superficiality of the image in postmodern culture and urban landscape and his ethical promotion of textual truth revives an old debate whose connections with the modern are complex and historically deep.

Finally, this comparison of landscape representations extends the search for appropriate metaphors to theorize landscape and society. The theatrical metaphor allows us to make a serious and critical response to certain features of the postmodern landscape, one that takes visual images seriously, regarding them as one among the many discursive fields in which we may represent truth, rather than merely as "a veil [obscuring] real geography through construction of images and reconstructions, costume dramas, staged ethnic festivals, etc."[28] The metaphor of theater allows us to place image into a dialectical unity with text and to approach ethical and political questions through analogical discourses rather than attempting, in vain, to construct a totalizing landscape theory.

DOLORES HAYDEN

9   Urban Landscape History: The Sense of Place and the Politics of Space

> Authentic knowledge of space must address the question of its production. —HENRI LEFEBVRE, *The Production of Space*

Every American city and town contains fragments of historic cultural landscapes intertwined with its current spatial configuration. Layered with the traces of previous generations' struggles to survive economically, raise children, and participate in community life, the vernacular landscape, as John Brinckerhoff Jackson writes, "is the image of our common humanity—hard work, stubborn hope, and mutual forbearance striving to be love."[1] His definition carries cultural geography and architecture straight toward urban history. At the intersection of these fields lies the history of the cultural landscape, the history of human patterns impressed upon the contours of the natural environment. It is the story of how places are planned, designed, built, inhabited, appropriated, celebrated, despoiled, and discarded. Cultural identity, social history, and urban design are here intertwined.

Indigenous residents as well as colonizers, ditchdiggers as well as architects, migrant workers as well as mayors, housewives as well as housing inspectors, are all active shaping the urban landscape. Change over time can be traced in incremental modifications of space as much as in an original city plan or building plan. This essay proposes a way to frame the history of urban space, a scholarly terrain where many fields overlap. It combines an approach to aesthetics (based on work dealing with the sense of place from the humanities, architecture, and landscape traditions in geography and environmental psychology) with an approach to politics (based on work on space in the social sciences and economic geography) and suggests how both apply to the history of urban landscapes.

The Sense of Place

Place is one of the trickiest words in the English language, a suitcase so overfilled that one can never shut the lid. It carries the resonance of homestead, location, and open space in the city as well as a position in a social hierarchy. The authors of books on architecture, photography, cultural geography, poetry, and travel rely on "sense of place" as an aesthetic concept but often settle for "the personality of a location" as a way of defining it. "Place" for such authors may engage mellow brick in an eighteenth-century building, the sweep of the Great Plains, or the bustle of a harbor full of sailboats, but such images can easily become clichés of tourist advertising. In the nineteenth century and earlier, "place" also meant the right of a person to own a piece of land, or to be a part of a social world, and in this older sense, "place" implies more political history. Phrases like "knowing one's place" or "a woman's place" still have both physical and political meanings.

People make attachments to places that are critical to their well-being or distress. An individual's sense of place is both a biological response to the surrounding physical environment and a cultural creation, as the geographer Yi-Fu Tuan has argued.[2] From childhood, humans come to experience and know places through all five senses, sight as well as sound, smell, taste, and touch. Extensive research on perception shows the simultaneous engagement of several senses in orientation and wayfinding. Children show an interest in landmarks at three or earlier and by age five or six can read aerial maps with great accuracy and confidence, revealing the human ability to perceive and remember the landscape.[3] Tuan also notes that cross-cultural studies reveal heightened sensitivities to certain kinds of places. The Aivilik of northern Canada can describe many kinds of snowy landscapes; the Puluwat Islanders of the Pacific can read minute variations in ocean currents. Yet it would be wrong to say that sense of place is primarily determined this way. Among the Aivilik gender accounts for marked differences. Settlements and trading posts appear on cognitive maps drawn by women, while coastline is the key to those made by men.[4]

Because social relationships are intertwined with spatial perception, human attachment to places attracts researchers from many fields. The environmental psychologists Setha M. Low and Irwin Altman define "place attachment" as a psychological process similar to an infant's attachment to parental figures. They also suggest that place attachment can develop social, material, and ideological dimensions, as individuals create ties to kin and neighbors, own or rent land, and participate in public life as residents of a particular community.[5] Some earlier sociological studies by Peter Marris of the aftermath of urban renewal convey the process of mourning for a lost neighborhood and use attachment theory to explain the power of human connections to places that may no longer exist physically.[6]

Cultural landscape studies, as the geographer Carl Sauer developed them, focused on the evolution of places and included the "combination of natural and man-made elements that comprises, at any given time, the essential character of a place."[7] Cultural landscape, as Sauer introduced it, had slightly more specific meanings than place. Yet the earliest cultural landscape methods for studying places and people's attachments to them were not adequate to convey fully the political dimensions of places. Unlike social history, which developed an urban bias from the 1960s on, cultural geography, from the 1940s on, leaned to the study of rural, preindustrial landscapes rather than the complicated urban variety, mapping ethnicity along with vernacular house types or patterns of cultivation, considering ecology but avoiding issues of political contestation.[8]

As the cultural landscape is more densely inhabited, the economic and social forces that shape it are more complex, change is more rapid, layers proliferate, and abrupt spatial discontinuities often result. Cultural landscape studies often seem unable to address these discontinuities adequately. One can't simply turn to economic geography or any other kind of quantitative analysis where the human experience of place is often lost. Rather, the cultural geographer's model of landscape needs to be better anchored in the urban realm, retaining the biological and cultural insights necessary to convey the sense of place while adding more focused analysis of social and economic conflict. This is the project of many politically sensitive geographers today.[9] At the same time, environmental historians such as William Cronon have laid claim to some of this same subject matter, with phrases that sound rather like Sauer: "if environmental history is successful in its project, the story of how different peoples have lived and used the natural world will become one of the most basic and fundamental narratives in all of history, without which no understanding of the past could be complete."[10] Yet for many environmental historians, the deployment of land and natural resources has been the central preoccupation, without much concern for the aesthetic and social aspects of the built environment, although the two are intertwined.

At the heart of Carl Sauer's definition of the cultural landscape was "the essential character of a place." It has often proved easier to study either the natural or the built components of a cultural landscape than to wrestle with the combination of the two in the concept of place. Today cultural landscapes are the subject of a good deal of academic research, but the authors are scattered in half a dozen disciplines (history, geography, architecture, urban planning, landscape architecture, art history, and folklore among them). At the same time that research on urban space is progressing, the authors of recent popular books about late twentieth-century urban landscapes have proclaimed the end of urban public space in sweeping, journalistic fashion, predicting that most Americans will soon live in a "placeless" commercial world of shopping malls and theme parks, a privatized, suburban "edge city" that can be contrasted with an anarchic, violent inner city, filled with new immigrants and long-term poor, especially people of color and female-headed households.[11] It is important to develop a more balanced body of scholarship in American urban landscape history as a response to this kind of polemic, a scholarship that explores inner-city neighborhoods and discusses what dimensions of political power are rooted in urban places.

If place does provide an overload of possible meanings for the researcher, it is place's very assault on all ways of knowing (sight, sound, smell, touch, and taste) that makes it powerful as a source of memory, as a weave where one strand ties in another. Place needs to be at the heart of urban landscape history, not on the margins, because the aesthetic qualities of the natural and built environments, positive and negative, are just as important as the political struggles over space often dealt with by urban historians and social scientists.

The Politics of Space

Henri Lefebvre, the French sociologist who began writing about the "production of space" more than two decades ago, provides a framework that can be used to relate the sense of place encountered in cultural landscape studies to the political economy. Lefebvre has argued that every society in history has shaped a distinctive social space that meets its intertwined requirements for economic production and social reproduction.[12] In terms of economic production, Lefebvre would be close to cultural geography in identifying spaces or landscapes shaped for mining, manufacturing, commerce, or real estate speculation. More original is his analysis of the space of social reproduction, which ranges over different scales, including the space in and around the body (biological reproduction), the space of housing (the reproduction of the labor force), and the public space of the city (the reproduction of social relations). Here he links the physical to the social in decisive ways. (More speculative are his analyses of the role of artists' representations of space and the role of popular political movements in creating what he calls "counter-space" in opposition to existing political structures.) The cultural critic Fredric Jameson has assessed Lefebvre's importance: Lefebvre "called for a new kind of spatial imagination capable of confronting the past in a new way and reading its less tangible secrets off the template of its spatial structures—body, cosmos, city."[13]

Lefebvre suggests that space is a medium through which social life is produced and reproduced. A small factory on a stream near a waterfall, with a boarding house and a couple of workers' cottages, announces New England in the earliest stages of industrial textile production; a vast aerospace complex next to a suburban tract of ten thousand identical houses exemplifies defense industries and their work force 150 years later. But Lefebvre also sees commonalities between the tract houses, the identical suites in corporate skyscrapers, and the identical shops in malls, suggesting that a quality of late twentieth-century capitalist space is the creation of many identical units—similar but not "placeless" places—by the large commercial real estate market that has become, in itself, a distinguishing feature of the economy. And just as analysts begin to count the environmental costs that this production of endless units of salable space may entail, so the cultural costs in terms of identity, history, and meaning can be weighed.[14]

Lefebvre's approach to the production of space can provide a framework for constructing some specific social histories of urban places. Depending on the kinds of arguments historians want to make (and the resources available in oral histories, social histories, and buildings), researchers might explore working landscapes, territorial histories of groups in the population, or political histories of building types. The first focuses on economic production as it is tied to social reproduction, the others make social reproduction the major theme.

Working Landscapes

The production of space begins as soon as indigenous residents locate themselves in a particular landscape and begin the search for subsistence. The place may grow into a town, inhabited by new waves of settlers. Many cities begin with farming, mining, fishing, or trading rather than manufacturing. The farm laborers, the miners, the fishermen, or the stall holders in the market, and their families, are the earliest builders of the economic enterprise that eventually becomes a city. Space is shaped both for economic production—barns, or mine shafts, or piers, or a factory—and for social reproduction—housing for the workers, managers, and owners, a store, a school, a church. As the town grows, the act of configuring streets and lots formalizes the earliest uses of land and path systems. Next comes the creation of infrastructure such as paved streets, bridges, water systems, streetcars, and railroads, all of which have substantial environmental effects.

All of these different kinds of private and public planning activities and public works have a social as well as a technological history.[15] Citizens fight for and against them. Workers construct and maintain them. The ditchdiggers and pile drivers, the streetcar workers and the railroad mechanics, the canal drivers and crane operators represent class, ethnic, and gender history shaping the landscape in ways that have barely been studied. As the environmental historian Patricia Nelson Limerick has observed: "Workers, often minority workers, provided the

FIG. 45. Workers' landscapes: Chinese-American railroad workers on the tracks, next to an Anglo-American supervisor, near Lang, Calif., 1876. Security Pacific Collection, Los Angeles Public Library.

essential labor of environmental change, and members of minority groups often absorbed a disproportionate share of undesirable environmental impacts . . . yet environmental history and ethnic history have been very separate enterprises."[16]

The history of the railroad in the nineteenth century offers just one of many possible examples. One can understand the railroad in engineering terms, as the history of trains and tracks, or in architectural terms, as stations and freight yards, or in urban planning terms, as the right and the wrong side of the tracks, without fully capturing its social history as the production of space. Limerick notes that twenty-nine Chinese workers died and dozens more were injured while building Wrights Tunnel for the South Pacific Coast Railroad through the Santa Cruz Mountains in California in 1879. Other historians have commented that the Chinese "contributed" to California's economic development. Limerick goes farther: the "'price of progress' had registered in the smell of burnt human flesh." She concludes, "In our times the rediscovery of the landscape hinges on just such recognitions as this one."[17] One could add that coming to terms with ethnic history in the landscape requires engaging with such bitter experiences, as well as the indifference and denial surrounding them.

Like a worker's dwelling, which may suggest how millions of people were sheltered, something as basic as a railroad or streetcar system reveals the quality of everyday life in the urban landscape, while marking the terrain.[18] For some it provides jobs in design, construction, operation, or maintenance; for others, it makes a journey to work through the city possible; for a few, it may be an investment that brings profits. John R. Stilgoe has shown how to study the clustering of different vernacular building types along railroad lines and the concept of the space of the railway as a "metropolitan corridor."[19] As Limerick demonstrates, there is also an important underlying story to tell about the labor force and the social space of the metropolitan corridor, from the people who blasted the tunnels and drove the trains right down to the workers who kept the cars clean and emptied the trash. From the perspective of social history, it is this second kind of story about the workers that can turn a set of nineteenth-century railroad tracks or a freight shed into a source for historians concerned with political meanings in the urban landscape.

Territorial Histories of Cities Based on Race, Ethnicity, Class and Gender

Lefebvre emphasized the importance of space for shaping social reproduction. One way to limit the economic and political rights of groups has been to constrain social reproduction by limiting access to space. For women, the body, the home, and the street have all been arenas of conflict, and examining them as political territories—bounded spaces with some form of enforcement of the boundaries—helps us to analyze the spatial dimensions of what nineteenth-century writers often called "woman's sphere." At the scale of bodily space, in the middle third of the nineteenth century, some women fought for dress reform and access to birth control, while others fought slavery as a system that required them to bear children as a source of new wealth for their owners. At the scale of housing space, by the last third of the century, some women, who were political activists and housewives, were looking for ways to reorganize the home economically as a domestic workplace, while others who were employed as domestics organized a major strike of household workers in Atlanta in 1881. And at the scale of urban space, in the late nineteenth and early twentieth centuries, some middle-class white women's campaigns for "municipal housekeeping" challenged corrupt government by men, while the suffrage movement brought broad coalitions of women, across lines of class and race, into public space to demand the vote.[20]

FIG. 46. Territorial histories: exclusion of Japanese-Americans from a residential neighborhood in Hollywood, Calif., took the form of signs as well as deed restrictions in the 1920s. Visual Communications.

Just as gender can be mapped as a struggle over social reproduction that occurs at various scales of space, the same is true of race, class, and many other social issues. As Michael Dear and Jennifer Wolch have written, the interplay between the social and the spatial is constant: "Social life structures territory . . . and territory shapes social life."[21] Ghettos and barrios, internment camps and Indian reservations, plantations under slavery and migrant worker camps can also be looked at as political territories, and the customs and laws governing them can be seen as enforcement of territory.[22] The territories of the gay and lesbian communities can be mapped. So can those of childhood or old age. The spatial dimensions of class can be illuminated by looking at other boundaries and points of access.[23] Since many of these territories intersect, analyzing both individuals' and groups' access to the urban landscape is always complex.

How can one find evidence about experiences of these overlapping territories? Frequently, observations about urban space are ignored by historians because the comments appear to be spatial description rather than social analysis,

FIG. 47. Territorial histories: segregated tract, with African-American observer, Los Angeles County, early 1950s. Southern California Library for Social Studies and Research.

but they can form the basis of a territorial history focusing on access to the public spaces of the city. For example, Loren Miller, Jr., an African-American lawyer who grew up in a middle-class family in Los Angeles in the 1940s, didn't see a segregated movie house until he went to Kansas in 1948. He could go to the beach any time on the streetcar. But, he observed, "As teen-agers, we knew not to drive into Compton, to Inglewood, not to drive into Glendale 'cause you would just be out, with your hands on top of the car, . . . LAPD did the same thing. You got too far south on Western, they would stop you." This man also remembered, as a child, having Japanese-American neighbors interned, going to visit them in temporary quarters at the Santa Anita race track, and finding that "soldiers with guns wouldn't let me go on the other side of the table, and they wouldn't let me play with my friends."[24] This is one individual account of spatial barriers about race. Another writer, Lynnell George, comments on this same city in the 1940s, "Off-limits for people of color in Los Angeles ran the gamut . . . not West of Main, not Glendale after dusk, never ever Fontana and its dusty flatlands dotted with burning crosses."[25]

Accounts like these begin to make it possible to map spatial segregation for the larger African-American community: not only accounts of streets and neighborhoods, but also reports about schools, hotels, stores, fire stations, swimming pools, and cemeteries would be some of the evidence to examine. Photographs often convey territorial history as well, documenting both residential segregation and communities' struggles against territorial exclusion.[26] Documentary photography, newspaper photography, commercial photography, and amateur snapshots all reveal different sides of a city. It can be revealing to consider the gender and ethnic background of the photographer as well as the architectural subject selected for the picture.

A territorial history based on limitations of gender in the public spaces of the city would use similar sources and interlock, but it would put buildings or parts of them off limits, more often than whole neighborhoods.[27] In the first two-thirds of the twentieth century, common types of gender segregation included private men's clubs, university faculty clubs, and programs in higher education. The segregation was not necessarily absolute—women might have been permitted to attend a class but sit separately, or they might have been allowed to enter a club as men's guests, provided they remained in a special room reserved for ladies. In the nineteenth century the list of gender-segregated spaces was much longer; forbidden activities for women included voting, entering a public saloon, or sitting in the main body of an assembly hall rather than the more restricted balcony.

To understand the intersecting segregation of race, class, and gender, the spatial dimensions of "woman's sphere" have to be studied in combination with the spatial limits imposed by race or class. Because white, middle-class women's clubs, charities, and suffrage organizations were often racially segregated, African-American women sometimes formed parallel groups, with their own meeting places, to help working women and girls in their own communities.[28] Or, to take another example, one photograph of a class at a state university open to women in the 1890s shows the men and women sitting separately. It is also important to ask: Are there any men and women of color present, segregated by gender and race, sitting at the very back of each group?

Political divisions of territory split the urban world into many enclaves, which are experienced from many different perspectives. Cognitive mapping is a tool for discovering fuller territorial information about contemporary populations. Urban planner Kevin Lynch studied mental images of the city by asking people to draw maps or give directions.[29] At the time, in 1960, Lynch suggested that such images could be combined into a composite portrait of a city, useful to urban designers, but not all Bostonians saw Boston the same way. Subsequent studies, including some of Lynch's own, explored class, gender, age, and ethnicity. Most striking was a study done in Los Angeles that showed graphically the differences

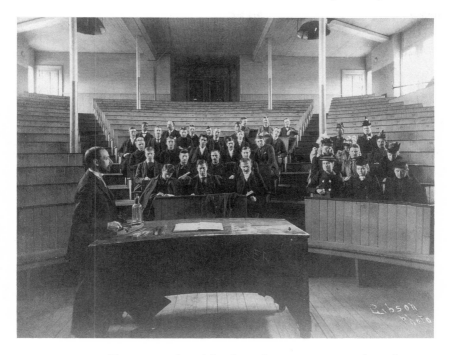

FIG. 48. Territorial histories: male and female students sitting separately at a lecture on physics, University of Michigan Medical School, late 1880s. Bentley Historical Library, University of Michigan.

between the residents of an affluent white suburb, an inner-city African-American neighborhood, and a mixed neighborhood close to downtown that had long been home to new immigrants working in downtown factories and using a few downtown bus lines.[30] The space of the city, as understood by these different groups, varied greatly in size as well as in its memorable features. The maps are striking images of inequality of access to the urban landscape.

Lynch's work from the 1960s and 1970s suggests not only that the sprawling, spatially segregated city is difficult for citizens to map, but also that architects and planners, as well as specialists in public history, have an important role to play in making the entire city more coherent in the minds of its citizens. Out of Lynch's work comes what Fredric Jameson has called "an aesthetic of cognitive mapping." Acknowledging some of the political limits of Lynch's work, Jameson applauds the potential of his insights about how to give individuals a heightened sense of place, and suggests that mapping can raise political consciousness.[31]

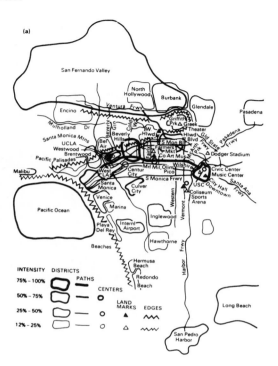

FIG. 49. Cognitive maps of Los Angeles as perceived by predominantly Anglo-American residents of Westwood. "Paths," "districts," "centers," "landmarks," and "edges" are elements of city form that Kevin Lynch concluded people used to organize their perceptions of the structure of cities. "Intensity" refers to the percentage of respondents to this study who identified each element. *The Visual Environment of Los Angeles,* Los Angeles Department of City Planning, April 1971, 9–10.

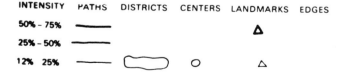

FIG. 50. Cognitive maps of Los Angeles as perceived by predominantly Latino residents of Boyle Heights. *The Visual Environment of Los Angeles,* Los Angeles Department of City Planning, April 1971, 9–10.

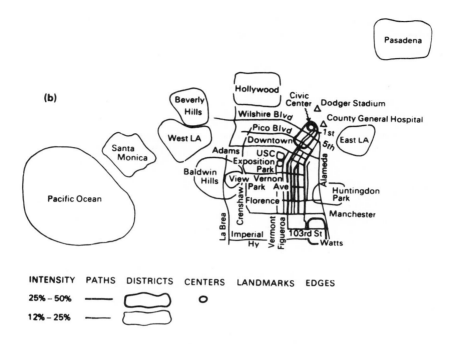

FIG. 51. Cognitive maps of Los Angeles as perceived by predominantly African-American residents of Avalon. *The Visual Environment of Los Angeles,* Los Angeles Department of City Planning, April 1971, 9–10.

The Political Life of Ordinary Buildings

Another way to analyze the production of space historically is to look at power struggles as they appear in the planning, design, construction, use, and demolition of buildings. While architectural history has traditionally been a branch of art history devoted to stylistic analyses of the works of a small group of trained architects, in recent years more attention has been given to vernacular buildings and to urban context.[32] Buildings offer rich sources for analyzing the material conditions of life in earlier times. When ordinary buildings—tens of millions of them—are being surveyed, identified, and classified according to shape and function, a larger sense of their political meaning is necessary.[33] Camille Wells, social historian of architecture, puts it this way: "most buildings can be understood in terms of power or authority—as efforts to assume, extend, resist, or accommodate it."[34]

Urban historians such as Sam Bass Warner, Jr., who studied Boston's streetcar suburbs, James Borchert, who looked at Washington's African-American alley dwellings, and Elizabeth Blackmar, who looked at the growth of Manhattan's rental housing from colonial times onward, have demonstrated how the built world's dimensions illuminate a larger urban economy.[35] Architectural historians interested in the political uses of design have also considered struggles over space: works on communitarian settlements and American company towns look at land use, siting, and processes of decision making as well as the design of buildings. Related studies using the archives of colonial planners and designers suggest how power can operate from the top down through the regulation of the built environment.[36]

Recent work on vernacular architecture, which has been heavily influenced by cultural geography, has often focused on rural or small-town subjects, such as agriculture or craft industries. More has been written about farmhouses and barns than urban boardinghouses, more about rural one-room schools than urban public high schools.[37] (Some scholars would still prefer to define the field this way. For them, the best vernacular building will always be the purest, the best-preserved, or the most elaborate example of its physical type.) A rural building, constructed by local people who may also own and occupy it, can illustrate the pro-

FIG. 52. Dwellings and social reproduction. Rural vernacular architecture and the building process: home in Chamisal, N.M., with women applying a new application of adobe, 1940. Photo by Russell Lee. Courtesy Library of Congress.

FIG. 53. Dwellings and social reproduction. A much less romantic vernacular: urban tenements and market on the Lower East Side of Manhattan, ca. 1900. Library of Congress.

duction of space more directly than an urban apartment house. It may still contain some surprises—such as women doing the construction. Yet greater potential lies in using the methods developed with preindustrial landscapes to look at urban building types like the tenement, the office building, or the public library to provide broad social interpretations of construction and habitation that represent the conditions of thousands or millions of people.[38]

Writing the social history of buildings can begin with material culture theory and method, identifying "mind in matter,"[39] but beyond evaluating an urban building as an artifact it is necessary to probe the complexity of habitation and finance. One must turn not only to building plans but also to all the public records of ownership, taxation, and regulation that may exist; one must consider the basic arithmetic of how much it cost to buy the land and construct the building versus how much rent was collected from how many tenants over how many years. For example, in a typical New York tenement at the turn of the century, many people's sordid habitat was one landlord's money machine, generating 25 percent return on investment per year.[40] There were few reasons to diminish profits through maintenance expenses, since enforcement of building codes and safety regulations was minimal.

The final results of research for an urban building type can be a complex social history linked to many ordinary buildings. Actors include not only the architect and the builder but also the developer, the zoning and building code writers, the building inspectors, and probably a series of tenants. The production of space on an urban scale involves them all. One social history research team associated with the Lower East Side Tenement Museum is working on a tenement located at 97 Orchard Street in New York City. (A fluke in the occupancy laws closed the units but kept small stores in the building operating, and thus saved it from any modifications for several decades.) Now the researchers are tracking the more than seven thousand immigrants of Irish, German, Italian, Russian, Greek, and Turkish descent who are known to have lived there between 1863 and 1935.[41]

What does this kind of history mean in terms of the sensory experience of place? One can read about unhealthy living conditions, but standing inside a tenement apartment—perhaps four hundred square feet of living space for an entire family, minimal plumbing, only one or two exterior windows—leaves a visitor gasping for air and looking for light. The claustrophobic experiences of immigrants living for decades in crowded, unhealthy space (as part of the reproduction of the labor force) are conveyed by the building in a way that a text or a chart can never match. Environmental history may come in the form of "black spot" charts of tenement residents dying of lung diseases, photographs of filthy communal privies serving hundreds of people, or sidewalks piled a yard high with uncollected garbage, but one intact building is the very best resource for conveying the experience. One tenement can tell the city-wide story of thousands of developers and millions of tenants. It represents daily urban life at the turn of the century far better than historic houses of refined architectural quality.[42]

From an Ordinary Dwelling to an Urban Residential Neighborhood

Dwellings are the basic, repeated units in an urban neighborhood. In a nineteenth-century or early twentieth-century American city, dwellings clustered along with related buildings such as public bathhouses, food markets, bakeries, factories, union halls, schools, clubs, nickelodeons, saloons, and settlement houses. All of these began to form historic urban working-class neighborhoods that now can be researched through sources such as fire insurance maps (Sanborn maps) and institutional records of trade unions and settlement houses, as well as records of individual buildings. There are patterns of gender segregation and types of places, such as saloons, where no respectable woman could go.[43] And there are patterns of ethnic and racial division, as well as distinctive ethnic building types.

The architectural historian Dell Upton once observed: "Large urban ethnic groups evidently built little that was distinctive but instead expressed their ethnicity through language, food customs, religion and social organizations."[44] However, ethnicity, as well as race, class, and gender, can be uncovered as a shaping force of American urban places, provided one looks carefully at the production of social space. In Eastern European Jewish neighborhoods, distinctive ethnic building types include synagogues; in Chinese-American neighborhoods, laundries, herb shops, and association boarding houses; in Japanese-American neighborhoods, temples, nurseries, and flower markets. (The researcher needs to be able to use sources not only in English but also in Yiddish, Chinese, and Japanese.)

Distinctive design traditions for outdoor spaces are associated with different ethnic groups—yards or gardens planted in certain ways identify Latino, African-American, Portuguese-American, Chinese-American, or Italian-American residents.[45] Stoops and porches, and the ways they are used, also speak about ethnicity and gender. Religious shrines do too, and so do street games for children. A world of shared meanings builds up, couched in the language of small semiprivate and semipublic territories between the dwelling and the street that support certain kinds of typical public behavior. The architect and planner James Rojas has analyzed the ways such spaces are created and used by residents in East Los Angeles, what he calls "the enacted environment."[46] Larger spatial patterns associated with ethnic groups have been studied in certain cities, such as Asian-American patterns of building and ownership in the state of Washington, Chinese-American gateways and underground passages in Vancouver, Canada, Latino public plazas in Los Angeles, African-American alley dwellings in Washington, D.C., or Puerto Rican *casitas* in New York.[47]

The story of the casita in New York City, is particularly fascinating. The casita represents a conscious choice by community organizers to construct the rural, preindustrial *bohio* (an eight-foot-by-ten-foot wooden house with a porch and a front yard) from the island as a new kind of community center in devastated tenement districts such as East Harlem, the South Bronx, and the Lower East Side. Here rural vernacular architecture was chosen to serve a polemical function, emphasizing the importance of what Rojas calls the "enacted environment" as a bridge between built and natural worlds. At the casitas, community organizers host political meetings, musical events, and classes. They often organize community gardening on vacant lots. Painted in coral, turquoise, or lemon yellow, these dwellings recall the colors of the Caribbean and evoke a memory of the homeland for immigrants who find themselves in Alphabet City or Spanish Harlem.

The casitas and their community gardens play against the context of aban-

FIG. 54. Counter-space, as a challenge to the reproduction of social relations. Dilapidated and abandoned tenements in New York City provide the context for a Puerto Rican *casita*, a rural house type built as a political gathering place. Photo by Martha Cooper.

doned tenements and litter-strewn lots. The organizers have produced their own public space, setting up a series of oppositions—past-present, inviting-uninviting, private-public. They offer an alternative kind of social reproduction within their space, at the same time that they critique the production of space, past and present, for Puerto Rican workers. As they attest the power of one cultural landscape to contradict another, they offer an example of Lefebvre's "counter-space." In this way, they resemble the political murals of East Los Angeles, which also set up a political dialogue with the surrounding city and its traditions of housing for Latino workers.[48]

Ethnic vernacular arts traditions have often operated in a similar way to instill community pride and signal the presence of a particular community in the city. Japanese-Americans have created flower decorations for streets. Anglos have made fruit, flower, and vegetable architecture for festivals. Mexican-Americans have developed hand-painted signs for both commercial buildings and trucks. Many communities enjoy more than one medium. A study of Italian Americans in South Philadelphia by Dorothy Noyes shows how Italian immigrants and their descendants made their presence felt through masonry, confectionery, window dressing, and street festival design.[49]

FIG. 55. Urban neighborhoods host many vernacular arts traditions that enable different ethnic groups to claim public space. In Los Angeles, Latino murals of the Virgin of Guadalupe and a more militant woman with a machine gun enliven the Estrada Courts housing project. Photo by Dolores Hayden.

Festivals and parades also help to define cultural identity in spatial terms by staking out routes in the urban cultural landscape. Although their presence is temporary, they can be highly effective in claiming the symbolic importance of places. They intermix vernacular arts traditions (in their costumes, floats, music, dances, and performances) with spatial history (sites where they begin, march, and end). African-American jazz funerals marching through the streets of New Orleans, Chinese New Year parades, saint's day processions in Irish-American or Italian-American Catholic communities,[50] and graveyard ceremonies for the Day of the Dead in Mexican-American communities are just a few examples of ethnic traditions with long histories. For a long time political parades have represented a range of communities, from workers to suffragettes, as the scholars Susan Davis and David Glassberg have shown.[51] In the last forty years, civil rights marches in southern cities, women's marches to "take back the night" or win abortion rights, and gay and lesbian pride parades in major cities have also established their participants in public space as part of campaigns to achieve greater political representation.[52]

An ordinary urban neighborhood will also contain the history of activists who have campaigned against spatial injustices. Whether one uses territorial histories, cognitive mapping, or some combination of the two, it is possible to identify historic urban places that have special significance to certain populations fighting spatial segregation of different kinds. Territorial history will point to a church where major civil rights meetings were held, a local newspaper that crusaded for fair housing, the first place in a city where women tried to vote, the first place where new immigrants were allowed to own land, or the first integrated primary school. There are also sites of assassinations, lynchings, massacres, and riots with political histories that should not be forgotten. In Memphis, the Lorraine Motel, where Martin Luther King was assassinated, is now a national civil rights museum, but every city and town has similar landmarks where territorial struggles have been waged. Finding these buildings and interpreting their history is one additional way to fuse the social and political meanings of space with the history of the urban landscape.

From the Urban Neighborhood to the City and the Region

As one moves from the scale of the neighborhood to that of the city, many works of urban history contribute to the understanding of cultural landscapes. A new American urban social history has begun to be written in the last two decades, a history that takes ethnic diversity as a starting point and recognizes disparate experiences of class and gender as well. For many years, urban history was dominated by a kind of city biography that projected a single narrative of how city leaders or city fathers—almost always white, upper- and middle-class men—forged the city's spatial and economic structure, making fortunes by building downtowns and imposing order on chaotic immigrant populations. This narrative tradition in urban history bore many similarities to the conquest histories of the American West.

In contrast, urban histories of the twenty-first century may begin by noting that in 1984 white males became a minority in the paid labor force in the United States.[53] Urban historians discovered workers in the 1960s and women in the 1970s. In the 1980s, as the history of suburban development became an essential part of urban history, spatial issues gained more attention.[54] In the late 1980s and 1990s, historians have been reconstructing the entire city, exploring the whole as seen from African-American, Latino, Chinese-American, or Japanese-American perspectives. While socially oriented studies of ethnicity and race have a long tradition, the new ethnic urban histories often emphasize the sharpness of spatial as well as cultural distinctions.[55] Soon the United States may have an urban history that encompasses the whole of the population, and the whole of the city, socially and spatially. Previous histories of American cities already seem dated if they focused only on the prosperous, white parts of cities—Manhattan without Harlem or the Bronx, Boston without Roxbury, the Westside of Los Angeles without East or South Central Los Angeles. As Toni Morrison's *Playing in the Dark* suggests, Anglo-American literature has often been constructed using the presence of African Americans to help define whiteness: "Through significant and underscored omissions, startling contradictions, heavily nuanced conflicts, through the way writers peopled their work with the signs and bodies of this presence—one can see that a real or fabricated Africanist presence was crucial to their sense of Americanness."[56] This could be said of some older urban histories as well.

New texts ask, "Who built America?"[57] Not only is the history of different ethnic communities becoming more fully represented, but historians also are increasingly placing women at the center rather than the periphery of economic and social life in the city. In contrast to the older city biographies that focused on city fathers and their conquest of the economic and physical obstacles to economic growth, women's history has brought a new emphasis on what might be called city mothers, the half of the city consisting of females of all races and classes, nurturing the rest of the population. Following the lead of scholars who worked on women of color a decade ago,[58] historians studying working women of every ethnic group have led the way to the broadest synthetic accounts of urban life, exploring textile mills and canneries, tenements and courtyards, where women struggled for sustenance for themselves, their families, and their communities.[59] Work in the home and paid work are complementary parts of women's urban economic activity, suggesting that urban history, ethnic history, women's history, and labor history are not separate categories. All of these studies of urban working women contain the outline of a larger urban narrative uniting women, children, and men in the struggle for survival, both in the market economy and in the home.

At the same time that social histories of the city are becoming more inclusive and spatial, environmental historians are showing how the old city biography tradition failed to convey the dynamic economic and spatial process of building a city, which depended on commanding natural resources far beyond the city limits. A city has a hinterland of economically dependent places. For Chicago, the cattle ranges of the West and the wheat fields of the Midwest were the environmental resources harnessed by the owners of railroads, slaughterhouses, grain elevators, and meat-packing plants headquartered in the city. For Los Angeles, the growth of the city required aqueducts reaching up through the Owens Valley and out to the Colorado River. An environmental analysis of both the central city and these far-flung places reveals the economic history of a city far better than a narrower look.[60]

Space as a Social Product: Local, Regional, National, and Global

"Space is permeated with social relations; it is not only supported by social relations but it is also producing and produced by social relations." So Henri Lefebvre sums up the complex, contradictory nature of space.[61] As the production of built space increases in intensity and scale during the later twentieth century, the politics of space becomes more difficult to map. Freeways connect dispersed locations of workplaces and dwellings, typical of contemporary working landscapes. As interstate freeways carry automobiles speeding at fifty-five miles per hour, it becomes more difficult to analyze the experience they provide in terms of human perception and memory, but easier to track the production of that American automotive space as the world's largest and most grandiose public works project.[62] At the same time a regional dispersion of activities is occurring, the global migration of capital leads to manufacturing processes scattered around parts of the world, while housing and factories lie abandoned in older, industrial inner cities of the United States.

In *The City and the Grassroots,* Manuel Castells has noted: "The new space of a world capitalist system, combining the informational and industrial modes of development, is a space of variable geometry, formed by locations hierarchically ordered in a continuously changing network of flows: flows of capital, labor, elements of production, commodities, information, decisions, and signals." He concludes that "the new tendential urban meaning is the spatial and cultural separation of people from their product and from their history." While suggesting that what "tends to disappear is the meaning of places for people," Castells finds many social movements mobilized against this loss of meaning in places.[63] In a similar vein, the geographer David Harvey describes the process of the "destruction, invasion, and restructuring of places on an unprecedented scale" caused by "changing material practices of production, consumption, information flow, and communication coupled with the radical reorganization of space relations and of time horizons within capitalist development."[64]

These changes attack older central cities with devastating architectural effect, and the inhabitants need to understand the complex forces that have led to present configurations. Territorial histories based on race, class, and gender can be illuminating, as well as the analysis of worker's livelihoods and landscapes. Today real estate developers are proliferating commercial space in suburban malls and edge cities while many inner-city neighborhoods struggle for economic viability. Both citizens and planners may find that urban landscape history can help to reclaim the identities of deteriorating neighborhoods where generations of working people have spent their lives. As Harvey suggests, paradoxically, "the elaboration of place-bound identities has become more rather than less important in a world of diminishing spatial barriers to exchange, movement and communication."[65] Understanding the history of urban landscapes offers citizens and public officials some basis for making political and aesthetic choices about the future. It also offers a context for greater social responsibility to practitioners in the design fields.

This chapter has explored some of the ways that social history is embedded in urban landscapes. This subject needs to be grounded in both the aesthetics of experiencing places with all five senses, and the politics of experiencing places as contested territory. Much the same can be said for organizations of historians, preservationists, or environmentalists, or of individual artists and designers, who wish to use the social history of places to make more resonant connections to public memory. Places make memories cohere in complex ways. People's experiences of the urban landscape intertwine the sense of place and the politics of space. If people's attachments to places are material, social, and imaginative, then these are necessary dimensions of new projects to extend public history in the urban landscape, as well as new histories of American cultural landscapes and the buildings within them.

ANTHONY D. KING

_____

10   The Politics of Vision

I begin with a story from a Brahmin colleague in India. A man, seeking enlightenment, asked his guru for advice. The man suggested, "I shall go to the highest mountain and there I shall open wide my eyes and look around." And the guru replied, "This will be your first mistake."

This brief story prompts a number of questions central to the theme of this book: What is the relation of sight or vision to belief, of belief to knowledge, and of knowledge to authority? In retelling this story from India's Brahmin tradition, I highlight the cultural specificity in which seeing and believing (and the ensuing construction of knowledge) take place, as well as the significance of particular topoi to this knowledge-making process: my story underlines the interrelated and interactive concepts of vision, culture, and landscape that are central to this book. It is these three concepts that I shall address.

Vision and Visualism

For some two hundred years in medieval Europe, from the late thirteenth to the late fifteenth centuries, the word *vision* meant "something which is seen otherwise than by ordinary sight, especially an appearance of a prophetic or mystical character, supernaturally presented to the mind in sleep or an abnormal state." A vision was "a mental concept of a distinct or vivid kind: an object of mental contemplation, a highly imaginative scheme or anticipation."[1]

Alternative to this objective sense of vision was a subjective one: "The action or fact of seeing or contemplating something not actually present to the eye, a mystical, supernatural insight." Only at the end of the fifteenth century did "vision" come to have the meaning of "the act of seeing with the bodily eye; the exercise of the ordering faculty of sight,"[2] which is now the commonly understood meaning of the word.

These two meanings, the one drawn from imagination and the other from a notion of bodily sight, provide a departure point for discussing the privileging of vision (what Johannes Fabian refers to as "visualism"[3]) in contemporary Western culture[4] and for considering some theoretical and practical implications of this privileging, especially for design fields.

A number of theoretical critiques in anthropology have directed attention to the inadequacies of a theory of knowledge that relies too much on the visual. James Clifford, for example, refers to the studies of Walter Ong, which draw attention to the ways in which the different human senses are hierarchically ordered, both in different cultures and in different epochs. In Western literate cultures, according to Clifford, the truth of vision has predominated over evidence provided by the other senses—sound, touch, smell, and taste. The main methodological metaphors in anthropology, he notes, have been "participant-observation," data collection, looking at, and objectifying. The taxonomic imagination in the West is likewise strongly visualist in nature, constituting cultures as if they were spatial arrays, set out especially to be seen.[5]

Fabian also has developed these critiques of overreliance on visual methods, discussing the implications of positing as cultural facts only those things that are observed rather than those that are heard, transcribed, or invented in dialogue. It is assumed by many anthropologists that the ability to visualize a culture is somehow synonymous with the ability to understand it. This assumption has grown out of certain methodological presuppositions, since the discourse about culture is generally anchored in real or mental spaces, with theoretical and conceptual propositions represented, for example, by reference to lesser-known cultures, such as the Kwakiutl, Trobriands, or Ndembu. More particularly, vision has been, as phenomenalism, a part of empirical and positivist theories of knowledge. The notion that until things are seen they cannot be properly known has, as a consequence, privileged the unknown Other as an object of knowledge. The Other must be separate and, preferably, distant from the knower. That which is close and, therefore, capable of being seen is both more easily knowable and, therefore, known.[6]

In historical and geographical terms, this emphasis on the use of vision in the construction of knowledge has depended on a particular political economy of the production of knowledge. Beginning in the 1880s, a combination of forces—the dominance of a colonial world political structure, the emergence of the scholarly discipline of anthropology, and the development of the technology of photography[7]—gave a new impetus to the notion of ethnography as observing and gathering and to a culturally unilateral use of photography that, in the act of appropriating visual images, constructed visually "other" cultures, the existence of which was useful for locating Europe or America in evolutionary time and civilization space. The monopoly of these technologies (not only photography but also a variety of printing and reproduction techniques) began a vast process of cultural accumulation—of archives of visual representations that yielded intellectual, cultural, and political profit. As the era of worldwide exhibitions dawned, this appropriation of images was translated into the reproduction of models of whole villages or towns, which purported to represent the colonized culture in its totality.[8]

In contemporary Western cultures, photography, cinematography, and television have, since the nineteenth century, combined with the political economy of market capitalism to construct representations of societies and cultures that exist through, and even depend on, the proliferation and consumption of visual images. In the late twentieth century, the era of emerging global capitalism, the proliferation of cameras and television has saturated populations with the consciousness of sight. Thus, the window, regarded in early medieval times as a device to let out smoke or ventilate the house (etymologically, "wind-eye"), has become, in modern times, a mechanism for consuming the landscape not only visually (as in the "picture window") but also economically and socially. The contemporary idea of space, in Henri Lefebvre's terms, presupposes and implies "a logic of visualization."[9]

In fact, the obsession with visual difference—in subcultural styles, product marketing, and consumption—is not only built into the foundations of contemporary capitalist economies (think of the common critique of socialist societies: how dull, boring, colorless, they look); it has also overeducated and overstimulated the eye in comparison to the mind and spirit, which, some would add, have become correspondingly impoverished.

In contemporary capitalist societies, in which the processes of cultural production are fragmented into compartments of knowledge and cultural practice, visualism, understood as the separation of the visual from culture as a whole, becomes a particular kind of conceit, a reification. It is this separation that makes a phrase like "visual culture" so problematic, full of contradictions and ambiguities. First, as I have already indicated, this attitude privileges what can be seen over what can be heard, touched, smelled, known, or merely experienced. We might pose a question: What kind of insight into art history can be gained from the perspective of a sightless person?

Second, the phrase "visual culture" is replete with ambiguity. For example, we must ask who is doing the visualizing, and what do they see? (This is the anthropological problem of the -emic and the -etic—that is, whether the seeing is from inside or outside the culture.) These questions are important whether we are considering our own visual consumption of other people's cultures or the production of seeable, material objects that are meant consciously or unconsciously for visual consumption either by the producers themselves or by other consumers.

Third, especially in relation to the built environment or landscape, the phrase "visual culture" segregates and privileges that which is seen from that which is thought, constructed, bought, sold, exchanged, inscribed in memory, or forgotten. It is this misapprehension that permits objects, be they paintings or buildings, to be seen as primarily visual rather than social, economic, or, ultimately, political objects that have a range of meanings[10] and that provide the basis for the construction of mystifying formalistic analysis. This privileging of vision, or of the pleasures of the eye, also encourages the de-education of architects, artists, and even landscape designers, who consequently believe that they are principally engaged in visual activity that is somehow divorced from the economic, social and political realms.

Culture and Ethnicity

The return of the topic of culture to the intellectual agenda in the late 1980s was both ironic and contradictory, particularly after a period in which the analysis of urban issues had been characterized by Marxist influences, the analytical primacy of capital, and strong doses of economic determinism. For some students of landscape, space, and environments, of course, culture had never left the agenda; even for them, however, the conceptualization of culture has had to change.

In much of the writing of this earlier period and in many of the explanations for social, urban, and environmental change, the problem seemed to be either that of undertaking a materialist approach or that of making a cultural analysis and positing explanations that prioritized world views, ways of life, values, and beliefs.

In the cultural analysis approach, culture was seen as some kind of separate analytical or explanatory variable that was either ignored or not given particular attention. Perhaps most representative of the cultural analysis approach was the collection of essays *The City in Cultural Context*, which was designed to confront and modify what was seen as the overly economic paradigms of the urban political economists.[11]

In the materialist approach, emphasis was placed on explaining the relationship between changing modes of production and the resultant urban and spatial forms, or, in a more localized and historically specific context, the relationship of space to the system of economic and social organization and political control. Representative of this tradition, in the urban field, would be the work edited by Susan and Norman Fainstein and others, or the earlier, paradigm-changing work of Manuel Castells and David Harvey.[12]

Neither approach offers an adequate theorization of culture, but both make it clear that there are cultural attributes that are common to particular modes of production, systems of economic and social organization, and types of political control—irrespective of the dissimilar and geographically disparate cultures in which they may appear.[13] These common cultural attributes have not yet received the attention they deserve—a result of the predominantly national context in which the majority of research, particularly cultural research, is frequently conducted (a point to which I shall return below).

More recently, this "either/or" situation has been modified. The conceptualization of culture as "values, beliefs, world views, ways of life" (which, as Peter Jackson points out, previously underpinned much of an older cultural geography and which depicted landscapes simply as reflections or recipients of the impact of given cultures[14]) has given way to more dynamic understandings that stress culture as the active construction of meaning, or the processes and codes through which meanings are constructed, negotiated, conveyed, and understood.

This emphasis on the cognitive and interactive also pays reference to the larger economic, social, and political context in which culture is produced. In Jackson's view, the absence of reference to these larger social and economic processes (to the influence of the state, for example) was characteristic of an earlier cultural geography, whose explanations ended with a reference to culture as some superorganic whole whose changing nature, however, no one was able to explain.[15]

What we now have, I believe, is a combination of both approaches in the notion of a political economy of cultural production, a recognition of the political and economic conditions in which cultures are produced, and an appreciation of the interactive nature of that process, whereby culture itself affects the conditions of production.

I would maintain that it is contemporary conditions in the capitalist world economy that have been largely responsible for putting culture (as well as ethnicity, with which culture is generally, though not necessarily, connected) firmly back on the intellectual and academic agenda. Our consciousness of culture and ethnicity has been sharpened by three factors: the rapid acceleration in international labor migration; the increasing degree of demographic displacement, much of it the result of the policies (as well as existence) of nation-states; and the growing importance of the cultural industries (and of cultural production in general) in the core economies of Western Europe and North America.

The rapid acceleration in international labor migration. International labor migration in the postcolonial era, one of the major elements in the global restructuring of capital, has been manifested particularly in Europe, North America, South America, the Middle East, and, to a lesser extent, Africa. Culture (as well as ethnicity), a phenomenon that, until the mid-twentieth century, was represented in the academy as being confined largely to the global periphery, has surfaced with a vengeance in the global core. The principal exception to this statement is, of course, the United States, with its long history of immigration, both forced and voluntary.

Culture is a reactive phenomenon; it is something which, in the first instance, others have. Culture as a realm of knowledge and practice initially developed in the context of power relations[16] and, typically, in colonial situations: in the United States, France, and Britain in relation to native Africans, Americans, Asians, or other Others.[17] Culture in this older anthropological sense[18] was, until the 1950s, a relatively esoteric subject that people studied at a distance, among populations over which one had political control. Moreover, when you caught some, you encased it (often literally) in ethnographic museums. Only in quite recent times have anthropologists seen their practice primarily in terms of offering cultural critique.[19]

Because the disciplines of social and cultural anthropology have had greater exposure to global heterogeneity, as Roland Robertson has pointed out, they have allowed culture (frequently conceived as a realm of values, beliefs, and symbols) into the analytical picture as a way of explaining social phenomena or as being explainable by the latter. The discipline of sociology, on the other hand, has generally tended to study aspects of modern societies and has had greater exposure to apparent homogeneity. Consequently, it has tended to see culture as important only in accounting for variation in the domain of social structure and social action. The different orientations to culture from sociology and social anthropology, and the initial separation between the two disciplines, is, in Robertson's words, attributable to "a particular conjuncture in the long-term process of globalization" (globalization being the processes by which the "world becomes a single place").[20]

Only with the ending of external (as well as internal) colonialism in the 1950s and 1960s (in the case of Europe) have the objects of this study moved out of the museum. According to Stuart Hall, cultural studies in the modern sense began in the mid-1950s with the work of Richard Hoggart and Raymond Williams.[21] These studies, however, focused for many years largely on the indigenous (British) population divided, economically and socially, along class lines, and they used the nation-state as a geographical boundary.

Cultural geography (which, according to Peter Jackson, comprises the study of the impact of "man" on the landscape[22]) can be considered as having started in the mid-1920s and, in a more sophisticated sense (including the work of Kroeber), in the early 1950s. The shift to a fully fledged conceptualization of what has subsequently been labeled "public culture"—which, quite exceptionally, recognizes cultural phenomena as resulting from transnational cultural flows and influences and which uses the new paradigms of cultural studies—emerged only in the late 1980s.[23]

Demographic displacement and cultural and ethnic identity. Closely related to the renewed interest in culture has been the heightened interest in race, class, and ethnicity, all of which we would recognize as socially constructed categories. While the use of the word *race* to refer to a group of people who share common physical characteristics may have no validity in science, race as a folk concept is both powerful and important in Western and non-Western societies, used both to classify and to exclude specific populations in specific racist practices. Of these, residential discrimination is the most obvious, though it is important to note the difference in degree, extent, and kind of residential discrimination, both historically and geographically. From these essentially social and linked economic and political practices, different cultures are produced. Whether we should refer to these as racial or ethnic cultures, or whether they are understood better in relation to class terms, is arguable; what is not arguable is that they are essentially social cultures that are materially affected by the policies of the state.

Like culture, ethnicity is a reactive phenomenon; the extent to which either category is mobilized depends on the structural context, be it political, economic, social, or, not least, geographic. There is, in short, a difference between a group that claims ethnic distinctiveness and one that has distinctiveness imposed upon it by some politically superior group in the context of political struggle.[24] The French in colonial Morocco or Algeria were no more conceptualized as an ethnic minority than were (or are) Europeans in India. Neither the English in the United Kingdom nor the Anglos in the United States are referred to as an ethnic majority.

Just why social groups or individuals located at various interstices in the social, spatial, and economic structure of any given state decide not simply to emphasize their supposed ethnicity but to construct and represent it (or construct *one*) actively is not subject to easy explanation, though a number of observations can be made.

In the first place, we might note that the original meaning of *ethnos* in Greek— tribe, people, or nation—was used to describe people other than the Greeks. Even in a relatively recent (1980) edition of the *Oxford English Dictionary* the meaning of *ethnic* is given first as "pertaining to nations not Christian or Jewish: gentile, heathen, pagan" and second as "pertaining to race or nation." Only in the twentieth century does the word *ethnic* take on the meaning "denoting nationality derived from . . . the name of a people or city."[25] So *ethnic* is a term with a long history in which sections of humanity are defined in difference, in we/they terms.

Moreover, as already suggested, ethnicity comes into existence either through adoption by the ethnic group itself or through imposition by others. As Seymour Smith defines an ethnic group as "any group who set themselves apart and"—we might ask whether this should be *or*—"are set apart from other groups with whom they interact or coexist in terms of some distinctive criterion or criteria which may be linguistic, racial or cultural." She continues, "The term is thus a very broad one which has been used to include social classes as well as racial or national minority groups in urban and industrial societies, also to distinguish different cultural and social groupings among indigenous populations." Most important: "The concept of the ethnic group combines both social and cultural criteria and the study of ethnicity focuses precisely on the interrelation of cultural and social processes in the identification of (and interaction between) such groups."[26]

Yet, as Immanuel Wallerstein points out, "minorityhood is not necessarily an arithmetically based concept; it refers to the degree of social power. Numerical majorities can be social minorities. The location within which we are measuring this social power, however, is not the world-system as a whole but the separate states. The concept of ethnic group is therefore as linked in practice to state boundaries as is the concept of nation, though this is never included in the definition. The difference being that the state tends to have one nation and many ethnic groups."[27]

In discussing ethnic groups, therefore, this clearly focuses our attention on the level of the state. In this context it might be argued that, in discussing "America's architectural roots," we might equally examine the "America that built ethnic groups" as the "ethnic groups that built America."[28]

As a socially constituted phenomenon, ethnicity flourishes to a greater or lesser extent in different economic and political systems. As capitalism lives and works through difference,[29] by encouraging segmentation and developing market niches, it follows that in market-oriented societies there is a greater commodification of ethnicity. Ethnicity can be used as a socially mobilizing vehicle to counter oppression, or it can be used by a culturally and politically hegemonic group to exploit the economically and socially disadvantaged. By emphasizing distinctive "identities," ethnicity masks people's common economic and social interests.

The boundaries of cultural production. Knowledge, like other aspects of culture, is largely organized, financed and produced by people and institutions in individual nation-states. We have only to walk into the nearest bookshop to see that the vast majority of scholars unquestioningly take their own nation-state as the unit of analysis.

In a (Western-influenced) world in which at least 50 percent of the population has an oral culture, but in which cultural hegemony rests with a scriptocentric West, the largest amount of established knowledge comes from the core states—those with the globally dominant economies. In the last twenty years, an era of postindustrialization, this tendency has increased as economies have shifted (as a result of a new international division of labor) to quaternary functions, whether banking, financial services, research, or higher education. Increasingly, more so-called international students come to study in institutions in the core states. The World Bank is based in Washington, not Dacca.

In these core states, interesting (even bizarre) developments in knowledge production take place. When the world is conceived (by the core states) as being divided into "developing/advanced," "Third World/First World," or "North/-South" countries rather than being broken down by nation or ethnicity, new courses of study emerge. These I can illustrate most easily by reference to the state (United Kingdom) and academic domain (built environment/planning studies) with which I am most familiar. Despite the obvious interconnectedness of the world's political economy, despite the conception of the world as a single, interdependent place, academic courses are taught and knowledge is constructed on topics like "architectural research and development *overseas*" or "building design in *developing countries*." The implication, despite the evidential contradiction in the presence of the students, is that the developing country or overseas is somehow other, different from and, most significant, not intrinsically connected to or necessary for the core states, historically, culturally, and, especially, economically. The parallel courses being offered to domestic students are not, as we might logically expect, "architecture and development *not overseas* or *at home*" or "building design in economically *advanced* countries"; rather, they are simply labeled "architecture." For the "overseas" student (more accurately, at the close of the twentieth century, a "through-the-air" student), the courses deal with "development," "political and economic factors," "cultural factors in design" and maybe even "ethnicity"—topics that rarely, though perhaps more recently, intrude into the architectural curriculum of domestic students.

Landscape

The obvious answer to these and similar problems (and here I slip into the third of my themes) is to find a unit of analysis larger than, and beyond, the boundaries of the state. Several approaches have been suggested, though each depends on the social, cultural, and, not least, political positioning and spatial location of its proponent. In recognizing the increasing degree of global compression, these approaches have attempted to find ways of conceptualizing and empirically charting the processes of the world as a single place.[30]

What is increasingly clear is that we need a frame of reference that recognizes,

FIG. 56. The global production of building form. Canary Wharf, London Docklands, July 1991. At the time of the photograph, the building on the left was designated as the European headquarters of the New York architectural firm Skidmore, Owens and Merrill; on the right is the European headquarters of American Express. The complex is a design product of the New York architectural firm Pei Cobb Freed and Partners. Photo by Anthony D. King.

in places where it is most relevant (which may not be everywhere), the global context in which built environments and other landscapes are produced and the equally global context in which they are consumed (not least in terms of internationally derived migratory populations). We need to develop a political economy of both world urbanization and the global production and consumption of the built environment. What this would show is the organization of economic and political power on a global basis: corporate headquarters buildings, international banks, and globalized investment buildings in New York, London, Los Angeles, Paris, and Tokyo; back office functions in the Caribbean; multinational chemical plants in Bhopal and Saõ Paulo; agribusiness fields in Mexico; and plantations in the Caribbean.[31]

Linked with this would be a history, geography, and political economy of global cultural production that would investigate, for example, where ideas, finance, and technology developed for the first high-rise office tower or skyscraper; the ideologies and theories of urban planning in capitalist and socialist societies;

the ideas of suburban development and the models of suburban houses; the institutions of mortgage finance; or transportation technologies—and how they have been transplanted to urban centers around the world, particularly to the postcolonial periphery.[32]

The purpose of such studies would be quite simple: the historical and empirical charting of universality and difference. We would no more suggest that the cultural form of the World Trade Center in New York resulted primarily from "American ethnic architecture" (not least because there are now similar skyscraper blocks in Asia, Latin America, and Europe) than we would suggest that the cultural form of white South African farms was primarily the result of Dutch or English ethnicity. In both cases, however, the economic and political power that is inherent in capitalist development and produces similar building forms all over the world—irrespective of *ethnos* or national culture—is nonetheless still marked, at a secondary level, with a particular cultural stamp. Likewise, at the broadest level of analysis, single-family suburban house developments around many cities are more alike, both in settlement and in house form, than they are different. Ethnicity may tell us why they are different. But we need a larger explanation to tell us why they are the same.

Culture is a problematic concept for conservatives and radicals alike;[33] it is also a double-edged sword. We can choose to undertake studies of cultural and ethnic difference at the level of the neighborhood, the nation, or the world. We can also choose to study house forms (or the absence of housing) in terms of the income available to their occupants, in terms of their size and function, or in relation to the place of their populations in the international division of labor. Each type of study will yield results. In different contexts, one will have more explanatory power than another.

In concluding, I would like to return to the two concepts of vision with which I began: vision as dream and vision as sight or observation. We can, as I have suggested, be beguiled by sight: The eye may be less reliable than the mind, or even the heart.

11 The Future of the Vernacular

Architecture, especially interior architecture, tends to formalize and institutionalize certain relationships. Why this should be the case I have no clear idea, but I am convinced that the Western world—in particular the United States—is in the midst of a radical shift in attitude toward architectural or designed spaces.

For centuries our civilization has relied upon enclosed spaces to establish relationships and identities, but now we are turning away from them in favor of ones that are either more natural or less formal. The vernacular or workaday spaces that we will use in the future will, of course, include buildings. But we will prefer open spaces such as streets, highways, fields, and even the desert.

For eighty years I have lived (along with other Americans) in a world largely composed of enclosed spaces, all of them well defined and characterized by a greater or lesser degree of accessibility: the church, the school, the library, the dwelling, even the workplace. All were careful to isolate themselves from the street and what it stood for. People of my generation can recall a time when all Americans of middle-class background were taught to distrust the street and street life, and to believe in the sanctity of the home.

We had heard of the fascinations of street life and had a highly romanticized image of its wickedness and its freedom, but we rarely ventured into it. Once we were home and had closed the front door, we had the happy feeling of being where we belonged. Home was where each room, each passage, had its own unique character and where every space, every hour of the day, imposed its own appropriate behavior. An important part of the joy of being home was that we could control who had access to it and who could be excluded.

My memories of the houses in which I have lived, and of the houses of friends and relatives, are still so vivid that there was a brief time when as a student of American domestic architecture I supposed that I could identify and describe the prototype exterior of the American dwelling. I soon found that I could do nothing of the sort. Take at random a dozen middle-class American families of a generation ago, all living in the same town, all with the same education and much the same income, and you will find one living in a white clapboard, two-story house, another in a Tudor cottage, another in their parents' Victorian house, and still another in a scaled-down version of a southern plantation.

But once I learned to think of the prototype interior, I was on safe ground. The middle-class home I learned to identify was simply a composition of rooms or spaces accommodating certain cherished domestic values: privacy, family continuity, undisputed possession, and, most cherished of all, the ability to offer formal hospitality.

In this type of house one would find the formal entrance lobby, very often the parlor, a so-called powder room and a guest room and bath upstairs (in those days most houses had two floors). The small dining room (rarely used by the modern middle-class family) would contain a handsome table and a set of chairs that would seat eight people (even though the family counted only four). There would be a display of silver and company china. The massive front door with its bell, chimes, or knocker was also part of the equipment for hospitality, and in those far-off days there even would be a place where guests could park their car. Many of the houses I am describing emphasized their limited accessibility by small signs saying "No Soliciting," "No Salesmen," or "Tradesmen's Entrance in the Rear," meaning at the kitchen door.

The custom of hospitality, the spaces it requires, and its various forms and schedules offer the best way of defining a dwelling and the status of its occupants. Standard middle-class hospitality indicates that the house is a territory, a domain with restricted access and its own rules and customs. Neither neighbors nor business associates are automatically invited. Formality in the shape of a sit-down dinner or a catered cocktail party implies no celebration or any ulterior motive; it is simply a tactful way of showing how you live and protecting the house from too much casual dropping in. Privacy is a precious commodity.

Formal hospitality of the kind that calls for invitations well in advance of the event and elaborate preparations in the kitchen is not common in working-class households, not only because of the expense of such meals, but also because the working-class home includes no special rooms for hospitality. If you are a friend you are made welcome even if your visit is a surprise. What takes the place of formal hospitality is a banquet or dance at a nearby restaurant or social organization, and such an event is usually a celebration of a family birthday or wedding or graduation. It calls for no reciprocity.

Among the rich and famous, hospitality is on a lavish, not to say boastful, scale and is meant to accomplish several well-defined objectives: to negotiate deals and alliances, social as well as in the business world; to display the owner's wealth and position; and to process people who might be candidates for membership in the power structure. If you pass muster, you will be invited to a smaller, more select party. If you fail, you are never invited again.

What do notions of hospitality have to do with the future of the vernacular landscape? I could answer in one word: territoriality. But a better answer involves the history of both concepts. I know of no study more fascinating for the amateur of landscape history than the evolution of the middle-class dwelling and its changing relationship with the land. That evolution has in my opinion come to an end, but we can see through history how the house developed not only architecturally but also in authority and prestige; how it gradually became a symbol of stability, attachment to the land, manners and codes of conduct and even morality.

When the Roman Empire had disintegrated as a landscape and the Dark Ages had overtaken northwestern Europe, the large agricultural estates, once worked by slaves, were abandoned or used for grazing. By the seventh and eighth centuries, a new kind of agricultural enterprise began to evolve on some of the extensive monastic estates. A suitable amount of farm land was granted in perpetuity to a family that agreed to live on it, work it, pay taxes, and perform occasional military service. These requirements created what is sometimes known as a "moral unit"—a permanent territory, with a religious and social and economic identity, capable of entering into an agreement with the sovereign power.

Most of those early medieval homesteads were small and poor. But if they ranked far below the larger feudal estates, they were much superior to the dwellings and plots of land of the rural proletariat or the urban worker. Their status was given official recognition: The crown granted them the right to "keep the King's Peace," that is, to enforce the law and maintain order without police interference, to discipline and protect their workers, to punish trespassers and defend their boundaries. We might call this privilege an early recognition of the right to domestic privacy; we might also call it an early recognition of the right to offer hospitality, for it meant the privileged landowner could control access to his house and land.

In its Dark Ages beginnings, the home of the yeoman farmer was simply a container, a house with no specific function other than that of providing shelter. But over time a number of radically new construction techniques evolved and combined with a better knowledge of local climate and materials to produce a house capable of withstanding the weather and of lasting for decades. This house could have a preconceived plan for both domestic needs and for large open, unencumbered interior spaces. It was well suited to local farming practices, to a self-contained family life, and to the public status of its occupants; it provided spaces for storage, privacy, work, and hospitality.

It would be a mistake to assume that this house is the only kind of dwelling there was throughout this thousand-year period. The nobility and the church had their own, more complicated architectural tradition, which the average yeoman farmer could only admire from a distance. There was also a tradition, far older, far more generally diffused, of a very different kind of dwelling: that of families possessing little land who supported themselves by working for others and who therefore had a different relationship to the land and its resources. This landless element seems to have constituted at least a third of the medieval population. Its size gradually increased until, in the late eighteenth century, it comprised almost half the population.

The house of the wage earner is what we now call vernacular, not only because it was crudely constructed out of local materials, but also because it was the dwelling of the poorest class. (Unfortunately, the word *vernacular* still suggests inferiority, the substandard version of the correct, and thus distorts the difference. But the term persists, and to be understood we must use it.)

The yeoman's farmhouse and the wage earner's house were unlike not only as to size and construction but also in the role each of them played in the lives of their occupants and how each was valued. The house of the laborer did not participate in the structural evolution of the middle-class house, remaining stubbornly loyal to a housing tradition originating in the remote, unchronicled pre-Roman past.

The typical house of those times, which we identify with the barbarian invasions of northwestern Europe, was crude, easily built, and without any individuality—a construction of vertical planks, quickly put together out of timber from the surrounding forest, with a heavy thatch roof supported by poles. There were a hearth and a fireplace on the dirt floor, but no chimney and no ceiling. There were usually two rooms, one of them occupied by livestock. Outside were a small, primitive garden and a number of sheds, outhouses, and barns.

An extended family would live in a cluster of such houses. All land and resources were owned in common; small wheat fields were allotted to each household. Raising cattle, hunting, fishing, and warfare were the main occupations. When the local resources of grass and timber were exhausted, or when an unfriendly group threatened invasion, the so-called village moved on. Mobility was so much a part of the lives of these people that their sacred structure was a small shed or shrine on wheels. A tribe in Scythia lived entirely in wagons on the move:

They were known as *hamaxobii* ("those who live in wagons"), a term that academics might adopt when discussing the mobile home.

Mobility was the ruling element. All things that moved—flowing water, vegetation, fire—were held in common. Even the grass that the cattle ate was common property, since it moved in the wind. Perhaps as a result of the notion that much of the natural environment belonged to everyone who used it, custom held that none of those spaces so necessary to survival were to be altered: no trees cut down or planted, no water damned, no wells dug, and no fences built, except around the fields to keep out livestock.

How much of this pagan tradition carried over among the rank and file of the Middle Ages is hard to say. It is easy to see resemblances between the primitive barbarian house and the medieval cottage, at least in construction. The cottage was a crude one- or two-room frame structure of mud and brush with a thatch roof. With no crops to store and no animals to feed, it was little more than a shelter, a container for the elementary needs of the family. It was easily disassembled and reassembled elsewhere, wherever there might be a job. It epitomized a vernacular culture based on mobility and a hand-to-mouth way of life.

The vernacular cottage, and the people who lived within it, were almost entirely dependent on the resources, social as well as material, of their immediate environment. The occupants spent much of the day outdoors. Village authorities or nobles offered (for a fee) a remarkable number of facilities—the public grist mill, the public wine press or brewery, the bathing establishment, the public outdoor laundry facilities, the market. Villagers had use of the common for grazing cows or geese, they could collect fallen branches in the communal forest for fuel, and they could cut a certain number of trees (under strict rationing rules) for building or repairing a house.

This philanthropic arrangement seems to have been intended to keep the vernacular element satisfied with its lot, for any attempt to live in a more private manner was discouraged. The police raided cottages without warning to put an end to too much hospitality. On the other hand, the ancient tradition of downplaying the role of the house accounted in part for the public delight in using (borrowing) public spaces for a brief time and then leaving them unaltered. The church, the churchyard, the village green, and even certain rooms in the houses of the nobility were freely used, on occasion, by all of the villagers.

The consequence of this prolonged outdoor living and absence from home was an animated and sometimes disorderly street scene. Medieval public spaces were used not only for sociability and relaxation but also for work, the exchange of goods and services and information, and even violent and competitive sports and games. When we now talk about the use of public space we usually have in mind friendly interaction and innocent recreation. We have forgotten that these spaces once served to supplement domestic life with all its needs and desires, just as we have forgotten the ancestral belief that all empty spaces were the property of the local families.

The sixteenth and seventeenth centuries brought a new, more complicated, more expensive architecture (of stone and brick with more specialized rooms and spaces) that all but eliminated the amateur home builder. The laborer's or peasant's house was the product of the crown or of a well-to-do employer, and much of the architecture that we label vernacular was the work of civil or military engineers or professional builders. This was true in colonial New England and in Virginia. The slave quarters, though built by the slaves themselves, were designed by the plantation owners, and a study of the houses of Massachusetts Bay suggests that many of them were built by professional carpenters and cabinetmakers.

It was a time of planned villages and uniform street facades, a time when people who traveled from town to town looking for jobs were severely punished and ordered to stay where they belonged, and a time when many spaces hitherto open to the public—gardens, forests, churches, palaces—were declared out of bounds. The street, once the scene of so much activity, was redesigned for through traffic and as a work of urban art.

Many of these reforms had the welfare of the public, particularly the poorer public, in mind, but the emphasis was on fostering middle-class standards in the home and public life, and the ideal was all too often the mythical village of self-sufficient households in a bucolic setting. Vernacular architecture meant village architecture, the architecture of landowners, who had clear-cut ideas of the sanctity of private property and the necessity for having roots in the land. The house became a shrine to this religion of permanence.

These attitudes toward vernacular architecture and the house prevailed in my youth a half-century ago. But by that time a reappraisal of the importance of the house had long been underway. Historians have pointed out that as early as the 1820s in this country the old triad, living on the land, working the land, owning the land—ways of celebrating the role of the house—was beginning to be meaningless. House and land and family, the moral unit first formulated in the Dark Ages ten centuries ago, was giving way to a separation between house and work and land. The old traditional landscape was beginning to crumble, first of all here in America.

The demise of the dwelling as a moral unit was connected to our growing taste for the exterior experience of architecture, our new street life here in America. All of these developments are leading to the spread of a new kind of landscape, based less on territoriality and specialized spaces with restricted access, and more on that vernacular liking for mobility and the temporary use of public or semi-public spaces.

I first noticed this great change in America when I came back after three years overseas during World War II. I was amazed by how our cities had grown, how crowded and full of life the streets were, how many new uses of public places had come into being, and how a new popular architecture was spreading across the country.

One of the first essays I wrote in *Landscape* was an attempt to understand the commercial strip. One of its characteristics was accessibility, another was the new-style exterior of the buildings: gaudy, unconventional, and obviously designed to attract the mobile consumer and lure him into stopping. The strip was merely the earliest example of a kind of architecture meant to be experienced from the outside and to appeal to the passing motorist: We soon invented the drive-in bank, the drive-in movie theater, and the drive-in church. Then there was the super truck stop, the super motel, the supermarket, and (what is still evolving) the super service center for automobiles—an elaborately planned landscape containing every possible auto-oriented business, from tire repair to paint jobs to auto sales.

Everywhere access was made easier and more alluring. The new architecture allowed us to have immediate contact with whatever we were looking for: no more waiting for a clerk to come and ask what you wanted, no more waiting for a server to take a request to the kitchen. Nor was there a need for the formality that governed our interaction with clerks or waiters, the social rituals that were to department stores or restaurants what hospitality was to the home. We helped ourselves; instant accessibility was the watchword.

The popularity of exterior architectural spaces—pedestrian walkways, mini-plazas, skyways and tunnels inserted between massive buildings—alerts us to the fact that the new kind of street culture has already made an impact on the urban scene and is telling us that the space of the street is the heart of the city, not green and spacious parks or the blocks of masonry in which people work and live.

Even contemporary urban parks and public squares have recently undergone a radical change in their functions.[1] The more our houses and tenements overflow into the street, the more the street will serve as a spacious extension and substitute for domestic activities and relationships. Public spaces are no longer quiet and respectable: they have become the setting for political confrontations, informal instantaneous contacts, buying, selling, and the exchange of ideas. Public spaces are more and more the setting for work, white-collar as well as manual. Our social position depends less on our ability to provide hospitality than on our ability to know the nuances of life on the street.

It is no longer realistic, it seems to me, to discuss the vernacular dwelling as having distinct architectural characteristics. More and more the dwellings of lower-income groups (wage earners and workers in many service industries) are all but identical, at least when seen from the outside, to the dwellings of the middle class. All that we can rely on as a definition of the vernacular house is the way it is lived in and its relationship with its immediate daily environment.

Nevertheless, I continue to look for some visual clue to the nature of the contemporary American vernacular house, and I think I have found one. I think a vernacular house is one that is surrounded by a large number of cars. They are parked on a driveway that leads to the garage, in the back yard, sometimes on the front lawn, and along the curb. The husband has a car to go to work in (often his car is a truck or van that he uses all day long—delivering, collecting, hauling, servicing, and transporting people and freight). The wife has a car to go to her job in. One of the children drives to school in his or her own car.

The cars, pickups, and Jeeps surrounding the house represent small-scale investment. Bought at a low price from a dealer or auctioneer, they are tuned up, modified, customized, and sold at a profit, a small beginning of capital accumulation. The spectacle in certain neighborhoods of the infestation of cars is not attractive, but I find consolation of a sort in the notion that all those automobiles stand for liberation from the constraints imposed by the house: the prospect of easier contact with the surrounding world, the prospect of showing off and—the most important prospect of all—achieving privacy.

Cars are not confined to the vernacular population; nine families out of ten possess them. But nowhere have they really improved a lifestyle as much as in blue-collar neighborhoods. The car has taken over, emptying the house of its noisy population, providing a privacy hitherto unknown and relieving the house of its burden of chores and responsibilities: taking the family to the day care center, the laundromat, the supermarket, the drive-in restaurant, the emergency room at the hospital. All that is left of the house is an environment dedicated to leisure and childhood pleasures.

The new landscape can be called the "auto-vernacular landscape." Though primarily urban, it is spreading across the country. (Even the old-fashioned rural and small-town vernacular that we recognize as "agro-vernacular," devoted to land and stability, is being replaced by a landscape devoted to mobility and short-term planning.) It is reminiscent not only of the medieval prototype but also of the barbaric prototype, with its obsessive wandering, its casual attitude toward the house and other traditional institutions, and, above all, its habit of sharing or borrowing public spaces.

The real challenge is defining the auto-vernacular landscape. At the moment I see it as composed of structures and spaces designed to accommodate the auto as distinguished from spaces designed to accommodate people: the interstate, the parking lot, the strip, the gas station, the downtown multiple level garage, the race track, and innumerable storage and transit facilities. The mobile consumer is at the wheel, but the layout of space is designed for vernacular movement, which does not occur at human scale. Similar places are by no means lacking in the countryside; a field modified to suit the tractors or a landing strip for planes has the same impersonal, empty beauty and attraction.

I am struck by the number of outdoor public spaces that owe their existence to the car and the number of structures and spaces, created by the automobile, that bring us together. Having worked in a gas station, I am aware of a very definite sense of place in many of them and of a sense of fraternity that can develop in even the least sightly of roadside installations. In spite of my weakness for truck stops and service stations, I hesitate to think of them as the modern equivalent of the "moral unit." Still, they are places where strangers come together and where they often turn for help, advice, and companionship. There is promise in many parts of the auto-vernacular landscape, with its emphasis on mobility and borrowed space, a promise of a place or institution that fosters what might be called a sodality, a society based not on territoriality and position and inaccessibility but on shared interests and mutual help.

The vitality of our car and street culture, its ability to evolve and to discipline itself, contrasts sharply with the decay of that part of our culture that is based on the dwelling and the permanent community. As our stock of houses decreases every year in quantity and quality, as our slums expand and the homeless can no longer be numbered, certain characteristics of our landscape seem to disintegrate before our eyes. One part of it sprouts new office buildings, superhighways, super parking lots, and condominiums, while the rows of shabby and crowded inner-city dwellings, abandoned tenements, abandoned schools, and churches wait to be bulldozed out of existence. No wonder we resent the new tyranny of the street and the automobile.

Yet on a certain very modest level these two elements sometimes come together to form what might be called a new kind of mini-urban landscape. You catch a glimpse of it in the fringe neighborhoods every American town and city now has: areas where the newest, the poorest and least skilled of minority families live. Often it is no more than several clusters of beat-up trailers, mobile homes, and campers, or sometimes hastily built shanties—much too crude to qualify as vernacular. Along a short, unpaved street or formless public space you find a convenience store, a laundromat, a day care center, a bilingual evangelical church, and a building called "Heart and Hands" or "Bright Tomorrow." That is where there are posters sternly warning us to lay off drugs. Inside volunteers listen to tales of beatings and dress knife wounds.

But there is also a gas station, a used car lot, a shop where radiators are repaired, and even a car wash. At the end of the day driveways and alleys are filled with cars and trucks being worked on, and low-riders or their equivalent with flashy paint jobs roar up and down the street, giving off clouds of blue exhaust. The neighborhood, such as it is, comes to life, and you begin to think this is a world where community and cars belong together, like bread and butter or ham and eggs.

A thousand years ago out of desperation we tried to devise a new arrangement: house and land. After a rough start it took hold, and, as we all know, it created a rich and beautiful landscape. Perhaps we can do it again.

Commentaries and
Future Directions

WILBUR ZELINSKY

12   Seeing Beyond the Dominant Culture

Perhaps the most useful contribution I can make to a discussion about "seeing beyond the dominant culture" is to offer a critical glance at the concept of ethnic landscapes with special reference to the American scene.

For most of our compatriots in recent times, the term *ethnic* has acquired a rather limited definition, but I prefer to frame it in a broader and, I believe, much more meaningful way by having it refer to "the ethnie" or, if you please, "the nation." Such a term identifies a fairly large real, or perhaps imagined, community of individuals who cherish a distinctive culture or history and regard their specialness as peculiarly important, setting them apart from other social groups. Such a community may—but often does not—aspire to some degree of political autonomy. If we adopt such a definition, what sorts of ethnic landscapes have ever existed, or are possible, in the United States?

What we find in geographic fact, in some three million square miles of territory sandwiched between Quebec and the borderlands of middle America, is a single dominant culture—one pervasive ethnic group—an entity we can properly label Anglo-American. (To simplify the argument, I am ignoring the closely related Anglo-Canadian community; the interrelationships between our two communities are close, complex, and not yet fully worked out.) The Anglo-American ethnic landscape is the product of the early transfer of various immigrant groups and their cultural baggage from northwest Europe, then a certain set of transformations under the impact of novel environmental and social conditions here, and, subsequently, the automatic acceptance of the resulting package by millions of later arrivals and their progeny.

The invading Europeans encountered in North America a varied set of genuine preexisting ethnic landscapes that were the result of many generations of cultural revolution. We have only a hazy perception of what most of these humanized places were like in visible, physical terms, and for too many virtually no information at all. Obliteration was the fate of nearly all Native American landscapes, with perhaps only one major regional exception—those scattered but reasonably authentic patches surviving in New Mexico and Arizona. (We can increase the count to two if we consider a large fraction of Alaska.) Elsewhere, the places inhabited or frequented today by Native Americans bear little resemblance to the homelands of their ancestors.

The supremely potent Anglo-American cultural system has its regional variety, of course, and with such variability a distinctive set of regional (but by no means ethnic) landscapes. As it happens, I have spent much of my career exploring these fascinating regional nuances. Thus we have the individualities of New England, the Pennsylvania culture area, the Middle West, southern California, the Mormon culture area, and other special tracts, but all are locked within a single unifying cultural embrace. The nearest approach to a genuinely autonomous ethnic—and it is a close call—is to be found in the persistent particularities of the South. There are also instances of partial hybridization with alien but related cultures, as in Louisiana's Acadiana and that ethnic shatter zone stretching from southern California to the mouth of the Rio Grande. And, of course, the entire system keeps on evolving in response to external stimuli and its own internal logic.

But, despite all the intriguing regional variations upon a central theme and the effects of time, there is really no serious challenge to a pervasive, if largely subconscious, code governing the proper ways in which to arrange human affairs over American space: how to cope with natural habitats; how to design towns, cities, houses, roads, other structures, or cemeteries; how to occupy rural territory; and, in general, how to relate to our surroundings.

If, for the sake of argument, you can accept this reasoning, what thoughts can we entertain concerning the sorts of landscapes set forth in the three previous papers? I discern two different situations, neither of which can inspire very much cheer among those who enjoy visualizing the United States as a multi-ethnic land.

Rina Swentzell's poignant account of the clash of two utterly different mind sets, two irreconcilable ways of dealing with the face of the earth and the things upon it, in Chapter 4 serves to remind us that a conflict that began in the American Southwest more than four hundred years ago has not yet completely played itself out; that there is no solution mutually acceptable to the two contending ethnic groups. When it comes to the crunch, can there be any question as to which party will prevail?

We can only hope, as much for the sake of our own enlightenment as for the general cause of ethnic integrity, that some pueblo landscapes will remain intact and endure. Clearly, there is no comfortable answer to the dilemma of such embattled groups surrounded and constantly assaulted by the intrusions of an overbearing national society. But in the setting of the American Southwest, there is the advantage of having some surviving shreds of the preexisting landscape around, in this instance one with special appeal even to outsiders, with which to marshal resistance.

No such advantage was available to those relative latecomers from Asia and Latin America (or the earlier ones from Africa) and from those sections of Europe beyond the zone nurturing the founders of our dominant culture. These immigrants confronted a preformed, predetermined set of rules, a settlement code already locked solidly into the ground and one they could modify only in the more trivial of details.

That was certainly true in the case of the large, reluctant influx of Africans. With a certain amount of luck you may be able to identify a few tangible items that may have had an African origin, or then again you may not. I have in mind such things as the style of some southern African-American church buildings, certain grave decorations, the bare-swept front yard, and some gardening practices. But even the most African of southern rural tracts does not replicate any portion of Nigeria or Ghana, and the urban African-American ghetto could never be mistaken for any neighborhood in an African metropolis.

I enjoy prowling through the so-called ethnic neighborhoods of our cities as much as anyone and looking at whatever is to be seen. But I must confess that I have never been able to identify any non-American ethnic landscape in any American city. There are, of course, particular sections of a city where a particular immigrant group, or its descendants, comprises all or most of the population. And, sure enough, one comes across what are called ethnic markers, such as distinctive shop signs, exotic religious objects in yards or on porches, ephemeral festival decorations, certain cemetery features, an occasional historical monument, or startling new color patterns for houses acquired by Portuguese-Americans and other chromatically adventurous groups (not to mention what the invading Québecois have done with old Yankee farmhouses in New England). Perhaps the closest approximation to an ethnic statement is in ecclesiastical architecture—those alien synagogues, mosques, and non-Protestant church buildings. Upon further scrutiny, however, these structures turn out to be compromised structures, a blending of styles and construction techniques from two contrasting ethnic worlds.

But whatever exotic tidbits one may glean in these "ethnic" neighborhoods are the handiwork of rather temporary sojourners, and we are dabbling with cosmetics instead of basics. The immigrants did not design or build the neighborhoods and almost inevitably will pass them on some day to other sets of newcomers. The same neighborhood (including its churches) can be recycled through a varied succession of immigrant groups. The textbook sequence of Irish, Germans, Italians, Eastern Europeans, Jews, African-Americans, Hispanics, and East Asians observed in several of our larger metropolises is only one of the actual scenarios.

Moreover, some of these transient groups were not aware of their so-called ethnic identity until they were briefed on the matter by 100 percent Americans. That is what seems to have been the experience of many Italian-Americans, German-Americans, Yugoslavs, African-Americans, and others who previously had little group consciousness beyond that of their village or region in the Old World.

The disconcerting truth would seem to be that we really have no Polish-American, Greek-American, Jewish-American, African-American, or other such ethnic landscapes in any meaningful sense. David Chuenyan Lai has served us well by classifying and describing the various types of Chinatowns in the United States and Canada (see Chapter 6), but here again I must question their authenticity as ethnic expressions. As a matter of fact, Lai reveals the essential visual fakery of such neighborhoods in a single pivotal sentence when he states that "Western architects or contractors built most of the old Chinatown buildings, but they tried to create 'chinoiserie' or exotica by modifying or manipulating standard Western architectural forms."

And, of course, an ever-increasing majority of Chinese-Americans reside in homes and neighborhoods that are outwardly quite indistinguishable from those of old-stock Americans. I invite the reader to inspect the upscale African-American sections of Greater Atlanta or Washington, the predominantly Jewish suburbs of Detroit or Chicago, those tracts of greater Los Angeles frequented by affluent Americans of Japanese or Korean origin, and then show me their ethnic specialness. The moral, of course, is that all these non-WASP folks were expected to conform and melt into the larger physical fabric of American life as fully and rapidly as possible. And the overwhelming majority were only too delighted to do just that.

What we seem to be getting in our latter-day Chinatowns, whatever their historical origins, is fantasy made tangible, a make-believe China as tourist or patron would like to imagine it or the China best calculated to separate the visitor from his cash. They are specimens of a larger tribe of roadside attractions that includes synthetic Wild West frontier towns and those garish Indian villages to be found in western North Carolina's Cherokee country and elsewhere. We also encounter their ilk vicariously, at an even further remove, in movies filmed in North African villages, Mexican plazas, or Polynesian paradises on the back lots of Hollywood movie studios. Any resemblance to cultural reality is strictly accidental.

This entertainment genre goes back to Chicago's Columbian Exposition of 1893, if not to even earlier events, when an array of exotic villages was concocted for the edification of the visitor. Still vivid in my recollection is the Belgian Village of Chicago's World's Fair of 1933–34 and other absolutely nonmidwestern villages magically erected along the shores of Lake Michigan. The tradition lingers on, after a fashion, in some of our newer theme parks.

In considering the Power of Place project in which Dolores Hayden has been so deeply involved (see Chapter 9), we confront a quite different phenomenon or question: How best to remember, or resurrect and celebrate, ethnic history? As it happens, I am in total personal and ideological sympathy with her didactic strategy and I applaud all such efforts to remind us of a largely forgotten, too often ignominious past—and thus, indirectly at least, to help mend a contemporary world that needs all the healing it can get. But again, I am obliged to express reservations about the ethnic authenticity of whatever landscapes we may be rescuing, restoring, or fabricating.

Hayden's chapter suggests a much vaster problem: How are we as a society to deal with the past in its entirety, not just the ethnic facets thereof? How much is to be preserved or rediscovered? To which fragments of the visible fabric of our daily lives should we cling, and which should we permit to change or disappear? Which elements, if any, should be museumized? How do we join together harmoniously the preservable past with an unruly present? But thereon hangs another book, or rather an endless series of discussions.

Yes, it is certainly important to look beyond the dominant culture, to learn how all those many alien peoples have fared as they tried to cope with that huge, absorbent phenomenon we call the American cultural system. What I question is the effectiveness of examining pseudo-ethnic landscapes as a strategy for getting at cultural adjustment or survival.

Just as is the case with our political and legal systems, we have in the built landscape something thoroughly public—and, to a certain degree, official. It does not take kindly to foreign intrusion or modification, for serious deviance from the norm is simply too offensive to the collective eye. If we wish to explore what is happening with the minority cultures within our borders, we must resort to less visible departments of cultural behavior, to those venues (such as worship, cuisine, social organizations, literature, and the arts) where there is space for experiment, improvisation, and cross-fertilization.

On the other hand, there are other motives for scrutinizing whatever passes for ethnic landscapes in America. Such places fall within the category of the landscapes of entertainment or fantasy. If we really wish to know more about Americans in general, they deserve our earnest attention.

RICHARD WALKER

13 Unseen and Disbelieved: A Political Economist among Cultural Geographers

After having spent almost two decades in Berkeley, past home of Carl Sauer and John Brinckerhoff Jackson, it is refreshing for me to be asked to comment on cultural geography and landscape studies. Times change hard. I was for many years treated as a viper in the bosom of geography by virtue of my affinity for economic analysis and Marxist theory.[1] This schism between cultural studies and political economy long stood in the way of a vital comingling of ideas. Now that the dam of old intransigences has broken, a fresh flow of ideas is washing over Berkeley geography.[2] More broadly, a new cultural geography is being forged by a generation of scholars—represented in this book by Denis Cosgrove, Deryck W. Holdsworth, and Paul Groth—who are widely schooled in social theory, willing to engage political economy, and who draw inspiration from the maverick cultural materialists within the Marxist camp, especially Raymond Williams.[3] Meanwhile, many of those raised on political economy and Marx have moved in the other direction, giving rise to a renaissance of urban cultural studies.[4]

In current approaches to landscape studies, there is an enormous creative tension between cultural and material studies. In the limnal zones of this encounter lie fertile places, yet it may be hasty to presume that mere declaration of good intent will suffice to warn of the dangers that the collision of theoretical frameworks and interpretative habits poses. My point of departure is Cosgrove's essay "Spectacle and Society: Landscape as Theater in Premodern and Postmodern Cities," Chapter 8 in this volume. Cosgrove's erudite essay, reminiscent of his extraordinary book *Social Formation and Symbolic Landscape,* raises a set of important issues, and his pirouette with David Harvey's *Condition of Postmodernity* hints at some of the difficult problems around which he finds it best to dance lightly.[5] I have organized my remarks around the key themes touched on by Cosgrove.

Theater, Spectacle, and Ordinary Landscapes

Theater is a valuable metaphor and analytic tool by which to understand the creation, display, utilization, and consumption of landscapes.[6] Cosgrove is well in line with recent thinking on the importance of social spectacle and the drama of urban life, an approach that breaks with strictly utilitarian or functional interpretations of landscapes. The icons of urban landscapes operate as common points of reference that are symbolically charged with the power of collective myth and involve history rewritten and futures anticipated.

Yet the current delight in fantastic and singular icons leaves a good deal out of the picture. What is the relation between spectacularly contrived venues and objects—whether piazzas, statues, or buildings—and everyday bits and pieces of the city—the uneventful and humble homes, factories, shrines, and pavements that bulk far larger than the special ones? What strikes me about, say, Orange County, California, is not its postmodern highlights, as elaborated by the iconographer Ed Soja, but the utter banality of yet another stretch of suburbia.[7] Guy Debord, from whom the catch-phrase "society of the spectacle" is taken, would be scathing in his criticism of an iconography that tries to gloss over the banality of everyday life by striking poses about high art or high kitsch.[8] But the interrogation of ordinary landscapes is not easy; it requires a deeper familiarity with the lives of common people and close attention to vernacular clues by humble archeologists of the contemporary. Here John Brinckerhoff Jackson's landscape school has shown the way.[9]

The sort of intellectual history practiced by Denis Cosgrove is perched precariously on the top of the social pyramid. Within the new cultural geography lies an unresolved contradiction between Cosgrove's perorations on grand piazzas and Palladian villas and declarations on the importance of popular culture by Peter Jackson or vernacular cityscapes by Paul Groth.[10] What is the intersection of landscape as high culture with the world constructed by ordinary people?

As Cosgrove points out, the idea of landscape in Europe was first of all a pictorial one that was applied systematically to the production of grand parks and lordly mansions. But not all manifest landscapes have such lofty origins. While the great artist like Claude Lorrain or Andrea Palladio may profoundly alter ways of seeing and conceiving of landscapes, the diffusion of ideas among the intelligentsia (much less the apprehension of ideas by the unlettered) runs an uncertain course that must be teased out from the swirl of ideas, in the manner of

Williams's effort to capture "structures of feeling" among the writers of an era.[11] Similarly, while the mighty burgher or aristocrat may be able to dictate the built form of large swaths of land (or impose a linear system of land survey across a whole country, as did Thomas Jefferson), the bulk of improvement and construction is carried out under lesser masters, yielding the incredible jumble of most ordinary cities and rural lands.

Similarly, one of the limits of the postmodern debate on cities has been an obsession with a form of modern architecture and planning that never triumphed over the vernacular portions of cities.[12] Even David Harvey is taken in by this high-end drift, when he defines postmodernism as "an eclectic mixture of styles, historical quotation, ornamentation, and diversification of surfaces."[13] Despite his awareness of counterflow within the culture of modernism, Harvey seems to forget that a historicist, romantic, eclectic form of urbanism has a long and distinguished presence in North American cities—as suburbia, the prized landscape of bourgeois consumption. As Robert Fishman says, "if . . . we are seeking the architecture that best reveals 'the spirit and character of modern civilization,' then suburbia might tell us more about the culture that built the factories and skyscrapers than these edifices themselves can."[14] An obsession with monumentality and modernity has caused people to overlook the crucial differences between the spaces of business and the spaces of consumption, two landscapes, two bourgeois utopias, often at odds with each other.[15] Suburbia is a landscape heavily infected with class denial with regard to urbanism and its capitalist roots; one did not have to wait for postmodern architecture to discover this streak in bourgeois landscape tastes. This systematic evasiveness in art and landscapes, the vision of absence, makes it doubly difficult to pin down the relations between material and ideational culture or between critique and affirmation of the dominant social order.

Ironically, the vernacularists are often just as guilty of rampant elitism and idealism as is the historian of ideas, despite their claim to go forth in sackcloth and ashes through the streets. A common ploy is to ascribe popular building styles to such transcendent notions as "the Jeffersonian ideal" without devoting sufficient attention to the practical bases for the popular acceptance of lofty concepts or the pragmatic constraints under which actual building goes forward.[16] By contrast, an exemplary blending of leading ideals and vernacular influences in landscape analysis is achieved by Fishman's *Bourgeois Utopias,* which traces the suburban form of homes-in-a-park from its origins in late eighteenth-century Britain to twentieth-century North America. While giving the designers John Nash and Frederick Law Olmsted their due, Fishman is careful to integrate these with the collective actions of the English Evangelicals and ultimately the whole class of suburbanizing burghers from Philadelphia to Los Angeles.

Yet even this remains on a fairly lofty plane and needs to be supplemented by studies such as Anthony D. King's *Bungalow,* which fill in essential details about the evolving aesthetics, production, and morphology of ordinary housing.[17] Furthermore, one has to recognize the tension between the suburban ideal and the dystopian effects of property markets, as the calculus of capital investment and speculation in land hems in the suburban dreams of most people trying to carve out humble living quarters.[18] Hence, traces of culture as symbol and sign, tradition, and ethnic signature must give due weight, as Deryck W. Holdsworth reminds us, to such mundane considerations as tenant-landlord relationships, inventories of property and possessions, and the like.[19]

Last, some account must be taken of the relation of residential districts to territories and landscapes of production in the city, as has only recently been taken up by economic geographers.[20] The landscape school has been altogether evasive about such systematic forces of political economy in mainstream capitalist America, and in answering the question of who and what, in fact, create urban and rural environments.[21]

Vision, Text, and the Ideology of Landscape

Cosgrove is surely right to argue for a dialectic of image and text and for taking the visual image seriously, in comparison to the literally textual strategies of so many postmodern commentators. Intellectuals raised on the written word can be mistrustful of other ways of knowing. He singles out Harvey, in particular, for a "distrust of image and faith in text."[22] At the same time, he chides cultural geographers for being spellbound by the purely visual qualities of landscape and for being captive to the dominance of the visual in European culture, tainted by the controlling sweep of an upper class, white, male outlook, or "Gaze."[23]

For landscape studies, visual command of space is of central importance. Cosgrove demonstrates in his book that the emergence of perspectivism in renaissance Italy provided a major axis for the organization of space in the modern world. He ties perspectivism to rationalized methods of survey and mapping appearing under the prod of commercial activity in the quickening European economy of the mercantile era.[24] He further observes that "an important effect of linear perspective is to arrest the flow of history at a specific moment, freezing that moment as a universal reality. Perspective, in structuring and directing universal reality at a single spectator, acknowledges only one, external subject for the object it represents. Thus, a landscape painted in accordance with pictorial rules, or nature observed by an eye trained to look at it as landscape, is in important respects far from being realistic . . . . The claim of realism is in fact ideological."[25]

These are powerful insights, but sweeping judgments about visual dominance and the emergence of perspectivism can whisk away the necessary subtleties of historical interpretation. The play of the visual and textual in European history is difficult to unravel—so difficult that Cosgrove and Anthony D. King (in his essay in this volume) appear to contradict themselves on which is truly dominant.[26]

To begin with, the reading of texts is itself a visual practice that triumphed, with the coming of the printing press, over oral traditions of knowing. Conversely, art historians regularly debate the presence of a textual mode within painting, and Svetlana Alpers even distinguishes between a southern European textuality and a northern ocularity.[27] Nor is the unfolding of perspectivism unproblematic over the course of European painting; Norman Bryson argues that as soon as perspectival painting had been invented, it was tinkered with and taken in unexpected directions; soon multiple perspectives and abstractions of viewpoint were introduced, with stunning and totally original results.[28] Indeed, the contrast between Gentile Bellini's fifteenth-century *Procession in the Piazza di San Marco* and Jacopo Tintoretto's sixteenth-century *Translation of St. Mark's Body,* of which Cosgrove makes much, is a good example of the dramatic manipulation of perspective to gain very different effects (Bellini is decidedly *not* a preperspective painter). So is the work of Claude Lorrain, the seventeenth-century master of the picturesque landscape.[29] Much later, perspective and the whole pictorial mode were ironically toyed with by the impressionists, then shattered fully by the cubists.[30]

David Harvey, elder political economist among the geographers, is keenly aware of the play of visual dominance and disintegration within the modernist stance. Harvey's concern with the capitalist manipulation of urban landscapes and pictorial representations for commercial gain is not, therefore, the same as a dismissal of images and postmodernism as inauthentic, as Cosgrove avers. It is more a question of "authentic for whom?" since images make for authentic profits and propaganda. Indeed, Harvey is at pains to show that postmodern theatrics are— for all their apparent chaos, fragmentation, and playfulness—purposeful constructs for the obfuscation of (and diversion from) urban squalor and class conflict.[31] On this point, Cosgrove should agree, judging by his analysis of the theatrics of Tintoretto, whose painting is full of myth making and melodrama, masking the less pleasant realities of social change in Venice.[32]

As Cosgrove knows full well and has written: "Landscape . . . is an ideological concept. It represents a way in which certain classes of people have signified themselves and their world through their imagined relationship with nature, and through which they have underlined and communicated their own social role and that of others with respect to external nature."[33] Built landscapes are robustly ideological, full of illusion as to their place in systems of power, profit, and passion.

(This is equally so whether they are the unified vision of an architect or the disparate art of many hands whose coherence is the unintentional result of common ways of imagining and living.) The city and its monuments are an unending procession of spectacle, high drama, low farce, and play of representations upon the rude stones—fraud on the grandest scale—from classical Athens to Islamic Cairo or from Baron Georges-Eugène Haussmann's Paris to Frank Gehry's Los Angeles. The urban fabric is a record of repeated efforts by the ruling classes to bring their kind of order and design to bear against the apparently inchoate patterns of myriad city-dwellers, involving a struggle between high art and low, the power-serving and the playful, and the monumental and the living tissue of the vernacular.

The play of image and text espoused by Cosgrove simply does not go far enough in pursuit of the antimonies of this accumulated urban symbolism and landscape ideology. Neither the false objectivism of positivist science nor noncommittal deconstruction of representational games is sufficient to uncover the play of consciousness and material life in the making of territories deeply instilled with cultural meaning and ideology.

Critical theory, by contrast, calls for the deconstruction of ideology by means of all available powers of analytical abstraction, given that prevailing representations are partial, distorted, and misleading manifestations of the full sweep of social life and material practices.[34] Harvey is well justified in saying that the argument of the eye is less trustworthy than that of the mind (in Cosgrove's paraphrase); one needs insight, a feeling for structure, and the hard work of critical deconstruction directed at a given discourse, painting, or landscape to reveal its many facets and levels of significance. An exemplary reading of the juncture of visual and textual modes of representation is that of John Barrell, dealing with the age of agricultural improvement and landscape aesthetics in England. He attends closely to the way literary strategies enact structures of feeling embedded in specific forms of agriculture and spatial organization and teases out the oppositions of viewpoint between and within class positions—whether the writer is the modernizer Arthur Young or the critical poet John Clare.[35]

To their credit, John Brinckerhoff Jackson and the old cultural geographers tried hard to educate the blind eye of the American public to the landscapes around them. But one must, as a part of ideology critique, denaturalize the everyday, not just appreciate it. Doing so requires a critical stance toward the disturbing social forces, from racism to capital accumulation, at work in the molding of contemporary material culture.[36] Deryck W. Holdsworth is correct to take landscape writers to task for this failing and to argue the necessity of penetrating the images of the landscape to reveal less obvious economic and political forces at work behind the immediate field of objects and representations.[37] Decoding the ideology of landscape and stripping away the cultural veil over the hard machinery of political economics is not easy, however, and a bracing dose of Marxist theory cannot do the job alone.[38] What is needed, again, is a sophisticated cultural materialism.

From Pillar to Post: In Search of the Modern

Cosgrove takes a postmodernist turn in his paper, adopting the grand narrative of premodern-modern-postmodern; but what is the analytic purchase of the concept of modernity on the landscape history he studies?[39] Grave errors can arise from hasty conclusions about the rise and fall of modernity without regard to the complications of internal class struggles, contending political positions, and uneven development. The difficulties can be suggested by a series of questions.

How substantial a break in visualization and landscape formation occurred with the emergence of a landscape way of seeing around 1500? Cosgrove presents as evidence for Venice the contrast between the extended narrative form of the Bellini painting and the focused drama of Tintoretto. Although we can clearly distinguish between the eyewitness spectacle of Bellini and the mannerist theatrics of Tintoretto as different forms of representational art,[40] it is harder to see a vast sea-change in the ideological relation of the art to the city it serves: both paintings are ideologically charged portraits, confirming the social order of the city through its leading icons. Cosgrove argues that one is more a participant in the Bellini type of urban panorama,[41] but that depends very much on one's position in the social hierarchy and ideological constellation. While Bellini's panoramic landscape is less individualistic and distanced than the Tintoretto, it takes its meaning no less from the observer's sense of command and participation in the spectacle. The key political difference is that his participants still include the small tradesmen and craft workers integrated through the corporatist system of the *Grand Scuole*.[42]

Is sixteenth-century Venice a valid case of emergent capitalism and an attendant move toward modernization? Cosgrove's essay gives the barest mention of Venice's changing social battleground, but his book is more explicit about "arrested capitalism in Renaissance Italy."[43] A feudal involution took place against the background of a disintegrating commercial empire, with the richest burghers investing in landed estates of the Veneto while the once-formidable corporate system of smaller masters and merchants of the *scuole* were economically decimated and politically marginalized. Despite an initial impulse toward agriculture improvements, agrarian capitalism did not break through in Italy as it did in the north.[44]

What is the relation of the Renaissance to the rise of capitalism? Cosgrove is quite aware of the mixed parentage of renaissance humanism, which, while undoubtedly stimulated by the commercial advances of Italy, in many ways represented a high tide of feudalism.[45] We have to be careful not to adopt the bourgeois stance of Adam Smith and his followers whereby cities and commerce are wholly alien bodies within the feudal system, birthplace of capitalism. To do so is to rob the past (the cavernous, vacuous premodern) of its history, dynamism, and human achievements.[46]

Are theater and spectacle strictly modern (let alone postmodern) phenomena? Surely not, as Cosgrove's work illustrates. Fifteenth-century Venice was saturated with pageantry, spectacle, and pastiche of an elaboration, richness, and calculation that put most puny postmodern efforts, such as Baltimore's Harbor Place, to shame. People still flock by the millions each year to view one of the greatest assemblages of urban icons on earth. The surviving landscape of Venice is the testament of a confident commercial class and probably the largest urban renewal effort before Hausmann's Paris.[47]

Is the formal landscape a product of the bourgeoisie and its form of modern rationality? Formal landscapes, whether of urban regimentation or Arcadian countryside, bear more than a whiff of aristocratic posturing, state authoritarianism, and rationalist intellectual arrogance, none of which is, strictly speaking, reducible to the modern or bourgeois. Baroque city plans were strongly associated with the Counter-Reformation in Rome, absolutism in northern Europe, and Federalist politics in America. Cosgrove has provided a wonderful analysis of the baroque arts as a species of romantic reaction to the Renaissance and Reformation, which one might say is politically akin to the romanticism in post-Napoleonic Europe or postmodern America today.[48] Even within renaissance humanism contradictions abound: Leone Battista Alberti had the same hubris as René Descartes, a kind of secularization of Divine Reason as the genius of a few Great Men (city planners and architects). Is this absolutist mentality essential to modernity, or does it represent a failure to go very far beyond the pious certainties of medieval Catholicism?[49]

How strong was the commonality across Europe in the modern landscape way of seeing? Cosgrove, in his book, is forced to negotiate his way through a shifting history of uneven development, as the center of mercantile capital shifted from Italy to the Low Countries, thence to Britain, and later to the United States. Dutch landscape paintings (and cities) of the sixteenth and seventeenth centuries show little of the pretentious idealism and aristocratic domination of the Italy of Alberti and Palladio, let alone that of Giovanni Lorenzo Bernini's Rome. While many English and Scots burghers shared the same Puritan and Leveler tastes as the Dutch, the gentrified bourgeoisie and commercialized aristocracy of eighteenth-century Britain looked further south to the Italians (or, rather, to French and Italian mythologized portrayals of the Baroque era by Claude Lorrain, Nicholas Poussin, and Salvator Rosa) for inspiration in organizing the "pleasing prospects" around their burgeoning country estates. A further twist in the shift from Italy to

Britain was that the urbanization of the countryside became the ruralization of the city, with the ultimate dominance of the Arcadian landscapes of suburbia. Italian rationalism in landscape imagination did not resonate deeply in the north, despite a few Georgian terraces and new town plans, and romantic tastes in wild landscapes carried the day.

Then there are the French, who have never given up on urban culture or their preference for formal gardens. And, despite the rationalist tenor of the U.S. cadastral survey, Jeffersonian revolutionary enlightenment soon became weighed down by land speculation and the romantic sensibilities of nineteenth-century America.[50] One can easily read too much homogeneity into these divergent histories, and too much political economy into their cultural variety.

Landscapes of Conflict: The Uneasy Marriage of Materialism and Culture

The engagement between political economy and cultural studies is unavoidable by the nature of the tug of war in human life between material restraint and popular creativity, between structure and agency, and between production and appropriation. Unfortunately, most of the participants in this engagement have treated it more as a war of good and evil, taking sides instead of working out the hard intellectual problems.[51] In the 1980s the culturalists were in the ascendant, and political economy became a dirty word in certain academic quarters. I am a bit uneasy, therefore, about Cosgrove's postmodernist drift back toward the old idiographic and romantic sins of cultural geography, even as he attempts to revive the field in several recent books.

I am equally uneasy about the relabeling in the currently fashionable postmodernist terminology—instability of meanings, disparity between signifiers and signified, representations, and all that—of the perfectly serviceable Marxist concept of ideology.[52] I grow more concerned when Cosgrove waxes rhapsodic over John Ruskin as prefiguring today's postmodern sensibilities—though he is perfectly aware of Ruskin's Tory colors and idealizations of mythological, idealized pasts.[53] I am further dismayed when Cosgrove begins to distance himself from John Berger and Raymond Williams's alleged "Marxist stratigraphy of economic base and cultural superstructure," as if that were all there were to cultural materialism.[54] And I simply cannot accept that a person of his analytic skills could conclude that "from such a postmodern perspective landscape seems less like a palimpsest whose real or authentic meanings can somehow be recovered with the correct techniques, theories, or ideologies, than a flickering text displayed on the word-processor screen whose meaning can be created, extended, altered, elaborated, and finally obliterated by the merest touch of a button."[55] Cosgrove cannot miss the meaning of my flickering text when I say that this is hogwash. Meanings are not merely the whisper of bats in the night; they cohere into flocks to sleep in the caverns of social thought and reemerge in thunderous flight to ignite a million imaginations together. These things can be understood and tracked, and that is the work of social science.

Arguments over culture and political economy, the particular and the universal, and necessity and resistance, have been considerably muddied, from a geographer's point of view, by their conflation with a quite different dialectic, that of the local and the global. Cultural geography has not come to grips with the ineluctable tension between the diversity of particular peoples and the universalizing embrace of global forces of the market, industrial technologies, and finance capital. The danger of essentialism in the Marxist tradition, much decried by the postmodernists, is particularly glaring at a moment of global recomposition that has left communism in shreds, capitalist industries in tatters, and the peoples of the world in new migratory and territorial alignments. As Anthony D. King indicates in "The Politics of Vision," the revival of interest in culture and multicultural visions has everything to do with these changes.[56] Yet these globe-straddling upheavals demand powerful and sweeping concepts to match their processes and consequences, concepts that political economy is prepared to offer. It is not sufficient to retreat into the fragments and to declare them to be all that is certain or all that is worthy against the tide of global integration.[57]

Especially contentious is the consumer realm—the encounter between commercialized selling, the expression of human desires, and the realization of human needs—where culture studies and political economy come together with a bang.[58] Marxists such as Harvey can be extremely distrustful of the manipulations of capitalist consumer culture, as Cosgrove points out, and thereby place themselves in odd juxtaposition to the Sauerian refusal of modernity in all its forms. Scholars of the landscape school, by contrast, have made a point of defying high-minded critics in their embrace of ordinary commercial and residential landscapes. Certainly, landscapes of consumption are much more than scenes of fleeting desire, manipulated fashion, and the shallow play of images, though they are that, too; they are sites of prodigious labor, creative human activity, and oppressive relations of gender and age, as well as vigorous engagement, playful and serious, with the commodities brought home from the abundant capitalist market.

This is where the studies of youth subcultures of the Birmingham School strike a resonant chord, providing a vibrant model for cultural geography, as Peter Jackson indicates. In the cultural analysis of Paul Willis, for example, contemporary subcultures are not simply victims of the homogenizing tendencies of capitalism, against which they cling to traditional values, but are capable of appropriating and revising dominant cultural terms and artifacts into unexpected avenues of self-assertion and solidarity.[59] Cultural geography need not be a celebratory encounter with the practices of modern consumption, however. On this score John Brinckerhoff Jackson and friends have often been too respectful in the face of the crass and disagreeable, indeed ugly, habits of the common folk. Populism can be either conservative or progressive, and respect for common people is not the same as adulation.[60]

Yet the old cultural geography had a healthy respect for the evidence of material culture, which is in danger of slipping away in the reinvention of the field. Peter Jackson repudiates the study of common landscape artifacts, refusing to indulge in the "obsessional interest in culture-as-artifact of the Berkeley School."[61] While artifacts must be seen in dialectical relation with the ideational side of cultural practices, it strikes me as hopelessly idealist, and insubstantial, to try to grasp culture without considering the objects it uses and produces. This is not just a matter of collecting evidence[62] but of recognizing the process of human development itself, which depends on the objectification of consciousness for the further evolution of ideas.[63]

Consider the potential unleashed by mass consumption, given the access to produced objects it has made possible. These spawn of the capitalist market are not mute objects but themselves representations, in both body and surface, from which may be crafted further representations, styles and fashions, high and low arts, where imagination, time, free spaces, and money are in supply. They are also material bearers of ideology and the dominant cultures of modern globalism. On this crucial point of the dialectics of consumption, I must chide all round: the landscape school for an overly static (and often antimodernist) view of culture, new cultural geographers for a reversion to cultural idealism, and political economists for a dismissive view of consumer cultures.

Conclusion: A Word on Style

Unlike people of a literary wit and theatrical cast, such as Denis Cosgrove and Catherine Howett, I am one of those mundane analytic types who want principally to know how things work, not how they strike the sensibilities. Of course, I am not fool enough to think that human beings labor without imagination and that materialism can be shorn of the dialectics of consciousness and action. Yet I have a jaundiced eye for the way the high-powered sensitivities of many academics in the culturalist camp can be used to convert the least bit of combustible material into billows of smoke spreading across the intellectual landscape. I become easily irritated with the posturing of the postmodernist and the mannered style of discourse that glibly condemns the linear, logical, and evidentiary essay in favor of fragments of literary allusion and freely tossed Lacanian word salads, which leave a faint and convoluted trail of simulacrumbs for the poor reader to follow.

I note Denis Cosgrove's reference to "soft metaphors" in place of "technical analogies" with some apprehension, therefore, because it continues a long habit of splitting what cannot be split in human reason.[64] Metaphor and the play of imagination are not something that only humanists and postmodernists can lay claim to: they are, in fact, essential to all mental activity and "reasoning." The creative mind is, at the same time, engaged in constant self-discipline, boundary drawing, stereotyping and logical sorting.[65] We are both humanists and scientists in the bud, and the divisions between the cultural and materialist turns of mind among intellectuals have more to do with divisions of labor in academia than with absolute and indelible schisms within human life. I therefore end with a plea for overcoming false dualisms in geography and neighboring disciplines, and for the promiscuous mingling and mutual education of cultural geographers and political economists.

DELL UPTON

14   Seen, Unseen, and Scene

What is the relation between the seen and the unseen in landscape? What relative weight should we give the seen and the unseen in studying the landscape? Underlying these questions, which lurk in the background throughout this book, is the issue of the primacy of vision in landscape studies.[1] Every chapter reminds us that there is more to the landscape than that which is visible. This point is essential and correct, and each chapter offers some clue to what that "more" might be. What unseen ought we to include in our analysis of the scene?

The characteristics of space and people's experience of space are curiously underplayed throughout these essays. Space takes a back seat to imagery in the conceptualization of landscape. But care for the landscape demands attention to both the seeable and the unseeable, particularly to the relationship between the seen scene and unseen space.

What is the connection between space and landscape? Are global space, social space, and psychological space themselves landscapes, albeit unseeable, or is landscape merely a scene, a neatly framed visual fragment of a larger spatial order? James Borchert, for example, observes that many houses of the Village section of Lakewood, Ohio, appear to be single-family residences but actually consist of several small rental units (see Chapter 2). That is, the visible order describes one sort of community and the spatial order implies another. Is the visual imagery meant simply to fool us, disguising tenements as suburban houses to avert hostility or gain respect, or is there some more complex relation between the space allotted to individual households and the public space organized by the exterior imagery? In another passage Borchert mentions that differing daytime and nighttime social worlds occupy the same space: social constructions of time of day turn the same visible terrain into very different places. A third passage offers the intriguing observation that apartment buildings (and consequently their developers) were the focus of middle-class hostility, while apartment dwellers were indistinguishable from other citizens on the streets of Lakewood and consequently escaped confrontation. In every instance, the disjunction between visible order and social space presents an intriguing but undeveloped opportunity for considering the relationships between seen and unseen.

The unresolved relationship of visual order to space, of the landscape's totality and the individual experience within it, that we observe in Borchert's Lakewood reminds us that many landscape studies obscure these tensions from us. Landscape is the product of many individual mental and physical acts, yet we describe it in collective terms. This paradox reveals much about our understanding of landscape production.

The approaches that Deryck W. Holdsworth labels "vernacular" or "cultural landscape" studies hold the individual and the collective in unacknowledged suspension. Many scholars take what Holdsworth calls a "populist" approach, celebrating individual ingenuity or cultural resistance over socioeconomic setting. Yet this approach is often proffered in the context of a concept of the collective—a culture, a society, a tradition, a class—that gives a consensual cast to the landscape. We look for large-scale patterns as though they were the projects of a unitary society, often failing to ask about their relationship to particular social groups and individual actors. Who or what creates these patterns? Who is the repository of the mentality that created them? Any large-scale description unavoidably freezes the dynamic process of culture within the morphological patterns that are the building blocks of cultural landscape studies.

Stressing pattern and continuity also tends to elide stratification and fragmentation in the creation of landscape. Visualism gives a deceptive unity to the scene, which Holdsworth seeks to undermine. Holdsworth is tempted to argue that the necessity of "understanding [economic and social transformations] that have restructured places and regions and landscape outcomes" might require one to "get behind and beyond landscape." As a corrective analytical strategy, he would have us give close scrutiny to the specific projects and conflicting values of the economic and political spheres. This requires attention to the more complex, less visible landscape recorded in the archive and described in terms of land prices, living standards, or construction costs. Even Borchert, whose reaction against "traditional historical sources such as census records and newspapers" reminds us of the excitement of the discovery of the material world by historians just fifteen or twenty years ago, turns to socioeconomic data to explain the ways in which Lakewood departed from the stereotypical suburban image.

But this strategy, which ignores detailed examination of the material land-scape, also gives the tension between the individual and the collective as short a shrift as cultural landscape studies do. Anthony D. King's discussion elsewhere of the "anti-personalist orientation" of the purely visual approach to studying the landscape, its "undervaluing [of] the motives, values, beliefs of subjects as per-sons," applies equally to Borchert's less visual urban morphology and Holds-worth's antivisual approach.[2]

To be sure, Holdsworth acknowledges that there is something to be learned from the artifact. He implicitly accepts the landscape's claims of visual unity as deceptive or irrelevant. But who is deceived? Seeing is not always believing be-cause we experience landscape through other organs than our eyes and because we have stories to apply to the landscape other than those it may tell us. One need not romanticize the folk or take a populist stance to suggest that, because the meaning and experience of landscape are fragmented and debated, the political and economic processes that shape landscape are not the final word on its mean-ing. Rather, fissures run through the landscape's unity at every scale, from the in-dividual on up. Thus, when Holdsworth denies that the individual building and the experience of traditional culture are improper starting points for under-standing social change, he is only partly correct.

Landscape—the scene—undeniably offers itself to us as a transparent total-ity, coherent and final. Compared with the ephemeral nature of human con-sciousness and social action, the continuity of the material world and its apparent unchangeability seem to promise constant or certain meaning. Yet the stability of physical form falsely certifies stability of meaning; there may be no meaning at all. But we need not fall back on the paradoxical antimaterialism of old-fashioned ma-terialist history. Rather, we might take a cue from recent neo-Marxist scholarship that treats ideology as part of the process through which realities are constructed.

A fruitful approach to landscape would be to start from its claim that it is a complete record of evidence and to inquire why that claim is effective—while demonstrating how much the scene demands that we not see. By picking apart seen and unseen, we can begin to get at the variety of human experience in a way that shatters the landscape's pretenses. This conjunction of seen and unseen, then, draws our attention to the experience of landscape as well as its initial cre-ation. It emphasizes the relative roles of vision and the intangible in the inter-pretation of landscape. It acknowledges the fissures and discontinuities revealed by archival studies while repersonalizing a landscape left unpeopled both by vi-sual and archival analysis.

Commemorative landscapes of the sort that Reuben M. Rainey addresses in Chapter 5 offer an opportunity for a close analysis of physical places that respects the centrality of the unseen. Commemorative landscapes take advantage of the vi-

sual claim of totality and transparency to support their own propositions about social unity and moral commonality. They demand acquiescence and deflect criticism.

Rainey accepts this claim. In recounting the transformation of the Gettysburg
battlefield into a memorial landscape, he concludes that "no society can continue
to flourish without perpetuating its fundamental values through rituals of remembrance and the making of monuments." But we have to ask what values a
memorial battlefield does commemorate and how it does so. In particular, what
specifically are the fundamental values represented by Gettysburg's landscape?
Are fundamental values equivalent to the dominant political ideology? Is it
equally noble to die fighting for slavery and against it, to support a particular government and to rebel against it, as long as one is sincere? Is there a fundamental
value in killing and dying that has no reference to the issues at hand? Is the experience of warfare in general an ennobling social value? These are questions that
this commemorative landscape, as Rainey depicts it, elides. To open them up, we
would need to investigate the ways the landscape frames our perception of battle
and inquire how we might reframe it.

Several unseen—physically absent or imaginative—landscapes come to mind
in scanning Rainey's Gettysburg. We might ask, for example, how the commemoration of war on battlefields relates to its commemoration at other sites: How does
Gettysburg differ from, for example, Monument Avenue in Richmond, that remarkable landscape that someone once called a banana belt of dead Confederate
generals? This is similar to asking, What is the distinctive story that Gettysburg's
monuments tell? What other stories might be told?

In Rainey's account, two things strike me. The first is his stress on large values—peace, national unity, freedom. Yet those words have no inherent meaning.
They have content only as they are acted out in specific settings. Rainey reveals
the selective memory of war that the monuments and their creators perpetrated,
a memory that omits atrocities committed by both sides, omits the atmosphere of
racism and the murderous actions toward black soldiers on both sides, and omits
the wanton viciousness of warfare. Rainey sees these as regrettable omissions,
contradicting the ideals of freedom and unity that the monuments promote. I say
that those issues are necessarily unseen. They are absences integral to the monuments, offering a glimpse of the monument builders' conception of peace, national unity, and freedom. The construction of monuments to reconciliation and
the passage of Jim Crow laws was not an embarrassing contradiction but the ac-
tualization of a particular vision of peace, nationhood, and freedom, as Kirk Savage and Catherine Bishir have shown in their recent work on Civil War monuments in their social and landscape contexts.[3] Selectivity and absence are the
content of these monuments, not unfortunate omissions: the unseen forces the
scene to confess.

This coyness in the scene goes to the second element of Rainey's Gettysburg that strikes me: the builders' obsession with physical specificity—with getting the placement just right, with the precise depictions of weapons and equipment, and with the representation of individual soldiers. Idealizing the citizen-soldier in this way creates a false specificity that finesses (to put it generously) questions about how and by whom the citizen-soldier was used. It avoids the globalizing perspective, burying the abstract in a distracting particularity. Like Mr. Goodwrench, Ronald McDonald, Joe Camel, or a host of other corporate fictions, the citizen-soldier personalizes large-scale political power, concealing it within the actions of relatively powerless individuals.

But the particularity is evasive. The individual soldier lacks personal identity, a history, a social standing, a life away from the battlefield. He exists only to fight, so we do not ask who he is or how he came to fight. His mythical individuality stands for equally mythical collective values. Yet the historians' big question of the last twenty years has been "who?" When we speak of national values, whose values do we mean? When we speak of national actions and decisions, whose actions, whose decisions do they represent?

Rainey points out that the soldier statues were insisted on by the citizen-soldiers themselves. The battlefield commemorative site indulged the citizen-soldier's memory of personal suffering, deflecting attention from the sites where conflicts arose and where decisions were made. It displaced "who" from council room to battlefield. It was the final step in mobilizing assent that began with volunteering, passed through the experience of combat, and ended at formalized memory. It would have us believe—and an unimaginative cultural landscape reading would accept—that the process was heartfelt, unanimous, and willing. But the Civil War's history of draft riots, bought substitutes, and desertion from military service; of the ambivalent, to say the least, response to warfare that soldiers' letters reveal; and even of lukewarm response to subscription drives for support for monument building tells a different, unseen story. It offers a richer reading of the monuments than the one that monumental images and inscriptions urge on us.

Gettysburg represents a common strategy for fashioning a so-called reconciliatory landscape. The same strategy can be found at the Vietnam Veterans' Memorial in Washington, D.C., where the issues of that war are reduced to the names of the American dead and glossed with a dissembling statement that these people had been taken from us. Taken by whom? Did the Vietnamese kidnap these men and women from their homes? If not, how did they get there? Why? This kind of reconciliation represents not the healing of wounds but the discounting of some people's wounds; not the assertion of fundamental values over incidental differences but the subordination of principles to generalities—and thus the denigration of belief, the removal of actions from scrutiny, the deflection of criticism.

To study the memorial landscape in a way that questions its values rather than endorsing them requires attention not only to the kinds of structural issues that Holdsworth rightly emphasizes but also to the landscape itself. Holdsworth notes that modern people and places are often marginalized and restructured by processes over which they have little control. Studies of sites like the Gettysburg battlefield can help us to understand how. Commemorative landscapes offer tangible abstractions as a substitute for the intangible but uncomfortable specifics of power and interest. Concreteness and specificity are relocated from the realm of human relationships to that of, well, concrete. This displacement invites suspension of rational inquiry and a faith in abstractions that political legitimacy requires. In this case the seen obliterates the unseen to our peril, for it promises that we will have occasion to visit more such scenes as Gettysburg.

DAVID LOWENTHAL

15 European Landscape Transformations: The Rural Residue

Suddenly landscape seems to be everywhere—an organizing force, an open sesame, an avant-garde emblem, alike in fiction and music, food and folklore, even for professors and politicians. Like the chroniclers of collective memory in Pierre Nora's *Lieux de mémoire*,[1] landscape experts now must gauge the very movement whose sole prophets and promoters they once were.

My coupling of landscapes with *lieux de mémoire* is purposive. The locus of memory lies more readily in place than in time, in locale than in epoch. In the shift from centralized history toward dispersed patrimony, landscape seems the seat of collective memory, rooted as it is in specific sites and suffused with the quotidian and the communal. Landscapes have become one of the most popular aspects of our diverse heritage. They are treasured not as elite masterworks but as familiar loci of daily life, precious for the personal and tribal memories they contain.

At this juncture in European affairs, France exhibits the most marked zeal for landscape appreciation and protection. Landscape concerns there loom large owing to the shock of scenic and social change on a scale so massive that intending visitors recently were urged to "see France while it is still there." But the predicament is not solely French: similar changes have already peaked in much of northern Europe and will sooner or later be fully felt in the south and east.

Rural landscapes attract increasing regard throughout Europe. Siting and milieu engage planners and architects; amenity groups and preservationists shift attention from specific objects and buildings to whole complexes and surroundings; ecologists are concerned not only with rare species but also with the whole fabric of ecosystems; landscapers move beyond parks and gardens to care for all the countryside. Yet agricultural transformation jeopardizes the social and physical fabric of all rural landscape.

The Changing Rural Landscape in Europe

With massive population shifts out of rural landscapes, most states lose intimacy with land as the seat of livelihood and everyday life. The pace of change, the endurance of old ties, new attachments to old milieus are diverse. But three points on the continuum of change reveal certain key traits.

Places where rural life still prevails are now rare in western Europe, and farm dominance is even challenged in the east. The Ukraine and Byelorussia, Bulgaria and Poland still look largely rural, and land commonly connects with labor; but many folk, if not yet most, are industrial or urban. Eastern Europe follows Portugal and Greece, Ireland and Spain, Denmark and Finland, where farmers have dropped from half to a quarter or less of the labor force in a generation. Albania and Kosovo alone remain almost wholly rural. Yet landscape attitudes remain essentially agricultural. Rural dwellers see landscape as hearth and livelihood. Farmers and herders find holiday-makers, folk-life tourists, and eco-cultists weird and alien. Pride in productive scenes is proprietorial.

In many parts of Europe rural life is still a recent memory. Despite a century or more of decline, rural abandonment has seriously hit Western Europe only since the last war. France, Scandinavia, Greece, Iberia, the Mezzogiorno, and Switzerland have lost most of their farm workers in just a few decades. As the French know best, intensive farming is crucial, but only a quarter to a twentieth of French, Danish, and Swiss workers remain farm-based. So recent is the exodus that most people in these places keep rural ties. Parents or grandparents are from the farm; rural scenes join personal with collective heritage. Recurrent visits, annual vacations, childhood memories sacralize countrysides that are sustained only by huge subsidies. Extolled as social paragons, farmers are an endangered breed cherished to save the nation's very soul.

Rural folkways are remoter memories in lands long urban and industrial. Britain is the prime exemplar, but few people in northern Italy, the Netherlands, Belgium, or much of Germany retain firsthand farm memories. Rural labor in Britain and the Low Countries, even in 1960 less than one-tenth of the total, has been reduced by more than half in the last thirty years.

These states' landscape legacy still sustains national identity and tourism. But it is shorn of obligations and rewards and embodies few direct memories. Even grandparents hark back not to rural but to urban and industrial roots. Factories and city streets frame personal recall. Hence industrial archaeology, urban heritage centers, factory and tenement museums multiply in Britain, France, and

Scandinavia. They attract those whose sense of purpose came from mill and mine and shipyard, not meadow and field and pasture. These rural realms retain some meaning, but what they signify connects ever less with everyday memory.

New Meanings for Rural Landscapes

Landscape values link with supposedly stable pasts. But the very concept of landscape is in flux. Five perceptions illumine landscape roles today:

Landscape as ecological paradigm. Rural areas are now spotlighted in Green ideals of man and nature. Diversity, complexity, fragile yet unbroken chains of being, humility about what cannot be known or controlled, frugality, and parsimony give old landscape deities new life. Pagan nature worship, classical pastoralism, romantic and postindustrial urban misgivings are not new. But their convergence in the cult of rurality reflects two changes: heightened concern for balance that equates nature with virtue, and a perceived split between traditional rural pursuits and rural landscapes.

Landscape and rural life are becoming ominously disjoined. Rural populations dwindle; crops need ever less human input. Landscapes get removed from social reality—they are less visibly distinctive where tillage is intensive, less economically viable elsewhere. As landscape is sundered from rural life, habitual rustic and pastoral folkways disappear. Bereft of social meaning, landscapes become vacant, vacuous, void of context.

Until recently, such scenes were the inherent domain of farmers and herders, traditional keepers of landscape health and appearance. That linkage is now being severed and is so seen by urban folk. Most of us are city dwellers, ever fewer rural; less landscape is under traditional care; ingrained views of farmers as natural stewards yield to views that landscape is all of ours and needs all our care.

The farmer-cum-ecologist dies hard; those still on the land are often so adulated. But intensive exploitation, uprooted hedges, mass use of commercial fertilizer, and vast tracts converted to prairies and to conifer forests erode this image. The farmer is no longer a demigod faithful to conserved tradition; stewardship passes from born countryman to anxious urbanite.

Landscape as the rightful realm of all. Ecologically correct, landscape is also the right place to live. Rural scenes promise a spacious plenitude and companionable solitude denied in cities. Such notions are, of course, not new; Arcadian myth dates back to ancient Rome. What *is* new is the widespread belief that it should be realized. Before, landscape longings were largely vicarious, indulged only briefly now and then on holiday, in weekend retreats, or at the close of life. Fleeting episodes are still the rule. But more and more townies think rural scenes and ways of life theirs by wish if not by right. Three out of four Britons in a 1993 survey opted for country life, foreshadowing an outflow of many millions. Absence of agriculture no longer impedes such prospects. Car and phone, personal computer and fax put rural life within urban reach.

The shift is breathtaking. A century or two back, rural life was routinely reviled as criminal idiocy. It was one thing to love nature and landscape, quite another to accept the folk who lived there, let alone to share that life. The dimwitted peasant then became the rural salt of the earth, a font of native wisdom and virtue. Both figures are now passé: farmers today are neither demons nor angels. Many are not even rural, but town dwellers who just work in the country. As the landscape sheds its social habits, *any* townsman may equally make his mark there.

Urbanites are held to know nothing of the rural milieus they crave—prizing the scenery while spurning the slurry. But landscape's old-time denizens, if any are left, know little more. No longer need the rural incomer feel shame because he milks no cow, sows no seed, reaps no corn. Often no one else does either, or only rootless hirelings. Of the rural economy little may be left but chopping wood and picking apples. The countryside is becoming a place for living, not for making a living.

Landscape as collective identity. Three traits commend landscapes for group bonds, above all local and provincial ones. As "natural" (not contrived or crafted), landscape reflects what is trusted; as the locus of everyday life, landscape matters more than linkages that are less often felt; as typical and commonplace, landscape expresses popular will. Two other traits make landscape a hallmark of local autonomy against centralized sovereignty. Landscapes are visible and viewable, hence delimited and small-scale, and they hark back to tribal attachments that predate the nation-state.

Landscape as art. In the Renaissance, a "landscape" was a sketch that depicted a scene. Painted landscapes made viewers aware of and then pleased with the landscapes thus caught. To draw or paint a scene was to possess and, hence, to love it. By being depicted, landscapes became alluring in their own right, alike for meadows and mountains, intimate scenes and grand tableaux.

Landscape art adorns Europe's best-loved rural scenes. French and British countrysides embody the uncontrived artistry of successive owner-occupants. And new art enhances existing scenes; aesthetic and ecological visions, garden fashion and town planning, private and public embellishment augment our sense of attachment. In Britain, the advocacy group Common Ground commends artists to patrons likewise sensitive to places. Such enhancements are not imposed; they are fostered by local consensus.[2]

Europe's countrysides remain visually coherent yet richly diverse. Rural landscapes in years to come will need to cater to manifold needs and tastes, artistic and agronomic; users must quarry not just salable commodities but also what is remembered of social culture.

Landscape as heritage. Patrimony now matters everywhere—it comprises everything from fossils and furniture to folklore and faiths. No longer are only aristocrats obsessed with ancestry, only the super-rich antiques collectors, only academics antiquarians, only a minority museum-goers; millions now hunt their roots, protect beloved scenes, cherish mementos, and dote on media visions of the past.

Heritage was once about grand monuments, great heroes, and unique treasures; it now applauds the vernacular and typical. Once confined to a remote past—buildings before 1750, antiques at least a century old, history back of Diocletian—it now embraces last year. Time barriers become lower: archives are open not in fifty years but in thirty, "historic" structures mean those of a mere generation ago, relics not only of long-dead monarchs but also of extant (if aging) pop stars are auctioned, school history concentrates on events that occurred within living memory.

Heritage transcends its old-time domain in two ways of moment here. One is the realm of ideas and expression. Folk life has long had devotees, but language and folklore are newly grouped *with* buildings and paintings, pewter and potsherds. Landscape is the other realm. Nature conservation has ancient roots, but landscapes are only now entering the patrimonial mainstream. Consider the landed estates of the National Trust for England and Wales. Twenty years ago, the trust's great houses and gardens alone were cherished; few gave a thought to the look of the estate's arable land, ruthlessly milked to feed these showpieces. Today the trust (whose membership has grown fivefold to more than two million) holds estate lands of equal concern.

Landscape as patrimony stresses three attributes. One is *materiality*. Visible and tangible, landscape's links with all our senses enhances its legacy appeal. A second attribute is *use as container*. Landscape is not just a thing in itself; it is a receptacle for manifold other things and uses, from homemaking to camping and cycling, from extracting gravel to harvesting crops. Composite use lends landscape more weight than artifacts made for single purposes. Third, landscape connotes *stability*: unlike objects and structures, landscapes are fixed, immovable, hence secure; we can rely on landscape to stay put. Seasonal flux aside, landscape also stays much the same over time.

Public Responses to the Changing Landscape

Landscape's continuing vital roles—*nature* as fundamental heritage, *environment* as the setting of human action, *sense of place* for local difference and ancestral roots—reflect three public concerns: safeguarding legacies of nature and culture, enhancing everyday settings, and sustaining distinctive communities.

Global environmental awareness is newly salient but not securely based; Green political support is highly volatile. Much Green advocacy seems hostile to vital enterprise; when jobs are threatened, the environment takes a back seat, as the Green Party's electoral collapse in Germany and Britain has shown. But *Silent Spring* made threats to the fundament globally familiar. Few people feel no fear of nuclear risk, global warming, depletion of the ozone layer, or species and ecosystem loss.[3]

Unlike our forebears, we now see life as a common legacy that needs common care. Huge gulfs yawn between risks faced and impacts understood, ecological *nous* and economic dogma, private greed and public need, doomsters and Pollyannas. These gulfs magnify fears that underlie much landscape awareness.

Landscape legacies are global heritage, exemplified by UNESCO's World Heritage Sites. Joint efforts are beginning to protect these scenic and natural treasures. Antarctica is a reserved continent, global pressure spared the Tasmanian wilderness, concern over space debris and marine pollution is shared worldwide. Europe is no island unto itself.

Setting requires attention not just to isolated icons but also to a greater framing landscape. Conservation areas and national parks, *espaces sauvegardés* and *écomusées* reflect awareness of this need. Schooling, the arts, and growing leisure reach beyond item to ensemble. Modern *philosophes* stress the shaping of humane domains, the convergence of natural with human milieu.

A sense of separate place becomes vital for identity in a world smudged by sameness. Landscape stands for what is innate to each locale; attachment grows with tending it. All over Europe, deracinated denizens of anonymous, ephemeral places mourn the loss of what is felt to be distinctive. Some seek links with their ancestral locales or childhood milieus. Others cherish or contrive scenery and social fabric that make locales *our* place rather than just any place.

Past workaday landscape is seldom recoverable; what lingers as scenery dies as social entity, much as bygone memories atrophy with disuse. Yet the urge to regain rural roots is now resulting in the restoration of some ancestral locales: resettlement can revivify local legacy. But new concerns are sketched on no tabula rasa; inherited attachments remain potent. Old habits echo how each people feels toward scenes its forebears shaped. In the past, tradition linked with terrain; kinship conjoined ancestry and acreage. Owning and working land were crucial while farming was the main livelihood. But local ties came to be overlaid by larger ones; landscapes became national symbols, so I append a fourth concern: landscape and nation.

Landscape attitudes link with embedded cultural habits that differ more than might be supposed. A sign in the Swiss village of Château d'Oex says in English: "Please do not pick the flowers." In German: "It is forbidden to pick the flowers."

In French: "Those who love the mountains leave them their flowers." These phrases all favor flowers but imply divergent landscape views—English good manners, German minatory prohibition, French aesthetic affection.

National attachments serve as cohesive stimuli. Countries commonly depict themselves in landscape terms, hallowing what they fancy uniquely theirs. Every national anthem praises special splendors or unique bounties. Patriotic feeling builds on talismans of space and place: "hills and rivers and woods cease to be merely familiar: they become ideological"[4] as sites of national battles and birthplaces.

The tenacity of national icons casts doubts on new regional and local emphases. National landscape tastes are rooted in populism. In landscape, as in language, regional power still recalls coercive privilege and landless labor. By contrast, nationalism in much of Europe spelled rural liberation and peasant emancipation. The new nation-state seemed a release from provincial and parochial bondage. And landscapes still remain compelling icons of *national* identity.

Rural Landscapes in the European Future

"The mass of mankind everywhere, except in a little workshop like England, must live by agriculture," observed a Briton a century ago. Time has reversed this. A Glastonbury rock festival has needed ever more land since it began in 1970. More is ever available. "The farmers love it. It's not worth growing anything these days, it is? You get a better return from parked cars for three days than rapeseed oil."[5]

Sooner or later we slough off rural life. Every decade distances the Parisian from Breton and Norman roots; the compote and calvados cease coming; the uncles retire; the farm is sold. Europe will soon be run by those severed from rural linkages and ancestral farms. No longer the font of home and family, métier or livelihood, landscapes are becoming the loci of vacation and avocation.

Much of Europe now needs landscape habitants. Farm machines and rural flight empty countrysides kept only as mines or icons. To reinvest them with resonance requires several acts of faith. One is to bow to the withdrawal of much arable and pastoral land yet not abandon it to neglect or greed. A second is to bequeath the public at large a major share in landscape legacies. As in times past, title to land again is held by very few. Yet we all have a stake in it. The most casual user should share in its stewardship—even weekenders wanting a quiet, odorless, pig-free countryside.

Possession is the impediment. "You swallows come and go but I'm always here and don't tell me what to do with my trees," says an irate English farmer. "I thought they were everybody's trees," muses an incomer, "but he thought they were his."[6]

Farmers still keep control over the scenery they sell. An Oxfordshire field from the train is marketed as a "private view for one of the best shows on earth," but landowners scorn "rural policy being dictated from the car window."[7] Yet it is from cars that most view the landscape. Though millions of highway travelers get only fleeting glimpses of Stonehenge, they are mesmerized by it. We need to ally those for whom landscape is a home, a locus of livelihood, and an inspiration, however sporadic.

The third act of faith is to augment car-window views of Stonehenge with sightings of France's Carnac and the Continent beyond. The landscape of the long-distance traveler, like that of walker and painter, weekender and pensioner, may yet become more fulfilling than the peasant grind of millennia past would ever lead us to expect.

"The countryside reassures us that not everything is superficial and transitory," concludes a social historian, "that some things remain stable, permanent, and enduring."[8] Rurality sanctions the status quo. Invoking rural roots, British prime minister Stanley Baldwin termed himself not "the man in the street even, but a man in a field-path, a much simpler person steeped in tradition and impervious to new ideas."[9] Elsewhere rural idiocy was an embarrassment; in England it spelled stability.

That was in 1924. Rural idiots give way to rural financiers. For two hundred years most English people have had no intimate links with green fields. Yet abiding affection for the landscape heritage valorizes farm subsidies as anachronistic as in France. Many farm landscapes survive largely through tourism. "In 20 years' time all Lakeland farmers will have given up farming," forecasts a local. "They'll be called field wardens. They'll build up dry stone walls, then knock them down again to amuse the tourists . . . . Sheep will become pets, never sold or killed."[10]

I end with two other visions of the rural future. The head of Britain's Nature Conservancy Council, Timothy Hornsby, envisions an outing in 2020 to:

Center Parc, a wonderful, enormous dome, under which private enterprise conserves rare and representative re-created countrysides and stunning holographs of romantic landscapes now lost. On the way back, I visit the small thatched mock Tudor cottage . . . with blown-up photographs of some striking buildings the National Trust used to run before they were either inundated or made way for the wonderful motorway. I sail over to a splendidly landscaped golf course for the senior Japanese businessmen whose microchip factories stretch to the horizon. Packed densely behind them lie corduroy stripes of Sitka spruce with an inviting notice to "Pick Your Own"; I garner some genetically manipulated bananas.[11]

The other millennial vision is from the famed Breton folklorist Pierre-Jakez
Hélias:

> After the peasant abandoned the countryside, all fell into ruins. But the
> new masters began living there. The richest acquired entire farms and vil-
> lages. But no one was around to keep up their estates or to serve them. So
> they were forced to cut their own lawns, prune their own trees, care for
> their animals, and fight against wild vegetation. And of course they began
> to love the land. They took pride in picking, harvesting, and eating what
> they themselves had grown. They rediscovered the taste of fruit and even
> bread. Their country homes became their only homes. Protected from the
> common people now locked up in the cities, they formed exclusive re-
> gional clubs where it was forbidden to speak anything but Provençal,
> Basque, and Breton. So the former bourgeoisie became professional peas-
> ants, while children of the former peasants consoled themselves with elec-
> tronic toys.[12]

Each image is terrifying, because it posits a continued, if not an aggravated,
chasm between rural and urban folk, natural and artificial scenes. It is better to
share William Cronon's recognition, in *Nature's Metropolis,* that "we all live in the
city; we all live in the country. To do right by nature and people in the country, one
has to do right by them in the city as well."[13] And soon, most rural folk will have
urban roots. In that future, to be a peasant one must have been a Parisian.

JAY APPLETON

16   The Integrity of the Landscape Movement

It can hardly be doubted that the resurgence of interest in landscape since World War II has by now reached a dimension that warrants the use of the term Landscape Movement, or that one of its most striking characteristics is the number and range of interest groups from which its activists have emerged to develop a common cause. The purpose of this chapter is to strike a note of warning about what I see as the principal danger implicit in this multidisciplinary origin and to suggest one or two ways in which advocates of the Landscape Movement can protect it from this danger, if only on the basis that forewarned is forearmed.

What characterizes this movement is not any particular discovery, theory, breakthrough, or philosophical position; it is, rather, a coming together of diverse minds trained in the thinking habits of different disciplines, many of them traditionally regarded as only remotely connected with each other. Figure 57 expresses this idea visually. Each triangle represents an area of human experience that can be equated with what has come to be recognized as the province of a particular scholarly discipline. My concern is not to enumerate these disciplines (we should each compile a different list, and those named here are merely examples), but for me they would include geography, biology, art history, literary criticism, and many others. Within each area there is a part which is specifically concerned with landscape. Often it is a minority interest, perceived by the majority as peripheral to the discipline as a whole—a fringe activity. Landscape architecture is, I suppose, an exception, in that no part of it is unconcerned with landscape.

If, however, we were to rearrange the triangles in such a way that the periph-

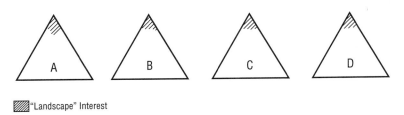

"Landscape" Interest

FIG. 57. Landscape interest as a minority or peripheral concern within separate disciplines. Drawing by Jay Appleton.

eral areas are all contiguous (fig. 58), we would create a distinctive area characterized by the unifying theme of landscape. Around this area would extend a succession of concentric zones indicating the diminishing effect of the landscape theme within each of the established disciplines. To tidy up the model we may be tempted to put a fence around this new territory to indicate that we have claimed it uniquely for ourselves, but it is a temptation we should at all costs resist. The free flow of ideas between this territory and what might be called the parent disciplines is essential if the movement is to continue to display the vitality that has been such a notable feature of its formative years. It is important that we at the core of the movement should maintain close personal contact with our colleagues who are working in the mainstream of each contributory discipline.

The danger, however, is that these liaisons, if allowed to become too strong or too limited in their breadth, may prove detrimental to the success of the movement itself. Let me give an analogy from my own discipline of geography. My ex-

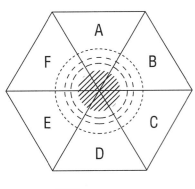

FIG. 58. Landscape interest in a cross-disciplinary view. Drawing by Jay Appleton.

"Landscape" Interest

perience is derived largely from teaching in universities in England, Australia, and New Zealand, whose syllabuses contain, to borrow a geological term, a kind of built-in fissile plane that renders them liable to a schism between physical and human geography. The vast majority of faculty in British university departments of geography would see themselves as quite clearly falling into one or other of these categories. Yet in the United States, the teaching of geomorphology seems to lie within the province of geology rather than geography; this may be taken to indicate either that the dangers of fission are less acute or that the process has already gone much farther. Either way, the concept of a world formed by natural processes that continue to operate while it is being modified by successive phases of human intervention cannot be helped by the conviction that we can reach a proper understanding of the whole phenomenon by looking at only one part.

A centralizing force that at one time held the subject of geography together was the study of regional geography, which directed the attention of students to the integration of all the phenomena, natural or human-made, that contributed to the identity of a selected area. But the importance of regional geography has now been so diminished that many geography syllabuses have no place for it at all. Much geographical research today is concerned with the study of phenomena, or even particular parameters of one phenomenon, abstracted from the totality and examined as an isolated topic that might just as well be studied under the aegis of, and published in the literature of, another discipline. Certainly one cannot complain when historical geographers talk to historians, social geographers to sociologists, or biogeographers to ecologists. Such bilateral liaisons have proven very fruitful, but, once it has become apparent that geographers of one brand can no longer talk to fellow geographers of another, it can hardly be conducive to the coherence of geography as a discipline.[1]

If we apply the same sort of critical analysis to ourselves as students of landscape, we can all too easily see the danger signs. I began by drawing attention to the diversity of our origins, and perhaps I hardly need to enlarge on the potential for fragmentation implicit in this. Let me briefly suggest several other dichotomies that seem to embody the same sort of potential.

First, there is the conceptual separation of landscape as encountered in the arts and sciences.[2] There is a widespread assumption that particular areas of human knowledge lend themselves to investigation by methodologies found in either the arts or the sciences, but not both. Artists have told us a great deal about the ways in which people have perceived landscapes at different times. Choices of subject, for example, have varied at different periods, and we can find a record of this in the catalogs of past exhibitions. Only recently, however, have attempts been made to subject this information to statistical analysis from which scientifically valid conclusions can be drawn about changing habits of perception.[3] Much scientific work involves the testing of hypotheses that are themselves the product of a kind of intuition that seems not to be far removed from the inspiration of the artist. We need to make a more serious attempt to integrate the activities of scholars working in what are still regarded as quite different fields of human experience.

Another dualism, which so perplexed the more gullible students of geography a few years ago, is that between nomothetic studies and idiographic studies. Nomothetic studies are those that lead to the formulation of general principles. They are literally lawmaking. Idiographic studies are those that concern themselves only with individual cases from which no such general principles can be extended. So far so good! But is not geography a science? Are not the sciences dependent on the application of general laws? For geographers, it would seem, nomothetic is therefore good and idiographic is bad! You may find it difficult to believe that such a simplistic argument could obtain any credence among intelligent students, but there was enough substance in the argument to furnish the material for at least one of the nails in the coffin of regional geography. In fact, or course, no general principles were ever discovered except from the study of data derived from individual cases.[4]

Many of the studies we have undertaken to establish general laws about landscape preference have fallen into this trap. Researchers ask very specific questions of numerous individuals about their aesthetic reactions to particular types or components of landscape and fit together the summation of the individual replies to form the basis of generalizations. This is fine; it is a cogent example of synthesis, or integration. But we must recognize the limitations of the methodology. The literature of this subject is woefully lacking in the sort of supporting individual case studies that one would expect to find in any branch of science that abstracts its raw material from the totality of individual personalities. There is an urgent need to make good this deficiency, to address the problem of integrity at the individual level, to develop a methodology analogous to the physician's holistic approach to the patient.[5]

Another troublesome dichotomy is that which separates what we may call theory from practice. I have noticed it as a conspicuous feature of a number of meetings organized by the Landscape Research Group in England, in which participants see themselves as falling quite clearly into one of two groups. In the first are the landscape architects, landscape managers, park superintendents, engineers of various kinds, and many others, whose professional occupations bring them into contact with situations in which their decisions have a direct impact on the landscape. In the second are the academics, the writers, and those journalists who, as a consequence of the growing interest in environmental issues, have increasingly found themselves required to cover public opinion on a whole range of landscape issues.

Meetings of this sort are extremely important and have resulted in some highly fruitful partnerships, but one sometimes detects a certain impatience on the part of the practitioners, who come to such meetings with an expectation that the theoreticians will be able to provide them with instant solutions to their day-to-day problems. The theoreticians, for their part, are sometimes reluctant to take the trouble to familiarize themselves, at more than the most superficial level, with the detailed nature of the problems with which the practitioners must contend.

Perhaps the most significant dichotomy, one that could prove dangerously divisive, is the separation of visual and cultural approaches to the study of landscape. A visual approach addresses the spontaneous visual impact of a landscape on the observer. It touches on such matters as aesthetic appreciation, landscape evaluation, and emotional response to scenic experience. Its academic study lies principally within such disciplines as environmental psychology, the philosophy of aesthetics, and the theory of art, though scholars in other disciplines, not least geography and landscape planning, have increasingly concerned themselves with various aspects of environmental perception as it impinges on their respective subjects.

A cultural approach is principally concerned with the study of landscape as a product of those evolutionary processes by which successive communities have left an imprint, whether by design or accident, on the land they have occupied. It is the domain of archaeologists, anthropologists, sociologists, historical geographers, and historians of various kinds (including social, economic, architectural, agrarian, and horticultural). Some researchers in these fields would describe themselves simply as landscape historians, while others would lay more emphasis on the importance of contemporary influences.

We can all understand very clearly the reason for accepting that this dichotomy is already a fact of life, but we should not accept it as inevitable. That the phenomenon of perception is central to the visual approach is self-evident, but it is no less important to the student of the cultural approach. Half a century ago geographers and others who were trying to explain the evolutionary origins of the landscape would speak of "an eye for country" as the most essential tool for the completion of their task. To impose a rigid line of separation between the study of the processes or perception and the phenomena perceived can hardly be productive.

Since the landscape at any one moment represents an interim stage in an ongoing evolutionary process, visual perception is not simply a necessity in the study of present landscapes. It is often a starting point for investigating past landscapes. Maurice Beresford makes the point that a number of distinguished economic historians between World Wars I and II discounted the view that the extensive abandonment of English medieval villages had ever happened, on the grounds that their remains were rarely to be found in the landscape.[6] Beresford was able to list no fewer than 118 such sites in the county of Yorkshire alone. The documentary evidence had been well enough known but nobody had seriously looked for the evidence in the field. It was the visual approach, in other words, that proved to be the key to the understanding of the cultural phenomenon.

An example from my own experience may serve to illustrate the interdependence of rational comprehension and emotional response. It fell to my lot to be raised in East Anglia, a part of England separated from the main body of the English Midlands by an expanse of flat terrain known as the Fens, and I have recollections of innumerable journeys of indescribable tedium across what seemed to me the dullest and most uninteresting landscape I had ever seen. When I became a historical geographer, I learned about the processes by which first the Romans, then the medieval monks, and later the seventeenth-century capitalist Adventurers drained this series of waterlogged surfaces—which, in spite of their apparent uniformity, contained important physical contrasts (peat and silt, with here and there low islands of geologically older material). I became compulsively fascinated by the Fens as a palimpsest on which the residual details of earlier phases could still be recognized by those who knew what to look for. The feelings this landscape evoked in me as an adult then became, and still are, as pleasurable as those that I experienced as a small child were antagonistic. The distinction between the visual and the cultural many be useful as long as it remains a conceptual one, but if we allow it to divide us into two categories of scholars, those who study one or the other, but not both, this will surely prove inimical to the integrity of the movement.

Another potential source of disruption is the very success scholars have achieved in recent years through new techniques of analysis. As in all branches of human knowledge, we have been able to call on the computer to process quantities of data that would have been quite impossible to handle in times past. The study of environmental perception itself is just one area in which our understanding has been greatly refined with the availability of new *analytical* techniques, but these have brought with them three dangers. The first two are well enough known. The first is the danger of being so preoccupied with the techniques themselves that we lose sight of the ultimate questions in the pursuit of which we are employing them. The second is assuming that the application of statistical measurements automatically replaces subjectivity by objectivity.

The third danger is perhaps less obvious but in the present no less important. It is the failure to recognize that analysis is only a part of the investigative process. Charles Darwin was a prodigious collector of field data and, though a lousy mathematician, was a pretty competent analyst; but so were dozens of other nineteenth-century scientists. What made him stand head and shoulders above most,

FIG. 59. Mildenhall Fen, Suffolk, England. View north-west along Hurdle Drove. Photo by Richard J. Appleton.

some might say all, of his contemporaries was his competence, not in analysis but in synthesis. Darwin was widely versed in the new discoveries in other branches of science, particularly geology, as well as in the work of the earlier evolutionary theorists, and he was able to revolutionize the biological sciences because he could see a common significance in what might at first seem to be a vast amorphous collection of apparently remotely related phenomena. It is a comparable breadth of sources from which we derive the raw material that distinguishes the study of landscape today, and if we fail to relate our several discoveries to the interpretation of landscape as a whole we shall be like the motorist who removes a faulty part from the motor and fixes it but forgets to put it back.

Here is an example of what I have in mind when I speak of "the integrity of the landscape movement." Ronald Paulson, in his book on the painters J. M. W. Turner and John Constable,[7] develops some ideas that I had communicated to him concerning the geographical basis of Constable's interest in the landscape of Hampstead Heath. Constable painted a number of landscapes looking over the edge of the heath toward the distant Chilterns, including at least four paintings (dating from 1819, 1825, 1828, and 1836) of Branch Hill Pond. The point at issue is the connection between the geological structure of these landscapes and the compositional structure of the paintings. Hampstead Heath is a small residual

FIG. 60. John Constable, *Branch Hill Pond, Hampstead* (ca. 1828). Courtesy of the Board of Trustees of the Victoria and Albert Museum, London.

plateau some five miles northwest of the City of London, formed by a cap of sandy material that overlies the heavy London Clay. Branch Hill Pond lies at the spring-line at the junction of the two. The weathering of these different materials has produced a flattish sigmoid curve, and the consequence of the juxtaposition of convex and concave surfaces has been to diminish the importance in the paintings of the middle ground. (See figs. 60 and 61.)

The geology is also significant because the sands in the foreground have proved too infertile for agriculture, and have later received legal protection from the enforcement of common rights or other quirks of land ownership. In three of the Branch Hill Pond paintings, workers can be seen quarrying the sand, an activity that has rendered the foreground not exactly natural, though it supports many of the characteristic plant species. Constable, like most other painters still living under the influence of the picturesque movement, shows a consistent preference for nonarable foregrounds. There is, of course, a long history of aesthetic rivalry between the cultivated and the uncultivated, going back at least as far as Virgil. Neither can be said to be intrinsically unaesthetic, but the smiling corn-

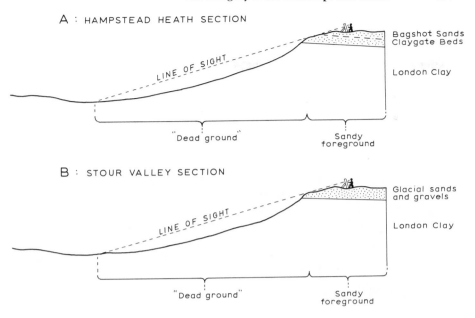

A : HAMPSTEAD HEATH SECTION

LINE OF SIGHT

Bagshot Sands
Claygate Beds

London Clay

"Dead ground"   Sandy
foreground

B : STOUR VALLEY SECTION

LINE OF SIGHT

Glacial sands
and gravels

London Clay

"Dead ground"   Sandy
foreground

FIG. 61. Geological sections of two favorite landscapes painted by John Constable: Hampstead Heath and the Stour Valley. Drawing by Keith Scurr.

fields and the haunts of beasts have discharged quite different roles in the history of environmental aesthetics and have been subjected to striking changes of fashion since they were presided over respectively by Ceres and Diana.

These interpretations of Constable's Hampstead Heath paintings become more convincing when we discover that the phenomenon is not confined to this one locality. If we turn to the numerous landscapes that Constable painted from the higher ground bordering his native Stour Valley, some fifty miles from Hampstead, we find a remarkably similar situation. (See fig. 62.) The caprock here consists of broad spreads of glacial sands and gravels rather than the Eocene sands of Hampstead, but the geomorphological influence of the sands has been the same. They provide a lip to the valley side, whose compositional function in the paintings is again to dramatize the separation of foreground and distance by diminishing the importance of the middle ground. The convex lower slopes are again formed in the same London Clay, while the sandy, podzolized surfaces of the foreground are again uncultivated.

Now, into which pigeonhole are we to place all this? Is it art or is it science? Is it illustrative of the visual or the cultural approach? In the last few paragraphs I

FIG. 62. John Constable, *Stour Valley and Dedham Church* (ca. 1815), also known as *View of Dedham*. Oil on Canvas. 55.5 × 77.8 cm. (21 ⅞ × 30 ⅝ in.). Warren Collection. Courtesy Museum of Fine Arts, Boston.

have touched on art history, geology, geomorphology, hydrology, soil science, biogeography, agrarian theory, and the regional geography of southeast England. Every one of these references could have steered the argument into the territory of some cognate discipline in which the whole cohesion of the argument would have been lost. If we want to understand the relationship between the art of the painter and the genius of the place, we cannot allow ourselves to be confined by the artificially imposed boundaries of conventional disciplines.

I am not, of course, arguing that we should all direct our researches to the whole field of landscape, but rather that, in pursuing our own individual interests within it, we should keep an eye on what our colleagues are discovering throughout the wider field and, not least, clarify our own minds about the significance of our own work within that wider field.

The literature on landscape has proliferated enormously within the last few years, but the publishing trade is only beginning to see the participants in the Landscape Movement as a recognizable market. With the exception, I suppose, of landscape architects themselves, those of us who are united in a common interest in landscape are still seen as small splinter groups pursuing minority interests within the accepted orthodox system of discrete disciplines. But we need, for our own good, to be perceived as a community of people who are brought together by a common interest in landscape and who just happen to be landscape architects or geographers or environmental psychologists or art historians or even freelance inquirers, unlabeled with any academic or professional designation. It is our job to replace the former image with the latter.

This will not be easy. It is true that the public is now displaying an unprecedented interest in environmental matters, but the very magnitude of its concern with pollution, the greenhouse effect and the hole in the ozone layer, and the plight of endangered species (along with the fear that we ourselves might be numbered among them) has tended to direct attention away from, rather than toward, landscape.

In 1988, at a relatively early stage in the U.S. presidential elections, I spent a wet Sunday afternoon watching a long television program in which the five aspirants still in the race for the Democratic nomination engaged in a discussion ranging over the whole field of public affairs. They devoted some twenty-five minutes to "the environment," in the course of which I do not recollect a single reference to its visual dimension. "Whatever happened to visual blight?" I thought, remembering how, on previous visits to the United States, I had been bombarded with this phrase from every side.

Maybe those of us who are interested in the landscape shall have to wait for the tide of public interest to turn before we can expect to be perceived as the entity that I believe we have become. In the meantime there is a good opportunity to look to our own house and put it in order, because we still have a long way to go. When we find the inspiration, as we shall, to pursue our own ideas and develop further our own individual research interests, let us not forget that there *are* potentially disruptive forces that, if we are not aware of them, may jeopardize the future of what I make no apology for calling the Landscape Movement.

ROBERT B. RILEY

17 The Visible, the Visual, and the Vicarious: Questions about Vision, Landscape, and Experience

Vision as a source for landscape interpretation is an important topic, but broad and frustratingly vague. Vision is our major source of information about our environment. But how far will it take us in understanding how and why our surroundings look as they do, or in understanding how and why people react to those surroundings as they do? The word *vision* is imprecise; *interpretation* is equally so. Does visual interpretation mean cognition, or affect, or evaluation? Meaning or scholarship? Or any of these?

I will define *interpretation* as the relation between the landscape, seeing the landscape, and experiencing the landscape. How do we, as designers and landscape scholars, begin to understand that relation?

A general approach would be to treat the landscape as a sensory stimulus and to investigate its relationship to perception, cognition, affect, evaluation, meaning, and memory in the human mind.[1] This is a subject for psychologists, not designers or landscape scholars. Even then, if we ask a question as basic as "Does affect precede cognition?" the answer will be "yes," "no," or "sometimes," depending upon the psychologist we ask. At the other extreme, we could attack vision as a source of landscape experience piecemeal by asking questions about specific landscape phenomena, such as preference for natural elements or landscapes in childhood,[2] hoping to shed fragmentary light on the larger role of vision and landscape experience. But however valuable the specifics of such scholarship, we seldom find much that can be generalized from such inquiries.

We might profit more by framing some general questions about vision and the landscape experience. I will suggest a few, neither discrete nor exhaustive, that are worth our attention.

Consider the dichotomy between the concepts of visual and cultural, the catchy publicity phrase for the symposium ("Vision, Culture, and Landscape") that produced this book of essays. Is this distinction intellectually valid? Is it useful? The terms *vision* and *culture* are broad and variable; depending on their definition, either could entirely subsume the other. Without more precise definition, in fact, the two terms would seem not even to refer to the same class of phenomena.

Why would vision versus culture be such an obvious dichotomy? The answer lies not in the subject matter but in the people who pursue it. The dichotomy between the visual and the cultural reflects the long debate between form and content in art, design, and planning, the ongoing quarrel between the aesthetic and the social. But it is also a specific reflection of the academic subculture of our time. Two major themes have dominated landscape architecture scholarship over the last quarter of a century: one is the tradition of visual assessment that grew out of the early work of R. Burton Litton, Jr., and Kenneth Craik at the University of California, Berkeley, who attempted to quantify landscape preference as a preliminary to understanding it. The other is a more humanistic tradition, personified in the landscape essays of Yi-Fu Tuan and John Brinckerhoff Jackson, who speculated on the cultural aspects of landscape.[3] The cultural-visual dichotomy may be an empty promise for developing reliable knowledge about the landscape experience, but it tells us a good deal about the socialization of disciplines in American universities.

Discussion of vision and landscape must begin with the recognition that vision dominates our immediate sensory and cognitive transactions with the landscape. How true this was in other times, evolutionary, or historic, and how true it is across cultures or occupations, are interesting questions that do not affect the dominance of the visual in contemporary society. But it is the very dominance of vision that makes its relationship with landscape an enormous, unwieldy subject for inquiry, and one that might include very different categories of human experience. To make discussion more manageable, focused, and, one hopes, more productive, let me arbitrarily isolate three relationships between vision, landscape, and landscape experience—distinguishing between vision as a source of sensory and mental information, vision as a source of pleasure from the landscape itself, and vision as the raw material from which internal landscape fantasies or narratives are composed. I will call these distinct phenomena the *visible*, the *visual*, and the *vicarious*.

ROBERT B. RILEY

The Visible

The relationship between vision and the landscape is less than simple, even when vision is considered only as a source of information about the real world, when human reaction to the visual stimulus is confined to perception and cognition. How reliable, for example, are the visible aspects of a landscape as a source of information that helps us understand the origin of a landscape and for understanding its role and meaning in the life of those inhabiting it? Within this book itself are different, but not necessarily contradictory, answers to this question. The absence of easy answers should come as no surprise, for the question is central to methodological debates in anthropology and archaeology, fields more intellectually advanced than the design disciplines.

A corollary to this question is, how adequately can visible displays—a museum exhibit, say, or an architectural or landscape reconstruction—communicate the origins and meanings of a cultural landscape? This is an important question, as the field of landscape archaeology grows and as living museums and the merchandising of landscape nostalgia become major social phenomena. What do consumers understand from these reconstructions, and does it bear any relation to the intended understanding?

FIG. 63. The visible: the ruins of a Roman aqueduct rise out of contemporary monoculture. Cilician plain, Turkey. Photo by Robert B. Riley.

The role of a stable, visible landscape in a world of rapid change and increasing mobility is another question. Does constant, unpredictable change in the environment erode cultural and personal sense of identity? Does environmental continuity, if not stability, support a personal and social sense of security?

Still one more question, less abstract than it might appear, is whether a landscape can be invisible. Jackson, Denis Cosgrove,[4] and others have pointed out that the conventional use of the word *landscape*, with its largely pictorial overtones, is a conceptual and visual abstraction from the real world. Today the word has moved beyond metaphor to generality and jargon. Pundits on television use terms such as "the economic landscape of Eastern Europe," and I have been guilty of referring to "the landscape of the CB Radio." If *landscape* means the interaction of human thought and behavior with the physical environment, then it obviously includes more than physical or visual components. The social landscape of a person, or a culture, is more than the sum of the buildings and exterior settings in which that person or culture inhabits. But how much more? What is that relationship between the physical and, therefore, visible setting and the more comprehensive and extensive social landscape? Clearly it must be variable.

Landscape, then, needs precise definition in a particular context. Within this volume, discrepancy in the use of the term is at the root of differences between Wilbur Zelinsky, who defines it one way, and Rina Swentzell and Dolores Hayden, who define it differently. The former caused a minor politically correct protest when he maintained that most ethnic groups in America had left no cultural landscape. Surely he did not mean that such groups lacked their own distinctive, vital, social landscape, but rather that it took place within a physical setting (that is, landscape) built, owned, and largely controlled by other groups. We should be wary of inconsistency and expansionism in the definition of landscape. It produces not only unnecessary intellectual squabbles but also an undue sense of importance among landscape designers, who should realize that while a landscape may be bigger than foundation planting, it needs to be smaller than the cultural landscape of North America if designers are to affect it.

The Visual

When we move beyond vision as a source of landscape information, when we move beyond the visible to the visual, we move into the realm of landscape experience, the realm in which visual stimulus goes beyond perception and cognition into affect, evaluation, and meaning. Here is where landscape, vision, and mind interact in the traditional realm of the designer. Here we derive pleasure from sights themselves and their cognitive ordering into texture, form, pattern, color, contrast, and, of course, meaning. Visual satisfaction is a large part of

FIG. 64. The visual: Stourhead, a composition of texture, color, and form, enriched by historical allusion. Photo by Robert B. Riley.

the total landscape experience, although probably not as large a part as designers assume. In fact, the question of just how much of the landscape experience is visual might be the most important that we might pursue, but one that I can only touch on briefly in this essay. There are, however, more limited, useful questions about the visual landscape.

How good a surrogate for the landscape experience can we achieve with two-dimensional visual representation? Designers, although aware of this question, are reluctant to pursue it. The issue becomes important in several specific contexts. One of these is design rendering. Most design education implicitly assumes that a potential three-dimensional, in-the-world event can be captured through plans, sections, elevations, and perspectives, often from a vantage point no human being will ever occupy. Some of these image classes, such as plans and sections, make no pretense at reproducing the participants' real-world experience; others, such as elevations, offer a very limited range of that experience. Some, such as perspectives or computer walk-arounds, assume that they capture it almost completely. These visual conventions are specific to a design subculture but they raise the issue of visual habits, assumptions, and conventions—in general, important issues in an image-merchandising society. We now carry these assumptions beyond the drawing board into the laboratory, praising visual simulation for its capacity to generate more alternative images and so improve evaluation and decision making. However, assumptions about validity as a surrogate for the real world remain the same.

There is no more extreme example of the assumed primacy of the visual than the field of quantitative research called visual assessment. The reader might trace in her own mind the steps and layers of extraction, abstraction, and simplification that lead from real landscape experience to the image used in visual assessment. The image is, of course, an abstraction from three dimensions to two, but think about some of its other characteristics. The experience is assumed to be entirely pictorial and unisensory (the sense being vision), the viewpoint is arbitrary and stationary, the field of vision equally arbitrary. Most important, perhaps, is that visual analysis is completely atemporal. The landscape pictured is assumed static. No ephemeral elements of light or weather are depicted. Length of exposure to the experience is assumed irrelevant. Last, it is atemporal in that neither the landscape, nor the viewer, nor the interaction between the two, is assumed to have history or future. But not all of these characteristics of visual analysis are inherent in two-dimensional visual representation of the landscape experience. Compare this contemporary work to the lengthy nineteenth-century debate over landscape painting, much of which centered on the methods and problems of going beyond those very assumptions to incorporate weather, light changes, cultural allusion, and mood.

The comparison of photographic computer imagery and painting raises several important issues. First, the difference between an actual landscape and a graphic landscape image is itself not simple, particularly for an image-dominated society in which the term *multimedia* has become a merchandising cliché. The real relationship between landscape-media and image-viewer not only is complex but also differs significantly from one medium to another. The literary image and the graphic image are so different as to be seldom related in thinking about landscape, although the relationships between Arcadian references in the paintings of Nicolas Poussin and Claude Lorrain and the pastoral poetry of Augustan England, or the interrelationship of Chinese calligraphy, scroll painting, and the scholar's garden show how close that link can be. Drawing, engraving, painting, photography, cinema, and computer simulation all interpose their own restraints and formats between the real and the viewed.

Second, fashions and canons within any medium change, and at a faster rate, than the lay audience assimilates or even recognizes. Until little more than a decade ago, for example, serious landscape photography was black-and-white, color being thought suitable only for calendars, travel brochures, and *National Geographic*. Surely the viewer brings different mental and emotional expectations to each medium, responding differently to a television show on the English landscape than to an exhibition of John Constable paintings.

Finally, the higher technology medium often is implicitly assumed to be the more objective, despite the fact that the higher the technology, the more processes, transformations, and manipulations fall between the original object and the ultimate viewer. It is a long journey, indeed, from the poor and backward landscape of ancient Arcadia through Virgil's *Eclogues,* the paintings of Poussin and Lorrain, and the landscapes of Stowe and Stourhead to coffee-table books and public television specials on the great gardens of England, and maybe even to strolls through virtual reality. It is a journey with many turns left untaken, but, even so, a journey in which the visual and the cultural are hard to distinguish one from another.

Visual assessment is meant to measure preference; it results in a judgment that a particular landscape is in some way better or more pleasing than others. Two basic questions about "preference" are seldom if ever asked. First, how does preference vary among individuals and across cultures? Much of contemporary visual assessment assumes, if implicitly, a large degree of constancy. But many landscape writers, from Tuan to Buttimer, emphasize individual or cultural variability.[5] Is this discrepancy only a difference in methodological subcultures? Speculative attempts to bridge or relate the two views in their implicit assumptions would seem an obvious step. Second, the nature, limitations, and operational purpose of preference are seldom discussed. What are the assumed relationships between preference, affect, and meaning? What, indeed, do preferences tell us about intervening in real landscapes or living in such landscapes? If there is indeed a high correlation between photographic and real-world preferences, then visual analysis would be extraordinarily useful for locating a scenic photo opportunity along a national forest roadside. What does it tell us about landscapes as places in which to live, work, make love, raise families, or enjoy other people?

A last speculation about the visual bears on the difference between "insider's landscape" and "outsider's landscape." The different experiences of inhabitants and visitors is a subject that has been well worked, in different ways, by David Lowenthal and Edward Relph.[6] This dichotomy makes common sense to us as well; we all know that a new city, experienced, say, the in first two hours after arriving by plane, is very different from the same landscape experienced even a day later. A classic example is Mark Twain's oft-quoted description of the difference between the Mississippi River landscape as experienced by a ship's passenger and by its pilot, the former enjoying scenery, the latter intent on currents, depth, and snags. Is the most important difference between the two experiences the fact that the outsider's, or first-glimpsed, landscape is almost entirely visual and that the customary, or insider's, landscape is experienced primarily in other terms and with other meanings? Does the visual wither as exposure, experience, and involvement grow? Both Lowenthal and Relph also attempt to link the visual with the cultural and the individual landscape experience with the collective, a job usually better done in fiction and journalistic essays.[7]

The Vicarious

With the insider's landscape, we move beyond the visual landscape experience but not necessarily beyond the role of vision. I have chosen the term *vicarious* for this last type of landscape experience, in which the real, observed landscape leads to an internally experienced landscape that is far richer and more personal than the "real" landscape. Vicarious is an inadequate name for this experience, but it does dramatically mark the distinction from the "real," or observable, landscape experience, and it is at least as adequate as the other terms that come to my mind—*fantasy landscape* or *internal landscape narrative*.

Landscape scholars have paid almost no attention to this vicarious, internally structured landscape—despite our fascination with deconstructionism, with its tenets of the indeterminacy of the text and the open-endedness of interpretation and its common sense–confirmed contention that such landscape readings will exist and will vary. These internal landscapes might well be central landscape experiences in a person's life. We might not all have the sensitivity to remembered and imagined landscapes of a Marcel Proust or a James Agee,[8] but we have such

FIG. 65. The vicarious: Monument Valley, the mythic setting for Native Americans and cowboys—and the Marlboro Man. Photo by Robert B. Riley.

FIG. 66. The visible, the visual, and the vicarious: an English cottage garden. . . .Photo by Robert B. Riley.

landscapes. We find them comforting and enriching in one degree or another. Vicarious landscapes might shape our experience of, our pleasure in, our preference for, external landscapes. How many American males, standing in a scenic overlook, viewing grassy range, Ponderosa pines, Alpine meadows, and the peaks of the Rockies, fantasize themselves as the mythic American cowboy? Even computer pinball games, essentially tests of eye-mind-hand coordination, offer rudimentary visual landscapes, presumably as cues for the players' own vicarious landscape. In both of these very different examples, what is viewed is not the direct producer of affect; it is a cuing device that produces an imagined, affective landscape. Could preference be largely a measure of vicarious potential, an indicator of the power of an image as a cuing device? Is vision different from other senses in such cuing? Think of Proust's *madeleines* and tea or Wallace Stegner's wolf willow,[9] or consider the power that the smells and sounds of your own life have to cue remembered landscapes and landscape experiences.

Relationships in Change?

Defining the visible, the visual, and the vicarious as elements of the landscape experience leads to a final question. Will a global, image-dominated society produce a drastic change in the roles of the visible, the visual, and the vicari-

ous and in the relationship between them? Our power as a society to ravage, transform, and create landscapes has grown so that many landscapes, landscape experiences, and maybe even our existence are threatened. But, compared to earlier ways of life, most of us have little individual experience in making landscapes.

Tourism, perhaps, is the essential condition of postmodern existence. Perhaps postmodern life is the triumph of the outsider's landscape over the insider's. While we make few landscapes, while we are seldom insiders, we are daily bombarded with hundreds of images of other landscapes, real and imaginary.

We have moved from a telling and hearing society to a writing and reading (and painting and hanging and viewing) society to—what? A flash-and-glimpse culture? That I can find no words to describe a phenomenon we all experience tells us something about that change. We were quick to adopt, a quarter of a century ago, Marshall McLuhan's glitziest terms,[10] but we have ignored his observations on the difficulty of separating image, meaning, and medium. The term *global village* has become common coin without our considering that it might have produced a global village landscape, in which images of landscapes we shall never visit are as familiar to us as those of our own village, or city. Surely we might wonder whether the experience of landscape, its role, and its interpretation are changing. Whatever the faults of nineteenth-century landscape painting, it generated a lively and stimulating debate about the nature of the landscape experience, its variety, and its relation to images and symbols. Maybe a contemporary John Ruskin could help us make sense of our imagineered world.

Notes

CHAPTER ONE
The writing of this chapter has been aided by close readings of earlier drafts by Todd W. Bressi, Margaretta Lovell, Kathleen Moran, Christine Rosen, Dell Upton, and Richard Walker.

1. The phrase "fish that can't see water," comes from an interview in San Francisco with communications consultant Tim Allen, 12 October 1987.

2. Jackson modeled *Landscape*'s variety of contributors and his approach to book reviews after the French quarterly *Revue de géographie humaine et d'ethnologie,* published in 1948–49 by the geographer Pierre Deffontaines and the anthropologist André Leroi-Gourhan.

3. On Jackson's biography, see Helen Lefkowitz Horowitz, "J. B. Jackson and the Discovery of the American Landscape," in Horowitz, ed., *Landscape in Sight: Looking at America* (New Haven: Yale University Press, 1997); Helaine Caplan Prentice, "John Brinckerhoff Jackson," *Landscape Architecture* 71 (1981): 740–745; and Donald W. Meinig, "Reading the Landscape: An Appreciation of W. G. Hoskins and J. B. Jackson," in Meinig, ed., *The Interpretation of Ordinary Landscapes: Geographical Essays* (New York: Oxford University Press, 1979): 195–244.

4. J. B. Jackson, "The Need of Being Versed in Country Things," *Landscape* 1:1 (Spring 1951): 1–5, quotation on p. 5.

5. See David Lowenthal, "The American Way of History," *Columbia University Forum* 9 (1966): 27–32.

6. Notable exceptions to this trend were James E. Vance, Jr., the urban morphologist, and Carl Sauer (both at Berkeley), and historical geographers Donald W. Meinig (at Syracuse University) and Andrew Clark (at the University of Wisconsin).

7. Classics are Margaret Byington, *Homestead: The Households of a Mill Town* (New York: Russell Sage Foundation, 1910) and the local and state tour books produced by the Federal Writers' Project of the Works Projects Administration.

8. Peirce Lewis, "Axioms for Reading the Landscape: Some Guides to the American Scene," in Meinig, ed., *The Interpretation of Ordinary Landscapes,* 12.

9. For samples of useful rural studies, see Allen Noble, "The Diffusion of Silos," *Landscape* 25:1 (1981): 11–14; and Henry H. Glassie, *Folk Housing in Middle Virginia: A Structural Analysis of Historic Artifacts* (Knoxville: University of Tennessee Press, 1975).

211

10. See John R. Stilgoe, *Common Landscape of America, 1580 to 1845* (New Haven: Yale University Press, 1982), 3, and David Chuenyan Lai's chapter in this collection.

11. Compare Stewart G. McHenry, "Eighteenth-Century Field Patterns as Vernacular Art," *Old-Time New England* 69:1–2 (Summer–Fall 1978): 1–21 to J. B. Jackson's treatment of fields in "An Engineered Environment: The New American Countryside," *Landscape* 16:1 (Autumn 1966): 16–20. See also Robert Blair St. George, "'Set Thine House in Order': The Domestication of the Yeomanry in Seventeenth-Century New England," in *New England Begins: The Seventeenth Century,* 3 vols. (Boston: Museum of Fine Arts, 1982), and Bernard L. Herman, *The Stolen House* (Charlottesville: University of Virginia Press, 1992). For many years, Jackson was one of the few writers to take on the more abstract aspects of the road and field.

12. Michael P. Conzen's *The Making of the American Landscape* (Boston: Unwin Hyman, 1990) is also strongly urban, with six urban chapters out of a total of eighteen. The urban chapters are written by James E. Vance, Jr., David Meyer, Edward Muller, John Jakle, Wilbur Zelinsky, and Conzen.

13. See Wilbur Zelinsky, "The Impact of Central Authority," in Conzen, ed., *The Making of the American Landscape,* 311–334; Hildegard Binder Johnson, *Order Upon the Land: The U.S. Rectangular Land Survey and the Upper Mississippi Country* (New York: Oxford University Press, 1976); and John R. Stilgoe, *Metropolitan Corridor: Railroads and the American Scene* (New Haven: Yale University Press, 1983).

14. On individual action and landscape, see Marwyn S. Samuels, "The Biography of Landscape," in Meinig, *The Interpretation of Ordinary Landscapes,* 51–88.

15. For a range of isolated as well as more nuanced studies, see Dell Upton and John Michael Vlach, eds., *Common Places: Readings in American Vernacular Architecture* (Athens: University of Georgia Press, 1986).

16. Dolores Hayden, *The Power of Place: Urban Landscapes as Public History* (Cambridge: MIT Press, 1995).

17. Meinig's book is cited above. Each of the chapters was based on a lecture in a series Meinig organized at Syracuse University.

18. For South Africa, see Margot R. Winer and James Deetz, "The Transformation of British Culture in the Easter Cape, South Africa, 1820–1860," *Kroeber Anthropological Society Papers* 74–75 (1992): 41–61; and Margot R. Winter, "Landscapes of Power: The Material Culture of the Eastern Cape Frontier, South Africa, 1820–1860," Ph.D. diss., University of California, Berkeley, 1994. On the Association of American Geographers, see, for instance, the twenty urban monographs of the Comparative Metropolitan Analysis project: John S. Adams, ed., *Contemporary Metropolitan America,* 4 vols. (Cambridge, Mass: Ballinger, 1977), especially the sections by Peirce Lewis (New Orleans) and Jean Vance (San Francisco). On the National Park Service, Robert Z. Melnick, Daniel Spann, and Emma Jane Saxe, *Cultural Landscapes: Rural Historic Districts in the National Park System* (Washington, D.C.: Park Historic Architecture Division, Cultural Resources Management, U.S. Department of the Interior, 1984).

19. A useful review of recent positions is Lester Rowntree, "Cultural/Humanistic Geography," *Progress in Human Geography* 10:4 (1986): 580–86.

20. On culture and its interpretation in social theory, see particularly Henri Lefebvre, *The Production of Space* (Oxford: Blackwell, 1991; first published in French in 1974); Raymond Williams, *Culture* (Cambridge: Fontana, 1981); Pierre Bourdieu, *Distinction: A Social Critique of the Judgment of Taste* (Cambridge: Harvard University Press, 1984); Allan Pred and Michael Watts, *Reworking Modernity: Capitalisms and Symbolic Discontent* (New Brunswick, N.J.: Rutgers University Press, 1992); John Clark, Stuart Hall, Tony Jefferson, and Brian Roberts, "Subcultures, Cultures, and Class," in T. Bennett et al., eds., *Culture, Ideology, and Social Processes* (Philadelphia: Open University Press, 1980); Michel de Certeau, *The Practice of Everyday Life* (Berkeley: University of California Press, 1984; first published in French in 1980); Michel de Certeau "Practices of Space," in Marshall Blonsky, ed., *On Signs* (Baltimore:

Johns Hopkins University Press, 1985); David Harvey, *The Condition of Postmodernity* (Oxford: Blackwell, 1989); Frederic Jamison, *Postmodernism, or the Cultural Logic of Late Capitalism* (Durham, N.C.: Duke University Press, 1991); Clifford James, *The Predicament of Culture* (Cambridge: Harvard University Press, 1988); Cornel West, *Beyond Ethnocentrism and Multiculturalism* (Monroe, Maine: Common Courage Press, 1993); Mary Douglas, *Natural Symbols: Explorations in Cosmology* (New York: Pantheon, 1970); Marshall Sahlins, *Culture and Practical Reason* (Chicago: University of Chicago Press, 1970).

In the face of the plethora of recent theoretical pronouncements, one might begin by interpolating from Clifford Geertz's "mentalist" position and defining culture to be the mental and physical webs of meaning that people themselves spin, not simply an ideational system but an adaptive and material system. See Clifford Geertz, "Thick Description," in Geertz, *The Interpretation of Cultures: Selected Essays* (New York: Basic Books, 1973), 3–30; Roger M. Keesing, "Theories of Culture," in B. Siegel et al., *Annual Review of Anthropology* 3 (1974): 73–97. Another very readable and cogent introduction is Cole Harris, "Power, Modernity, and Historical Geography," *Journal of the Association of American Geographers* 81:4 (1991): 671–83.

21. For classic examples, see: Joan Didion, *The White Album* (New York: Simon and Schuster, 1979); Wallace Stegner, *Mormon Country* (New York: Duell, Sloan and Pearce, 1942); George R. Stewart, *U.S. 40: Cross-Section of the United States of America* (Boston: Houghton Mifflin, 1953); William Faulkner, *Light in August* (Norfolk, Conn.: New Directions, 1932); Louise Erdrich, *Love Medicine* (New York: Holt, Rinehart and Winston, 1984); Philip Langdon, *American Houses* (New York: Stewart, Tabori and Chang, 1987); Suzannah Lessard, "The Suburban Landscape: Oyster Bay, Long Island," *New Yorker* (11 Oct. 1976): 44–79.

22. Carl Sauer, "The Morphology of Landscape" (1925) and "The Education of a Geographer" (1956), repr. in John Leighly, ed., *Land and Life: A Selection from the Writings of Carl Ortwin Sauer* (Berkeley: University of California Press, 1963): 315–50 and 389–404. See also James S. Duncan, "The Superorganic in American Cultural Geography," *Annals of the Association of American Geographers* 70 (1980):181–98.

23. Geography departments that are or have been known for cultural landscape work include the University of California, Berkeley; Pennsylvania State University; Louisiana State University; University of Minnesota; University of Chicago; Syracuse University; University of British Columbia; and University of California, Los Angeles.

24. Wilbur Zelinsky, *The Cultural Geography of the United States,* rev. ed. (Englewood Cliffs, N.J.: Prentice-Hall, 1992; first published in 1973).

25. On place and phenomenology, Yi Fu Tuan, *Topophilia: A Study of Environmental Perception, Attitudes, and Values* (Englewood Cliffs, N.J.: Prentice-Hall, 1974). See also Edward Relph, *Place and Placelessness* (London: Pion, 1976); David Seamon, *A Geography of the Lifeworld: Movement, Rest, and Encounter* (London: Croom Helm, 1979); and Irwin Altman and Setha M. Low, eds., *Place Attachment* (New York: Plenum, 1992). On more recent theoretical positions, the sources on definitions of culture (see n. 20 above) are a reasonable starting list.

26. W. G. Hoskins, *The Making of the English Landscape* (London: Penguin, 1985). On Hoskins and Jackson, see Meinig, "Reading the Landscape," 195–244; see also Barbara Bender's *Landscape: Politics and Perspectives* (Oxford: Berg, 1993).

27. For a record of the discussion at one of these conferences, see Edmund C. Penning-Rowsell and David Lowenthal, eds., *Landscape Meanings and Values* (London: Allen and Unwin, 1986).

28. William Norton, *Explorations in the Understanding of Landscape: A Cultural Geography* (New York: Greenwood, 1989); see also Peter Jackson, *Maps of Meaning: An Introduction to Cultural Geography* (London: Unwin Hyman, 1989).

29. On the close links between Stilgoe and Jackson, see Helen Lefkowitz Horowitz, "Toward a New History of the Landscape and Built Environment," *Reviews in American History* 13:4 (December 1985): 487–93. After teaching as a lecturer for at least one year in geography

at Berkeley, Jackson taught in Berkeley's College of Environmental Design from 1967 to 1978. He taught in the Graduate School of Design at Harvard from 1969 to 1977 and lectured at dozens of universities, most often in environmental design or geography departments.

30. Architecture and landscape architecture departments known for cultural landscape courses include Harvard, Yale, Rhode Island School of Design, University of California, Berkeley, University of Syracuse, Rice University, University of Oregon, University of Illinois, and University of Georgia.

31. See the *Vernacular Architecture Newsletter*, with its notable bibliographies, and the Vernacular Architecture Forum serial (currently published every other year) *Perspectives in Vernacular Architecture*. See also Chris Wilson, "When a Room Is the Hall," *Mass* [Journal of the School of Architecture and Planning, University of New Mexico] 2 (Summer 1984): 17–23; and Eric Sandweiss, "Building for Downtown Living: The Residential Architecture of San Francisco's Tenderloin," in Thomas Carter and Bernard Herman, eds., *Perspectives in Vernacular Architecture* 3 (Columbia: University of Missouri Press, 1989): 160–75.

32. Paul E. Johnson, *A Shopkeeper's Millennium: Society and Revivals in Rochester, New York, 1815–1837* (New York: Hill and Wang, 1978); William Cronon, *Nature's Metropolis: Chicago and the Great West* (New York: W. W. Norton, 1991); Elizabeth Blackmar, *Manhattan for Rent, 1785–1850* (Ithaca, N.Y.: Cornell University Press, 1989); Sally Ann McMurry, *Families and Farmhouses in Nineteenth-Century America: Vernacular Design and Local Change* (New York: Oxford University Press, 1988).

33. Prominent American studies scholars with landscape studies interests include John R. Stilgoe, Leo Marx, Annette Kolodny, and Thomas Schlereth.

34. Donald W. Meinig, "Environmental Appreciation: Localities as Humane Art," *Western Humanities Review* 25 (1971): 1–11; and Peirce Lewis, "Axioms for Reading the Landscape: Some Guides to the American Scene," in Meinig, ed., *The Interpretation of Ordinary Landscapes: Geographical Essays* (New York: Oxford University Press, 1979). For more purely aesthetic visual positions, see John Jakle, *The Visual Elements of Landscape* (Amherst: University of Massachusetts Press, 1987), and Tadahiko Higuchi, *The Visual and Spatial Structure of Landscapes* (Cambridge: MIT Press, 1983; first published in Japanese, 1975).

35. David Lowenthal, "Is Seeing Disbelieving?"—comments at *Vision, Culture, and Landscape*, the Berkeley symposium on cultural landscape interpretation, March 1990.

36. See Martin Jay, *Downcast Eyes: The Denigration of Vision in Twentieth-Century French Thought* (Berkeley: University of California Press, 1993).

37. Peter Jackson, *Maps of Meaning*, 19.

38. Lowenthal, "Is Seeing Disbelieving?"

39. Peirce Lewis sets forth the uses and limits of visual clues in "Axioms for Reading the Landscape," 11–32.

40. Lowenthal, "Is Seeing Disbelieving?"

41. Ervin Zube, ed., *Landscapes: Selected Writings of J. B. Jackson* (Amherst: University of Massachusetts Press, 1970); J. B. Jackson, *American Space: The Centennial Years, 1865–1876* (New York: W. W. Norton, 1972); *The Necessity for Ruins and Other Topics* (Amherst: University of Massachusetts Press, 1980); *Discovering the Vernacular Landscape* (New Haven: Yale University Press, 1984); *The Essential Landscape: The New Mexico Photographic Survey* (Albuquerque: University of New Mexico Press, 1985); *A Sense of Place, a Sense of Time* (New Haven: Yale University Press, 1994); and Helen Lefkowitz Horowitz, *Landscape in Sight: Looking at America* (New Haven: Yale University Press, 1997).

42. J. B. Jackson, "Preface," *Discovering the Vernacular Landscape*, x, xii.

43. Ibid., x.

44. See Meinig, "Reading the Landscape," 215–17.

45. On Jackson's first urban writing in *Landscape*, see the "Notes and Comments" section of issue 1:2 (Autumn 1951), 1–2. On alienation from cultural environment, see Jackson, "The

Non-Environment," *Landscape* 17:1 (Autumn 1967): 1. For longer and early urban studies by Jackson himself, see "The Stranger's Path," *Landscape* 7:1 (Autumn 1957): 11–15; and "Southeast to Turkey," *Landscape* 7:3 (Spring 1958): 17–22.

46. On Gottmann, I rely on an interview with Jackson in Berkeley, Calif., 14 March 1978.

47. On landscapes of economic difficulty, see J. B. Jackson, "To Pity the Plumage but Forget the Dying Bird," *Landscape* 17:1 (Autumn 1967). On processes that are "by no means rational," see J. B. Jackson, "Notes and Comments: Tenth Anniversary Issue," *Landscape* 10:1 (Fall 1960): 1–2. On the psychological and religious approaches as the "only ones with promise" for deriving landscape meaning, see Jackson, "Human, All Too Human, Geography," *Landscape* 2:2 (Autumn 1952): 2–7.

48. J. B. Jackson to Paul Groth, letter of 25 June 1994; before its recent change in editorial policies, the *New Yorker* would probably have been on Jackson's list.

49. Early in his career, Jackson found the dictum on being "straightforward and little systematized" in Maurice le Lannou; he quotes Lannou in "The Vocation of Human Geography," *Landscape* 1:1 (Spring 1951): 41. The exploratory challenge comes from Jackson's last issue as editor, in J. B. Jackson, "1951–1968: Postscript," *Landscape* 18:1 (Winter 1969): 1.

50. Meinig, "Reading the Landscape," 229. Some of Jackson's most resolute statements on method are in the preface to *Discovering the Vernacular Landscape,* ix–xii.

51. An exception, in which specific case studies are central, is Jackson's *American Space*. On explicit theory, see Bonnie Loyd, "The Saga of an Academic Outlaw Tamed and Branded by the Law of the Scholarly World," unpublished paper given at the Association of Pacific Coast Geographers, June 1979.

52. Jackson's notion of abstract landscape orders was partially developed in *American Space* and seems to draw, in part, on Michel Foucault, *The Order of Things: An Archeology of the Human Sciences* (New York: Pantheon, 1971; first published in French in 1966), and on J. P. Vernant, *Mythe et pensée chez les grecs* (Paris: F. Maspero, 1965). See also a later variant in J. B. Jackson, "Concluding with Landscapes," in *Discovering the Vernacular Landscape,* 145–57. The full development, never published, was part of his survey courses. On recreation categories, Roger Caillois, *Man, Play, and Games* (New York: Free Press, 1961).

53. Jackson's windshield tours often consisted of his annual trips between Harvard, Berkeley, and Santa Fe. Classic examples using detailed fieldwork for larger interpretations include Fred B. Kniffen, "Folk Housing: Key to Diffusion," *Annals of the Association of American Geographers* 55 (1965): 549–77; and Dell Upton, "Vernacular Domestic Architecture in Eighteenth-Century Virginia," *Winterthur Portfolio* 17:2–3 (Summer–Autumn 1982): 220–44.

54. On telling details making the landscape unforgettable, see J. B. Jackson, "By Way of Conclusion: How to Study the Landscape," *The Necessity for Ruins,* 119. On seeing landscape as a "political or cultural entity," see J. B. Jackson, "The Order of a Landscape: Reason and Religion in Newtonian America," in Meinig, *The Interpretation of Ordinary Landscapes,* 153. On landscape not being a work of art, see J. B. Jackson, "Goodbye to Evolution," *Landscape* 13:2 (Winter 1963–64): 1–2; on focus on the practical, R. B. R. [Jackson], "The Urban Cosmeticians or the City Beautiful Rides Again," *Landscape* 15:3 (Spring 1966): 3–4, and J. B. Jackson, "Limited Access: The American Landscape Seen in Passing," *Landscape* 14:1 (Autumn 1964): 18–23. On landscape being regarded in terms of living, J. B. Jackson, quoted in Meinig, "Reading the Landscape," 236.

CHAPTER TWO

The author wishes to thank Richard Walker and Todd W. Bressi for their helpful criticisms and suggestions for revising this essay.

1. In this paper, the word *landscape* means the network of places that results from individuals' efforts to make and remake environments to fit their needs. To the extent that individual decisions become common responses, a cultural pattern begins to emerge; and when pat-

terns take hold, they produce a distinct landscape. The landscape includes both physical forms, such as buildings and open spaces, as well as the way those forms are used—both of which give meaning to the environment.

2. Kenneth T. Jackson, *Crabgrass Frontier: The Suburbanization of the United States* (New York: Oxford University Press, 1985). The "weave of small patterns" that Sam Bass Warner documented in Boston's suburbs does not reflect the extent of diversity found here. Warner, *Streetcar Suburbs: The Process of Growth in Boston,* 2d ed. (Cambridge: Harvard University Press, 1978), 67–116.

3. Later in this article, I use *urban village* to mean a landscape that combines elements of rural village and urban life. Herbert Gans used the term to refer to an inner-city ethnic enclave whose life "resembled that found in the village or small town, or even in the suburb." See Gans, *The Urban Villagers: Group and Class in the Life of Italian-Americans* (New York: Free Press, 1962), 15.

4. These are probably undercounts. Census tracts cut across landscapes, making precise numbers hard to determine. Howard Whipple Green, *Population Characteristics by Census Tracts: Cleveland, Ohio, 1930* (Cleveland: Plain Dealer Publishing, 1931), 57, 116; and U.S. Census, Population Schedules, 1910.

5. The historian Margaret Marsh has described turn-of-the-century suburbs as "lushly landscaped, safe, homogeneous, and purged of the poor, the radical, and the ethnically suspect." See Margaret Marsh, "From Separation to Togetherness: The Social Construction of Domestic Space in American Suburbs, 1840–1915," *Journal of American History* 76 (September 1989): 522. In contrast, students of visual and spatial analyses have demonstrated other kinds of suburbs. John R. Stilgoe describes elite "borderlands" of wealthy homes "so far apart that . . . they cast shadows only on their own lots," while Roger Barnett identifies "libertarian suburbs" as a "disorderly array of houses" built mostly by "the poor or those of modest income." See John R. Stilgoe, *Borderland: Origins of the American Suburb, 1820–1939* (New Haven: Yale University Press, 1988), 11; and Roger Barnett, "The Libertarian Suburb: Deliberate Disorder," *Landscape* 22 (Summer 1978): 44–48. For a discussion of working-class suburbs, see Richard Harris, "American Suburbs: A Sketch of a New Interpretation," *Journal of Urban History* 15 (November 1988): 98–103.

6. The research in this chapter draws on several years of field study and participant observation. For historical visual analysis methods, see James Borchert, "Analysis of Historical Photographs," *Studies in Visual Communication* 7 (Fall 1981): 30–63. On multiple confirmation, see Eugene J. Webb et al., *Unobtrusive Measures: Nonreactive Research in the Social Sciences* (Chicago: University of Chicago Press, 1966), 5.

7. Jim Borchert and Susan Borchert, *Lakewood: The First Hundred Years, 1889–1989* (Norfolk, Va.: Donning, 1989), 40, 109, 129.

8. Green, *Population Characteristics,* 5.

9. Ibid.

10. Borchert and Borchert, *Lakewood,* 108, 133.

11. Green, *Population Characteristics,* 1. Lakewood could be considered a "city-suburb." This type of urban settlement, which I have identified elsewhere, has a large, heterogeneous, densely settled population; see "Residential City Suburbs: The Emergence of a New Suburban Type, 1880–1930," *Journal of Urban History* 22 (March 1996): 283–307.

12. Elsewhere I have reported on two additional Lakewood landscapes—a neighborhood of successful farmer-developers and a west-end, native-born, working-class enclave; see "Cities in the Suburbs: Heterogeneous Communities on the U.S. Urban Fringe, 1920–1960," *Urban History* 23 (August 1966): 223–24.

13. U.S. Census, Population Schedules, 1910; Fred McGunagle, "Millionaires' Row Falls to More Modern Era," *Cleveland Press* (19 Jan. 1961); Tom Barensfeld, "Lakewood Salutes the Arts," *Cleveland Press* (5 Aug. 1978); Tom Barensfeld, "Lakewood's Largest Home Was a Castle," *Cleveland Press* (22 July 1978).

14. See Robert L. Vickery, Jr., *Anthrophysical Form: Two Families and their Neighborhood Environments* (Charlottesville: University Press of Virginia, 1972), 1–40. Bowditch's Cleveland associate, Myron Vorce, probably prepared the Clifton Park plan.

15. "The Clifton Park Land Improvement Company" (Cleveland: Clifton Park Land Improvement Co., no date).

16. Clifton Park Land Improvement Company incorporation papers, as quoted in Blythe Gehring, *Vignettes of Clifton Park* (Cleveland: private printing, n. d.), 25.

17. Cuyahoga County Treasurer's Department, tax duplicates, 1894–1923. James Borchert and Susan Danziger-Borchert, "Migrant Responses to the City: The Neighborhood, Case Studies in Black and White, 1870–1940," *Slovakia* 31 (1984): 8–45; and James Borchert and Susan Borchert, "The Bird's Nest: Making of an Ethnic Urban Village," *Gamut* 21 (Summer 1987): 4–13.

18. Although the neighborhood is now known almost exclusively as "Birdtown" (five of the eight streets are named for birds), residents used to refer to it as "the village." Margaret Manor Butler, *The Lakewood Story* (New York: Stratford House, 1949), 228.

19. Jan Pankuch, *Dejiny Clevelandskych a Lakewoodskych Slovakov* (Cleveland: no publisher, 1930), 22; Cuyahoga County Auditor, Tax Maps; U.S. Census, Population Schedules, 1910.

20. Pankuch, *Dejiny Clevelandskych*, 24.

21. City of Lakewood Building Department, building permits, 1900–1982.

22. Howard Whipple Green, *An Analysis of Population Data by Census Tracts* (Cleveland: Cleveland Health Council, 1927), 11–12.

23. Building permits indicate that many builders constructed their own homes or hired neighbors to do so; Slavic surnames dominate both property records and building permits. See City of Lakewood Building Department, building permits, and Borchert and Borchert, "Migrant Responses," 23–24.

24. Green, *Population Characteristics*, 116. Even perceptive observers missed the extent of multifamily units: Eric Johannesen, "The Architecture of Cleveland's Immigrant Neighborhoods," in Edward M. Miggins, ed., *A Guide to Studying Neighborhoods and Resources on Cleveland* (Cleveland: Cleveland Public Library, 1984), 109–13; and Steve McQuillin, *Birdtown: A Study of an Ethnic Neighborhood* (Lakewood: Ohio Historical Preservation Office, 1991), 3, 5.

25. I discovered this arrangement only by penetrating the side doors. Today exterior electric meters and city directories suggest the number of units. On its origins, see McQuillin, *Birdtown*, 8.

26. Early housing reformers, such as Jacob Riis, attacked common corridors as a danger to social order and urged limiting the number of units per entry. Jacob Riis, *How the Other Half Lives* (1890; reprint, New York: Dover Publications, 1971), 228–29.

27. *Cleveland City Directory, 1930* (Cleveland: Cleveland Directory Co., 1930).

28. G. M. Hopkins Co., *Plat Books of Cuyahoga County, Ohio, 1927*, vol. 6 (Philadelphia: G. M. Hopkins, 1927; revised to 1937).

29. Borchert and Borchert, *Lakewood*, 130. William H. Whyte described similar responses in a post–World War II suburb in *The Organization Man* (Garden City, N.Y.: Doubleday, Anchor, 1956), 365–404.

30. Clifford Edward Clark, Jr., *The American Family Home: 1800–1960* (Chapel Hill: University of North Carolina Press, 1986), 99.

31. Borchert and Borchert, *Lakewood*, 130–32. Herbert Gans described a similar process and social patterns in *The Levittowners: Ways of Life and Politics in a New Suburban Community* (New York: Vintage, 1967), 44–48, 51, and 124–25, and in "Park Forest: Birth of a Jewish Community," *Commentary* 11 (April 1951): 330–39. The concept of communities of limited liability is from Gerald D. Suttles, *The Social Construction of Communities* (Chicago: University of Chicago Press, 1972), 44–81.

32. For example see *Cleveland Plain Dealer* (1 January 1917): 16, and (26 January 1928): 7.

33. *Lakewood Suburban News*, 1920. See also *Lakewood Post* (22 May 1930): 1, and (26 June 1930): 1.

34. *Lakewood Post* (22 March 1928): 1, 6.

35. On the other hand, even careful observers can misread the past from present landscapes. A recent article on Lakewood began with the incorrect observation that "the grand mansions along Lake Erie here are still splendid." Karen DeWitt, "Older Suburbs Struggle to Compete with New," *New York Times*, 26 Feb. 1995: x10.

CHAPTER THREE

1. This opening sentence is a summary response to the invitation from Paul Groth to participate in the 1990 symposium "Vision, Culture, and Landscape." The invitation included a list of questions such as: "Consider the reliability of visual information, and when and whether other sources of information are more important." My working draft was included in the conference volume *Vision, Culture, and Landscape: Working Papers from the Berkeley Symposium on Cultural Landscape Interpretation* (Berkeley: University of California, Center for Environmental Design Research, 1990) in a section titled "Limits, Potentials, and Dangers of Vision."

2. Torsten Hägerstrand, "The Landscape as Overlapping Neighborhoods" (Carl Sauer Memorial Lecture, Berkeley, 1984), in Gösta Carlestam and Barbro Sollbe, eds., *Om Tidens Vidd Och Tingens Ordning: Texter av Torsten Hägerstrand* (Stockholm: Byggforskningsradet, 1991), 50.

3. Deryck W. Holdsworth, "House and Home in Vancouver: The Emergence of a West Coast Urban Landscape, 1886–1929," Ph.D. diss., University of British Columbia, 1981. The argument is summarized in "House and Home in Vancouver: Images of West Coast Urbanism, 1886–1929," in Gilbert A. Stelter and Alan F. J.. Artibise, eds., *The Canadian City: Essays in Urban History* (Toronto: McClelland and Stewart, 1977), 186–211.

4. This is a tradition of urban analysis that I learned as an undergraduate with Prof. M. R. G. Conzen at Newcastle. For him, the morphological approach had three elements: town plan, building types, and land use. Any one of those by itself involved a significant research challenge, and few have been able to bring all three detailed elements together. In an age prior to computerized geographical information systems, this was a mammoth task and rarely satisfactorily accomplished. Even so, the mixture of detailed landscape record and historical evidence provides a powerful signpost. For a summary of Conzen's important contributions, see Jeremy W. R. Whitehand, ed., *The Urban Landscape: Historical Development and Management: Papers by M. R. G. Conzen,* Special Publication 13 (London: Institute of British Geographers, 1981). Whitehand summarizes a morphological period as a "phase of social and cultural history creating distinctive material forms in the cultural landscape," 14. With the significant exceptions of the work of James Vance and M. R. G. Conzen, the tradition never really transferred across the Atlantic, partly because many American urban geographers were far more interested in a more functional and ahistorical view of urban pattern. Some people find Grady Clay's more journalistic *Close-up: How to Read the American City* (New York: Praeger, 1973) useful.

5. A good role model is Michael J. Doucet and John C. Weaver, "Material Culture and the North American House: The Era of the Common Man, 1870–1920," *Journal of American History* 72:3 (December 1985): 560–87.

6. David Harvey, "Labor, Capital, and Class Struggle around the Built Environment in Advanced Capitalist Societies," in Kevin R. Cox, ed., *Urbanization and Conflict in Market Societies* (Chicago: Maaroufa, 1978), 9–37.

7. A working-class Brit from Newcastle-upon-Tyne in northern England; a product of a neighborhood of terraced houses who knew where he was and wasn't when visiting semidetached and detached houses in garden settings; an immigrant traveler with curiosity and ambivalence about home.

8. Clare Cooper, "The House as Symbol of Self," Institute of Urban and Regional Development, Working Paper 120 (Berkeley: University of California, 1971).

9. See Fred B. Kniffen, "Louisiana House Types," in *Annals, Association of American Geographers* 26 (1936): 179–93; "Folk Housing as the Key to Diffusion," ibid. 55 (1965): 549–77; Estyn Evans, *Irish Folk Ways* (London: Routledge and Kegan Paul, 1957); a broad summary of this approach can be found in the entries in Dell Upton, ed., *America's Architectural Roots: Ethnic Groups That Built America* (Washington: Preservation Press, 1986).

10. John A. Jakle, Robert W. Bastian, and Douglas K. Meyer, *Common Houses in America's Small Towns: The Atlantic Seaboard to the Mississippi Valley* (Athens: University of Georgia Press, 1989).

11. Anne E. Mosher and Deryck W. Holdsworth, "The Meaning of Alley Housing in Industrial Towns: Examples From Late-Nineteenth and Early-Twentieth Century Pennsylvania," *Journal of Historical Geography* 18:2 (1992): 174–89.

12. Richard Harris, "Household Work Strategies and Suburban Home Ownership in Toronto, 1899–1913," *Environment and Planning D: Society and Space* 8 (1990): 97–121.

13. Michael Steinitz, "Rethinking Geographical Approaches to the Common House: The Evidence from Eighteenth-century Massachusetts," in Thomas Carter and Bernard L. Herman, eds., *Perspectives in Vernacular Architecture III* (Columbia: University of Missouri Press, 1989), 17.

14. Ibid., 23.

15. Another example is provided by the work of Bernard Herman, who draws on archival sources such as estate inventories, orphan court property valuations, tax assessments, and the manuscript census to clarify the class relations of the transforming agrarian landscape of eighteenth- and nineteenth-century Delaware. Bernard L. Herman, *Architecture and Rural Life in Central Delaware 1700–1900* (Knoxville: University of Tennessee Press, 1987); *The Stolen House* (Charlottesville: University Press of Virginia, 1992). For further discussion of the diffusion approach to housing by cultural geographers, see Deryck W. Holdsworth, "Revaluing the House" in James Duncan and David Ley, eds., *Place/Culture/Representation* (London: Routledge, 1993), 95–109.

16. A recent example is Larry R. Ford, "Reading the Skylines of American Cities," *Geographical Review* 82:2 (1992): 180–200.

17. The arguments for an alternate approach are presented in Gunter Gad and Deryck W. Holdsworth, "Looking Inside the Skyscraper: Size and Occupancy of Toronto Office Buildings, 1890–1950," *Urban History Review/Revue d'histoire urbaine,* 16:2 (1987): 176–89; and "Corporate Capitalism and the Emergence of the High-Rise Office Building," *Urban Geography* 8:3 (1987): 212–31.

18. Ford, "Reading the Skylines," 199.

19. Ibid., 193.

20. Metropolitan Life continued to expand on these two blocks adjacent to Madison Square, and five more components of the complex were built in decades to come. A similar preoccupation with this fifty-story tower built in 1909 is evident in Mona Domosh, "Corporate Cultures and the Modern Landscape of New York City" in Kay Anderson and Fay Gayle, eds., *Inventing Places: Studies in Cultural Geography* (Melbourne: Longman Cheshire, 1992), 77–82.

21. Most of the tower was blocked by the giant City Investing Building, built immediately adjacent at some 43 stories and providing, by 1908, some 13 acres of office space. See Deryck W. Holdsworth, "Morphological Change in Lower Manhattan, 1893–1920," in Jeremy W. R. Whitehand and Peter J. Larkham, eds., *Urban Landscapes: International Perspectives* (London: Routledge, 1992), 114–29.

22. Gail Fenske and Deryck W. Holdsworth, "Corporate Identity and the New York Office Building, 1895–1915" in David Ward and Oliver Zunz, eds., *The Landscape of Modernity: Essays on New York City, 1900–1940* (New York: Russell Sage, 1992).

23. Individual buildings, even landmark structures, can still offer a wealth of insight. For example, Mona Domosh offers an effective interpretation of Pulitzer's decisions surrounding the construction in 1890 of the towering, 16-story New York World Building; Mona Domosh, "A Method for Interpreting Landscape: A Case Study of the New York World Building," *Area*

21:4 (December 1989): 347–55. Similarly, Oliver Zunz uses Metropolitan Life archival material to look "inside the skyscraper" to get at a fascinating range of issues around corporate management, gender, and design. See *Making America Corporate, 1870–1920* (Chicago: University of Chicago Press, 1990).

24. John R. Borchert, "Major Control Points in American Economic Geography," *Annals, Association of American Geographers,* 68 (1978): 214–32; Michael P. Conzen, "The Maturing Urban System in the United States," *Annals, Association of American Geography,* 67 (1977): 88–108.

25. For Toronto, for example, see Gunter Gad and Deryck W. Holdsworth, "Building for City, Region, and Nation: Office Development in Toronto, 1834–1984" in Victor L. Russell, ed., *Forging a Consensus: Historical Essays on Toronto* (Toronto: University of Toronto Press, 1984), 272–322; "Streetscape and Society: The Changing Built Environment of King Street, Toronto" in Roger Hall, William Westfall, and Laura Sefton MacDowell, eds., *Patterns of the Past: Interpreting Ontario's History* (Toronto: Dundern Press, 1989), 174–205; "The Emergence of Corporate Toronto," plate 15 of Donald Kerr and Deryck W. Holdsworth, eds., *Historical Atlas of Canada,* vol. 3: *Addressing the Twentieth Century* (Toronto: University of Toronto Press, 1990).

26. For a sense of the redirection, see David Ley and Marwyn S. Samuels, eds., *Humanistic Geography: Prospects and Problems* (Chicago: Maaroufa, 1978).

27. David Lowenthal, "Geography, Experience, and Imagination: Towards a Geographical Epistemology," *Annals, Association of American Geographers* 51 (1961): 241–60; "The American Scene" *Geographical Review* 58 (1968): 61–88; David Lowenthal and Hugh C. Prince, "English Landscape Tastes," *Geographical Review* 54 (1964): 309–346.

28. Donald W. Meinig, ed., *The Interpretation of Ordinary Landscapes: Geographical Essays* (New York: Oxford, 1979).

29. Meinig, *Interpretation of Ordinary Landscapes,* 5.

30. Ibid., 13.

31. John Eyles, "The Geography of Everyday Life," in Derek Gregory and Rex Walford, eds., *Horizons in Human Geography* (Totawa, N.J.: Barnes and Noble, 1988), 102–17.

32. One exception might be Mona Domosh, whose work on the nineteenth- and early twentieth-century American city draws on landscape imagery, although she writes largely as a historical geographer; she is also concerned about the absence of feminist thought.

33. Vera Norwood and Janice Monk, "Perspectives on Gender and Landscape," in Vera Norwood and Janice Monk, eds., *The Desert Is No Lady: Southwestern Landscapes in Women's Writing and Art* (New Haven: Yale University Press, 1987), 4.

34. Dolores Hayden and Peter Marris, "The Quiltmaker's Landscape," *Landscape* 25:3 (1981): 39–47.

35. Heather Huyck, "Beyond John Wayne: Using Western Historic Sites to Interpret Western Women's History," in Lillian Schlissel, Vicki L. Ruiz, and Janice Monk, eds., *Western Women: Their Land, Their Lives* (Albuquerque: University of New Mexico Press, 1988), 303–29.

36. Gillian Rose, *Feminism and Geography: The Limits of Geographical Knowledge* (London: Polity, 1993), 86–112. She titled chapter 5 "Looking at Landscape: The Uneasy Pleasures of Power."

37. Stephen Daniels, "Landscaping for a Manufacturer: Humphrey Repton's Commission for Benjamin Gott at Armley in 1809–10," *Journal of Historical Geography* 7 (1981): 379–96.

38. Stephen Daniels, "Marxism, Culture, and the Duplicity of landscape" in Richard Peet and Nigel Thrift, eds., *New Models in Geography: The Political-Economy Perspective* (London: Unwin Hyman, 1989), 197.

39. Donald M. Mitchell, "State Intervention in Landscape Production: The Wheatland Riot and the California Commission of Immigration and Housing," *Antipode* 25 (1993): 91–113; "Fixing in Place: Progressivism, Worker Resistance, and the Technology of Repression," *His-

torical Geography 23 (1993): 44–61; James Parsons, "A Geographer Looks at the San Joaquin Valley," *Geographical Review* 76 (1986): 371–89.

40. Paul L. Knox, "The Restless Urban Landscape: Economic and Sociocultural Change and the Transformation of Metropolitan Washington, D.C." *Annals, Association of American Geographers* 81:2 (1991): 181–209.

41. See, for example, Stuart Hall et al., *Culture, Media, Language: Working Papers in Cultural Studies 1972–79* (Birmingham, U.K.: Centre for Contemporary Cultural Studies, University of Birmingham, 1980); Paul Gilroy, *"There Ain't no Black in the Union Jack," The Cultural Politics of Race and Nation* (London: Hutchinson, 1987).

42. Kay J. Anderson, "The Idea of Chinatown: The Power of Place and Institutional Practice in the Making of a Racial Category," *Annals, Association of American Geographers* 77 (1987): 580–98. Note that this is not to diminish the careful work of David Lai (this volume) and his *The Forbidden City within Victoria: Myth, Symbol and Streetscape of Canada's Earliest Chinatown* (Victoria, B.C.: Orca, 1991).

43. Peter Jackson, "The racialization of Labour in Post-war Bradford," *Journal of Historical Geography* 18:2 (1992): 190–209.

44. Sarah Deutsch, "Landscape of Enclaves: Race Relations in the West, 1865–1990," in William Cronon, George Miles, and Jay Gitlin, eds., *Under an Open Sky: Rethinking America's Western Past* (New York: Norton, 1992), 110–31.

45. Thomas Carter, "Building for the 'New Time': Global Economics and the Scandinavian Three-part House in Nineteenth-century Utah," session on the political economy of vernacular architecture, Vernacular Architectural Forum, Portsmouth, N.H., May 1992.

46. Peirce Lewis, "Facing Up to Ambiguity," *Landscape* 26:1 (1982): 21.

47. Ibid., 22.

48. David Harvey, *Consciousness and the Urban Experience* (Oxford: Blackwell, 1985); Richard Walker et al., "The Playground of U.S. Capitalism? The Political Economy of the San Francisco Bay Area in the 1980s," in Mike Davis et al., eds., *Fire in the Hearth: The Radical Politics of Place in America* (London: Routledge, Chapman, and Hall/Verso, 1990), 3–82; Neil Smith, "New City, New Frontier: The Lower East Side as the Wild, Wild West," in Michael Sorkin, ed., *Variations on a Theme Park: The New American City and the End of Public Space* (New York: Noonday, 1992); John Fraser Hart, *The Land That Feeds Us* (New York: Norton, 1991).

49. Mary Beth Pudup, "Arguments within Regional Geography," *Progress in Human Geography* 12 (1988): 369–390.

50. David Harvey, "Monument and Myth," *Annals, Association of American Geographers* 69:3 (1979): 262–81.

51. Barbara Rubin, "Aesthetic Ideology and Urban Design," *Annals, Association of American Geographers* 69:3 (1979): 339–61.

52. Denis E. Cosgrove, "Towards a Radical Cultural Geography: Problems of Theory," *Antipode* 15 (1983): 1–11; *Social Formation and Symbolic Landscape* (London: Croom Helm, 1985); Denis E. Cosgrove and Peter Jackson, "New Directions in Cultural Geography," *Area* 19 (1987): 95–101; Peter Jackson, *Maps of Meaning: An Introduction to Cultural Geography* (London: Unwin, 1989).

53. An important early step in this transition was Jim Duncan's critical examination of the underpinnings of Sauerian or Berkeley School cultural geography; see James S. Duncan, "The Superorganic in American Cultural Geography," *Annals, Association of American Geographers* 70 (1980): 181–98. For Derek Gregory and David Ley, "Culture's Geographies," *Environment and Planning D: Society and Space* 6:2 (1988): 115–16, landscape is "a 'concept in high tension,' one which contains multiple and competing claims about the constitution of social order," 115. See also James S. Duncan, *The City as Text: The Politics of Landscape Interpretation in the Kandyan Kingdom* (New York: Cambridge University Press, 1990).

54. Among his many works, see Raymond Williams, *Culture and Society, 1780–1950* (New

York: Columbia University Press, 1958); *The Long Revolution* (New York: Harper and Row, 1961); *The Country and the City* (New York: Oxford University Press, 1973); *Keywords: A Vocabulary of Culture and Society* (New York: Oxford University Press, 1976); *Marxism and Literature* (New York: Oxford University Press, 1977); *Culture* (London: Fontana, 1981). A further indication of the Commonwealth axis in the new cultural geography is a collection of essays mostly written by Australian, Canadian, and British geographers: Kay Anderson and Fay Gayle, eds. *Inventing Places: Studies in Cultural Geography* (Melbourne: Longman Cheshire, 1993).

55. Paul Duncum, "Approaches to Cultural Analysis," *Journal of American Culture* 10:2 (1987): 1–16.

56. Peter Jackson, *Maps of Meaning,* ix.

57. Allen Pred, *Lost Words and Lost Worlds: Modernity and the Language of Everyday Life in Late Nineteenth-Century Stockholm* (Cambridge: Cambridge University Press, 1989).

58. Michael Watts, "Struggles over Land, Struggles over Meaning: Some Thoughts on Naming Peasant Resistance and the Politics of Place," in R. E. Golledge, H. Couclelis, P. Gould, eds., *A Ground for Common Search* (Santa Barbara: Santa Barbara Geographical Press, 1988), 32.

59. Barney L. Warf, "Regional Transformation, Everyday Life and Pacific Northwest Lumber Production," *Annals, Association of American Geographers* 78 (1988): 326–46.

60. Derek Gregory, *Regional Transformation and Industrial Revolution* (London: MacMillan, 1982).

61. Jon Goss, "The Built Environment and Social Theory: Towards an Architectural Geography," *Professional Geographer* 40 (1988): 392.

62. Donald W. Meinig, "Reading the Landscape: An Appreciation of W. G. Hoskins and J. B. Jackson," in Meinig, *Interpretation of Ordinary Landscapes,* 228.

63. See for example David Lowenthal, *The Past Is a Foreign Country* (Cambridge: Cambridge University Press, 1985); Peirce F. Lewis, "Taking down the Velvet Rope: Cultural Geography and the Human Landscape," in Jo Blatti, ed., *Past Meets Present: Essays about Historic Preservation and Public Audiences* (Washington: Smithsonian Institution Press, 1987), 23–29; Peirce F. Lewis, David Lowenthal, and Yi-Fu Tuan, *Visual Blight in America* (Washington: Association of American Geographers Commission on College Geography, 1973).

64. Anthony D. King, *The Bungalow: The Production of a Global Culture* (London: Routledge and Kegan Paul, 1984). See also his edited volume *Buildings and Society: Essays on the Social Development of the Built Environment* (London: Routledge and Kegan Paul, 1980).

65. Mike Davis, *City of Quartz: Excavating the Future in Los Angeles* (New York: Vintage, 1990); Richard Walker et al., "The Playground of U.S. Capitalism? The Political Economy of the San Francisco Bay Area in the 1980s," in Mike Davis et al., eds., *Fire in the Hearth: The Radical Politics of Place in America* (New York: Verso, 1990), 3–82; Sharon Zukin, *Loft Living: Culture and Capital in Urban Change,* 2d ed. (New Brunswick, N.J.: Rutgers University Press, 1989; Sharon Zukin, *Landscapes of Power: From Detroit to Disneyland* (Berkeley: University of California Press, 1991); Paul Knox, *The Restless Landscape* (Englewood Cliffs, N.J.: Prentice-Hall, 1993).

66. R. Cole Harris, "Power, Modernity, and Historical Geography," *Annals, Association of American Geographers* 81 (1991): 671–83.

67. Denis Cosgrove, *The Palladian Landscape: Geographical Change and Its Cultural Representation in Sixteenth-century Italy* (State College: Pennsylvania State University Press, 1993); and Denis Cosgrove and Stephen Daniels, eds., *The Iconography of Landscape* (Cambridge: Cambridge University Press, 1988).

68. Perhaps the best example is the work of Ted Relph as he progressed from *Place and Placelessness* (London: Pion, 1976) to *Rational Landscapes and Humanistic Geography* (London: Croom Helm, 1981) to *The Modern Urban Landscape* (Baltimore: Johns Hopkins University Press, 1987).

69. Mona Domosh, "Method for Interpreting Landscape," 34.

70. Jeanne Kay, "The Future of Historical Geography in the United States," *Annals, Association of American Geographers* 80:4 (1990): 618–21; "Hornsby's Reply," 622–23.

71. Richard Dennis, "History, Geography, and Historical Geography," *Social Science History* 15:2 (1991): 265–84.

CHAPTER FOUR

1. Committee on Labor and Public Welfare, *Indian Education: A National Tragedy—a National Challenge* (Washington: U.S. Government Printing Office, 1969), 10.

2. Ibid., 13.

CHAPTER FIVE

1. David Lowenthal, "Age and Artifact, Dilemmas of Appreciation," in Donald W. Meinig, ed., *The Interpretation of Ordinary Landscapes: Geographical Essays* (New York: Oxford University Press, 1979), 104.

2. William Hubbard, "A Meaning for Monuments," in Nathan Glazer and Mark Lilla, eds., *The Public Face of Architecture, Civic Culture, and Public Spaces* (New York: Free Press, 1987), 124–41.

3. The most comprehensive study of these monuments is Michael Wilson Panhorst, "Lest We Forget: Monuments and Memorial Sculpture in National Military Parks on Civil War Battlefields, 1861–1917" (Ph.D. diss., University of Delaware, 1988). I am especially indebted to this work for its information on the design and construction of regimental monuments. See also Wayne Craven, *The Sculptures at Gettysburg* (N.p.: Eastern Acorn Press, 1982).

4. A useful brief history of the development of Gettysburg battlefield as a memorial landscape is Kathleen Georg Harrison, "'A Fitting and Expressive Memorial': The Development of Gettysburg National Military Park," in *The Gettysburg Compiler* 1:1: 28–34. McConaughy began his effort a scant four weeks after the battle and used his own funds to purchase its first parcels of land.

5. See John Brinckerhoff Jackson, "The Necessity for Ruins," in *The Necessity for Ruins and Other Topics* (Amherst: University of Massachusetts Press, 1980), 91–92.

6. See especially *Pennsylvania at Gettysburg: Ceremonies at the Dedication of the Monuments Erected by the Commonwealth of Pennsylvania* (Harrisburg, Pa.: E. K. Meyers, State Printer, 1893), 2:595, 675; William F. Fox, *New York at Gettysburg: New York Monuments Commission for the Battlefields of Gettysburg and Chattanooga, Final Report on the Battlefield of Gettysburg* (Albany, N.Y.: J. B. Lyon, 1900), 1:295, 340, 525, 555, 621, and 2:928, 115.

7. For a detailed description of the fiftieth-anniversary celebration, see *Pennsylvania at Gettysburg,* vol. 3.

8. See Panhorst, "Lest We Forget," 44–80, for details.

9. This was especially true of New York and Pennsylvania, which had more troops engaged at Gettysburg than the other states. Pennsylvania delayed its vote until it knew New York's appropriation and then matched it. They ended up deadlocked at $1,500 per monument. Official state seals were affixed to most monuments.

10. The three-volume set *New York at Gettysburg* is a typical example.

11. A regiment was allowed only one monument, to be erected on a battlefield of its own choosing. Gettysburg, because of its importance as a major turning point of the war, was the most frequent choice. At Gettysburg, 172,000 troops were engaged for three days, and they suffered 51,000 casualties.

12. "Official Minutes of the Gettysburg Battlefield Memorial Association, 1872–1895," unpublished manuscript in the Gettysburg National Military Park Library. I am indebted to Robert H. Prosperi, historian, the Gettysburg National Military Park, for calling this and other primary source materials to my attention.

13. John M. Vanderslice, *Gettysburg Then and Now* (1889; rpt., Dayton, Ohio: Press of Morningside Bookshop, 1983), 400–468, esp. 451.

14. In addition to specializing in Civil War monuments, these companies also produced cemetery monuments and building materials. See Panhorst, "Lest We Forget," 92–98.

15. The following summary is based on the dedication speeches found in *New York at Gettysburg*, vols. 1–3, and *Pennsylvania at Gettysburg*, vol. 2.

16. *New York at Gettysburg*, 1:237; and *Pennsylvania at Gettysburg*, 2:703, 904.

17. *Century* 50 (May–October 1895): 795–96.

18. There are numerous records of regimental monument committees visiting sculptors' studios to correct errors in uniform detail. See Robert M. Green, *History of the One Hundred and Twenty-fourth Regiment Pennsylvania Volunteers in the War of the Rebellion, 1862–1863* (Philadelphia: Ware Brothers, 1907), 343–52.

19. *Dedication Service at Gettysburg of Pennsylvania's Sixth Reserves Volunteer Infantry* (Athens, Pa.: Gazette Printing and Engraving, 1892), 6–7. A copy of this document can be found in the Gettysburg National Military Park Library.

20. *Pennsylvania at Gettysburg*, 2:772; Frederick W. Hawthorne, *Gettysburg: Stories of Men and Monuments* (Hanover, N.H.: Sheridan Press for the Association of Licensed Battlefield Guides, 1988), 118.

21. *New York at Gettysburg*, 3:1024–1025.

22. *Pennsylvania at Gettysburg*, 2:500; Hawthorne, *Gettysburg*, 28.

23. Garry Wills, *Lincoln at Gettysburg: The Words that Remade America* (New York: Simon and Schuster, 1992), 169–72. Wills has observed that Lincoln's Gettysburg Address, with its telegraphic succinctness, set a new precedent for political oratory. This precedent apparently did not affect the veterans, whose speeches resembled the longer, more theatrical oratory of Lincoln's cospeaker Edward Everett.

24. Members of a few regiments composed of German immigrants gave their dedication speeches in their mother tongue. See *New York at Gettysburg*, 1:281. Typical orders of service will be found throughout this volume.

25. Personal communication from Robert H. Prosperi, historian, the Gettysburg National Military Park.

26. I am indebted to Gary Wills for this insight. See Wills, *Lincoln at Gettysburg*, chap. 2.

27. These themes are summarized from speeches in *Pennsylvania at Gettysburg*, vol. 2 and *New York at Gettysburg*, vols. 1–3.

CHAPTER SIX

1. Alastair W. Kerr, "The Architecture of Victoria's Chinatowns," *Datum* 4:1 (Summer 1989).

2. David Chuenyan Lai, *Chinatowns: Towns within Cities in Canada* (Vancouver: University of British Columbia Press, 1988).

3. Nelson Chia-Chi Ho, *Portland's Chinatown* (Portland, Ore.: City of Portland, Bureau of Planning, 1978).

4. David Chuenyan Lai, *The Forbidden City within Victoria: Myth, Symbol, and Streetscape of Canada's Earliest Chinatown* (Victoria: Orca, 1991), and Christopher L. Salter, *San Francisco's Chinatown: How Chinese a Town?* (San Francisco: R & E Research Associates, 1978).

5. David Chuenyan Lai, *Arches in British Columbia* (Victoria: Sono Nis Press, 1982).

CHAPTER SEVEN

Epigraph: Marshall McLuhan and Quentin Fiore, *The Medium Is the Massage* (New York: Bantam, 1967)

1. Marshall McLuhan, *The Gutenberg Galaxy: The Making of Typographic Man* (Toronto: University of Toronto Press, 1962); Marshall McLuhan, *Understanding Media: The Extensions of Man* (New York: McGraw-Hill, 1964); McLuhan and Fiore, *Medium*.

2. McLuhan and Fiore, *Medium*, 53.

3. John White, *The Birth and Rebirth of Pictorial Space* (New York: Harper and Row, 1972), 190.

4. John Brinckerhoff Jackson, "Landscape as Theater," *Landscape* 23, no. 1 (1979): 3–7.

5. René Descartes, *Discourse on Method* (1637), quoted in David Pepper, *The Roots of Modern Environmentalism* (London: Croom Helm, 1984).

6. Pepper, *Roots*, 5, 46–52.

7. J. Alexander Gottlieb Baumgarten, *Aesthetica* (1750), quoted in Arnold Berleant, "Toward a Phenomenological Aesthetics of Environment," in Don Ihde and H. J. Silverman, eds., *Descriptions* (New York: State University of New York Press, 1985), 112.

8. Berleant, "Toward a Phenomenological Aesthetics," 113.

9. Ibid., 115.

10. See, for example, John Dixon Hunt, *The Figure in the Landscape: Poetry, Painting, and Gardening During the Eighteenth Century* (Baltimore: Johns Hopkins University Press, 1976), 39–48.

11. Edmund Burke, *A Philosophical Inquiry into the Origins of Our Ideas of the Sublime and the Beautiful*, quoted in David Watkin, *The English Vision: The Picturesque in Architecture, Landscape, and Garden Design* (New York: Harper and Row, 1982), 68.

12. Letter of Rev. Joseph Spence to Rev. Mr. Wheeler, Sept. 19, 1751, quoted in Ann Leighton, *American Gardens in the Eighteenth Century: "For Use or for Delight"* (Boston: Houghton Mifflin, 1976), 333–36.

13. Raymond Williams, *Problems in Materialism and Culture* (London: Verso/New Left Review Editions, 1980), 80–81.

14. Ibid., 81.

15. William Bradford, *History of Plymouth Plantation,* 1606–1646, ed. William T. Davis (New York: Barnes and Noble, 1908), quoted in Leo Marx, *The Machine in the Garden: Technology and the Pastoral Ideal in America* (London: Oxford University Press, 1964), 41.

16. Andrew Jackson Downing, *A Treatise on the Theory and Practice of Landscape Gardening, Adapted to North America. . . .* , 6th ed. (New York: A. O. Moore, 1859), 18.

17. R. Burton Litton, Jr., "Visual Assessment of Natural Landscapes," in Barry Sadler and Allen Carlson, eds., *Environmental Aesthetics: Essays in Interpretation*, Western Geographical Series, no. 20 (Victoria, B.C.: University of Victoria, 1982), 99.

18. Ibid., 103.

19. Gary Zukav, *The Dancing Wu Li Masters: An Overview of the New Physics* (New York: Morrow, 1979), 211.

20. David Ray Griffen, "Introduction: The Reenchantment of Science," in David Ray Griffen, ed., *The Reenchantment of Science* (Albany: State University of New York Press, 1988), 14.

21. Robert Irwin, *Being and Circumstance: Notes Toward a Conditional Art* (Larkspur Landing, Calif.: Lapis Press in conjunction with the Pace Gallery and the San Francisco Museum of Art, 1985), 12.

22. Barry Sadler and Allen Carlson, "Towards Models of Environmental Appreciation," in Sadler and Carlson, *Environmental Aesthetics*, 162–63.

23. James Wines, *De-Architecture* (New York: Rizzoli, 1987), 38.

24. Manfredo Tafuri, quoted in Wines, *De-Architecture*, 38.

25. Ibid., 26.

26. Robert Venturi, *Complexity and Contradiction in Architecture* (New York: Museum of Modern Art in association with the Graham Foundation for Advanced Studies in the Fine Arts, 1966), 104.

27. Martin Filler, review of *The Most Beautiful House in the World*, by Witold Rybczynski, *New York Review of Books* 37 (1 Feb. 1990): 26.

28. Kenneth Frampton, "Toward a Critical Regionalism: Six Points for an Architecture of

Resistance," in Hal Foster, ed., *The Anti-Aesthetic: Essays on Postmodern Culture* (Port Townsend, Wash.: Bay Press, 1983), 26, 28.

29. McLuhan, *Understanding Media*, 4–5.

CHAPTER EIGHT
1. David Harvey, *The Condition of Postmodernity* (Oxford: Blackwell, 1989), 93.
2. Harvey, *Condition*, cites various examples; see also David Ley and Kenneth Olds, "Landscape as Spectacle: World's Fairs and the Culture of Heroic Consumption," *Environment and Planning D: Society and Space* 6 (1988): 191–212.
3. Harvey, *Condition*, 328.
4. John Brinckerhoff Jackson, "Landscape as Theater," *Landscape* 23, no. 1 (1979): 3–7.
5. Manfredo Tafuri, *Venice and the Renaissance* (Cambridge, Mass., and London: MIT Press, 1989), and Denis Cosgrove, *The Palladian Landscape: Geographical Change and Its Cultural Representation in Sixteenth-Century Italy* (University Park: Pennsylvania State University Press, 1993).
6. Yi-Fu Tuan, "Thought and Landscape: The Eye and the Mind's Eye," in Donald W. Meinig, ed., *The Interpretation of Ordinary Landscapes* (Oxford: Oxford University Press, 1979), 89–102; and "Surface Phenomena and Aesthetic Experience," *Annals, Association of American Geographers* 79 (1989): 233–41.
7. James S. Duncan and Nancy Duncan, "(Re)Reading the Landscape," *Environment and Planning D: Society and Space* 6 (1988): 117–26; James S. Duncan, *The City as Text: the Politics of Landscape in the Kandyan Kingdom* (Cambridge: Cambridge University Press, 1990).
8. Brian Vickers, Introduction, in *Occult and Scientific Mentalities in the Renaissance* (Cambridge: Cambridge University Press, 1984), 1–56; Robert S. Westmann, "Nature, Art, and Psyche: Jung, Pauli and the Kepler-Fludd Polemic," ibid., 177–230.
9. Svetlana Alpers, *The Art of Describing: Dutch Art in the Seventeenth Century* (London: John Murray in association with the University of Chicago Press, 1983).
10. James Macarthur, *Foucault, Tafuri, Utopia: Essays in the History and Theory of Architecture* (Brisbane: Queensland University, Department of Design Studies, 1984).
11. Frances Yates, *The Art of Memory* (London: Routledge and Kegan Paul, 1966); Jonathan D. Spence, *The Memory Palace of Matteo Ricci* (London: Faber and Faber, 1984).
12. Walter S. Gibson, *"Mirror of the Earth": The World Landscape in Sixteenth-Century Flemish Painting* (Princeton: Princeton University Press, 1989).
13. G. Ferrari, "Public Anatomy Lessons and the Carnival: The Anatomy Theatre of Bologna," *Past and Present* 117 (1987): 50–106; Jonathan Sawday, *The Body Emblazoned: Dissection and the Body in Renaissance Culture* (London: Routledge, 1995), esp. 54–84.
14. Edward Muir, *Civic Ritual in Renaissance Venice* (Princeton: Princeton University Press, 1981); E. Muir and R. F. E. Weissman, "Social and Symbolic Places in Renaissance Venice and Florence," in John Agnew and James S. Duncan eds., *The Power of Place: Bringing Together the Geographical and Sociological Imaginations* (London: Unwin Hyman, 1989), 81–104; Åsa Boholm, *The Doge of Venice: The Symbolism of State Power in the Renaissance* (Göteborg: Institute for Advanced Studies in Social Anthropology, 1990).
15. Richard Mackenney, *Tradesmen and Traders: The World of the Guilds in Venice and Europe c. 1250–c. 1650* (London: Croom Helm, 1987).
16. Denis Cosgrove, "The Myth and the Stones of Venice: The Historical Geography of a Symbolic Landscape," *Journal of Historical Geography* 8 (1982): 145–69; Boholm, *Doge of Venice*; Boholm, *Venetian Worlds: Nobility and the Cultural Construction of Society* (Göteborg: Institute for Advanced Studies in Social Anthropology, 1993).
17. Mackenney, *Tradesmen and Traders*, 147.
18. Ibid.
19. Tafuri, *Venice and the Renaissance*, 161–96; Cosgrove, "The Myth and the Stones."
20. Harvey, *Condition*, 91.

21. Mackenney, *Tradesmen and Traders,* 145.

22. Patricia Fortini-Brown, *Venetian Narrative Painting in the Age of Carpaccio* (New Haven and London: Yale University Press, 1988), 79. My interpretation of Bellini's *Procession* is based on Fortini-Brown's work.

23. On Venetian historiography, see William S. Bouwsma, *Venice and the Defense of Republican Liberty: Renaissance Values in the Age of the Counter-Reformation* (Berkeley: University of California Press, 1968); on painting, see Fortini-Brown, *Venetian Narrative Painting,* and David Rosand, *Painting in Cinquecento Venice: Titian, Veronese, Tintoretto* (New Haven and London: Yale University Press, 1982).

24. Donald M. Nicol, *Byzantium and Venice: A Study in Diplomatic and Cultural Relations* (Cambridge: Cambridge University Press, 1988), 24–25.

25. Daniele Barbaro, *La Practica della Perspettiva di Monsignor Daniel Barbaro eletto Patriarcha d'Aquileia, opera molto profittevole ai pittori, scultori, et architetti* (Venice: Camillo and Rutilio Borgominieri, 1569). See also Giuseppe Barbieri, *Andrea Palladio e la cultura veneta del Rinascimento* (Rome: Il Veltro, 1983), 45–106.

26. Tafuri, *Venice and the Renaissance;* Cosgrove, *Palladian Landscape,* 163–87.

27. Harvey, *Condition,* 258–59.

28. Ibid., 87.

CHAPTER NINE

This text is adapted from a chapter in Dolores Hayden, *The Power of Place: Urban Landscapes as Public History* (Cambridge: MIT Press, 1995).

Epigraph: Henri Lefebvre, *The Production of Space,* trans. Donald Nicholson-Smith (Oxford: Blackwell, 1991).

1. John Brinckerhoff Jackson, *Discovering the Vernacular Landscape* (New Haven: Yale University Press, 1984), xii.

2. Yi-Fu Tuan sees both biology and culture forming the human connection to place, in *Space and Place: The Perspective of Experience* (Minneapolis: University of Minnesota Press, 1977), 6. He also notes that these terms may be elusive: "Architects talk about the spatial qualities of place; they can equally well talk about the locational (place) qualities of space." Tuan describes place as a pause in the flow of time: "If we see the world as a process, constantly changing, we should not be able to develop any sense of place."

3. Ibid., 30, 79–84.

4. Ibid., 79–84.

5. Irwin Altman and Setha M. Low, eds., *Place Attachment* (New York: Plenum, 1992). Also see Denise L. Lawrence and Setha M. Low, "The Built Environment and Spatial Form," *Annual Review of Anthropology* 19 (1990): 453–505, a review essay covering several hundred works.

6. Peter H. Marris, *Family and Social Change in an African City* (Evanston, Ill.: Northwestern University Press, 1962); Peter H. Marris, *Loss and Change,* 2d ed. (London and New York: Routledge and Kegan Paul, 1986). Also see Herbert J. Gans, *The Urban Villagers: Group and Class in the Life of Italian-Americans,* 2d ed.(New York: Free Press, 1962).

7. Sauer said: "Culture is the agent, the natural area is the medium, the cultural landscape is the result." See "Landscape" in Robert P. Larkin and Gary L. Peters, eds., *Dictionary of Concepts in Human Geography* (Westport, Conn.: Greenwood, 1983), 139–44.

Among the scholars who have helped shape cultural landscape studies are John Brinckerhoff Jackson and Donald Meinig. See Jackson's *Landscapes* (Amherst: University of Massachusetts Press, 1980), *Discovering the Vernacular Landscape* (New Haven: Yale University Press, 1984), and *A Sense of Place, a Sense of Time* (New Haven: Yale University Press, 1994); and Meinig's edited volume *The Interpretation of Ordinary Landscapes* (New York and Oxford: Oxford University Press, 1979), as well as *The Shaping of America* (New Haven: Yale University Press, 1986).

More recent edited volumes include Dell Upton and John Michael Vlach, eds., *Common Places: Readings in American Vernacular Architecture* (Athens: University of Georgia Press, 1986) and Michael Conzen, ed., *The Making of the American Landscape* (New York: Harper-Collins, 1990), both with extensive bibliographies. Conzen's is the more urban of the two and the broader. Also see Wayne Franklin and Michael Steiner, eds. *Mapping American Culture* (Iowa City: University of Iowa Press, 1992).

The landscape architect Anne Whiston Spirn, in a forthcoming book, *The Language of Landscape*, will provide a more thorough grounding in aesthetics and environmental science for landscape studies and design. See her articles "From Uluru to Cooper's Place: Patterns in the Cultural Landscape," *Orion* 9 (Spring 1990): 32–39, and "The Poetics of City and Nature: Towards a New Aesthetic for Urban Design," *Landscape Journal* 7 (Fall 1988): 108–27.

8. Two collections of essays on ethnic spatial patterns and vernacular architecture in the American rural landscape exist, but there is nothing comparable focusing on vernacular building in urban ethnic places: Allen G. Noble, ed., *To Build in a New Land: Ethnic Landscapes in North America* (Baltimore: Johns Hopkins University Press, 1992) and Dell Upton, ed., *America's Architectural Roots: Ethnic Groups That Built America* (Washington, D.C.: Preservation Press, 1986).

9. See Michael Dear and Jennifer Wolch, eds., *The Power of Geography* (Boston: Unwin Hyman, 1990); Kay Anderson and Fay Gale, eds., *Inventing Places* (New York: John Wiley, 1992); John A. Agnew and James S. Duncan, eds., *The Power of Place: Bringing Together Geographical and Sociological Imaginations* (Boston: Unwin Hyman, 1989); James Duncan and David Ley, eds., *Place/Culture/Representation* (London and New York: Routledge, 1993); Derek Gregory, *Geographical Imaginations* (Oxford: Blackwell, 1994); Neil Smith, *Uneven Development: Nature, Capital, and the Reproduction of Space* (Oxford: Blackwell, 1990).

10. William Cronon, "A Place for Stories: Nature, History, and Narrative," *Journal of American History* 78 (March 1992): 1347–76.

11. Michael Sorkin, ed., *Variations on a Theme Park: The New American City and the End of Public Space* (New York: Noonday, 1992) is uneven but contains a wonderful essay on shopping malls by the historian Margaret Crawford. The journalists Joel Garreau (*Edge City: Life on the New Frontier* [New York: Doubleday, 1991]) and James Howard Kunstler *(The Geography of Nowhere: The Rise and Decline of America's Man-Made Landscape* [New York: Simon and Schuster, 1993]) agree with Sorkin that Americans face the end of meaningful places and public space.

12. Lefebvre, *Production of Space*.

13. Fredric Jameson, *Postmodernism, or, The Cultural Logic of Late Capitalism,* (Durham: Duke University Press, 1991), 364–65.

14. For a more complex look at these issues, see Gregory, *Geographical Imaginations,* and David Harvey, *The Condition of Postmodernity* (Oxford: Blackwell, 1989), esp. table 3.1.

15. To list just a few examples of works that deal with political contestation: on housing, Margaret Crawford, *Building the Workingman's Paradise: The Architecture of American Company Towns* (London: Verso, 1995); on city plans, Gwendolyn Wright, *The Politics of Design in French Colonial Urbanism* (Chicago: University of Chicago Press, 1991); on parks, Galen Cranz, *The Politics of Park Design* (Cambridge: MIT Press, 1982), and Roy Rosenzweig and Elizabeth Blackmar, *The People and the Park* (Ithaca: Cornell University Press, 1992).

16. Patricia Nelson Limerick, "Disorientation and Reorientation: The American Landscape Discovered from the West," *Journal of American History* 79 (December 1992): 1021–49.

17. Ibid., 1031–34.

18. Denis Wood's atlas of the Boylan Heights neighborhood of Raleigh, N.C., is a wonderful example of the evocation of an entire urban neighborhood, achieved through drawings that record the contours of its landscape and the patterns of its roads, alleys, bridges, sewers and water mains, manhole covers, street trees, street signs, and stop signs. Denis Wood, *Dancing and Singing: A Narrative Atlas of Boylan Heights,* proof copy from the author, 1990, School of De-

sign, North Carolina State University, Box 7701, Raleigh, N.C. 27695–7701. A basic text that explores some of these materials for teachers undertaking school projects is Gerald Danzer, *Public Places: Exploring Their History* (Nashville, Tenn.: Association for State and Local History, 1987.)

19. John R. Stilgoe, *Metropolitan Corridor: Railroads and the American Scene* (New Haven: Yale University Press, 1983).

20. Two historical studies that deal with women and space are Dolores Hayden, *The Grand Domestic Revolution: A History of Feminist Designs for American Homes, Neighborhoods, and Cities* (Cambridge: MIT Press, 1981) and Mary Ryan, *Women in Public: Between Banners and Ballots, 1825–1880* (Baltimore: Johns Hopkins University Press, 1990). Recent geographical works on women and space include Gillian Rose, *Feminism and Geography: The Limits of Geographical Knowledge* (Minneapolis: University of Minnesota Press, 1993); and Doreen Massey, *Space, Place, and Gender* (Minneapolis: University of Minnesota Press, 1994). For a discussion of "women's sphere" unsympathetic to geographic analyses, see Linda Kerber, "Separate Spheres, Female Worlds, Woman's Place: The Rhetoric of Women's History," *Journal of American History* 75 (June 1985): 9–39.

21. Dear and Wolch, *Power of Geography*, 4.

22. There are many essays that address one or more aspects of these places, for example, Rina Swentzell's essay in this volume; Dell Upton, "Black and White Landscapes in Colonial Virginia," in Robert Blair St. George, ed., *Material Life in America, 1600–1860*, (Boston: Northeastern University Press, 1988), 357–69; Manuel Castells, "Cultural Identity, Sexual Liberation and Urban Structure: The Gay Community in San Francisco," in *The City and the Grassroots* (Berkeley: University of California Press, 1983), 138–72; and George Chauncey, *Gay New York: Gender, Urban Culture, and the Makings of the Gay Male World, 1890–1940* (New York: Basic Books, 1994).

23. For example, Allen Scott and Michael Storper, eds., *Production, Work, and Territory: The Geographical Anatomy of Industrial Capitalism* (London: Allen and Unwin, 1986); Dear and Wolch, *Power of Geography*.

24. Interview with Loren Miller, Jr., in Charles Perry, "When We Were Very Young," *Los Angeles Times Magazine* (4 February 1990): 13–14.

25. Lynell George, *No Crystal Stair: African Americans in the City of Angels* (London: Verso, 1992), 222–23.

26. Such photographs are often surprisingly difficult to locate since only certain archives are willing to preserve them. Lonnie G. Bunch's *Black Angelenos* includes a good selection (Los Angeles: California Afro-American Museum, 1989).

27. For a sociological look at these spatial issues in world perspective, see Daphne Spain, *Gendered Spaces* (Chapel Hill: University of North Carolina Press, 1992).

28. Miller, in Perry, "When We Were Very Young," 13, includes a photograph of an African-American women's social club his mother belonged to in Los Angeles in the 1950s.

29. Kevin Lynch, *The Image of the City* (Cambridge: MIT Press, 1960).

30. Peter Orleans discusses this study by Tridib Bannerjee and others in "Urban Experimentation and Urban Sociology," in *Science, Engineering, and the City*, publication 1498 (Washington: National Academy of Sciences, 1967), 103–17; also see Peter Gould and Rodney White, *Mental Maps* (Boston: Allen and Unwin, 1986).

31. Jameson, *Postmodernism*, 54. But how this could operate in terms of global capitalism is more difficult to say. Also see Doug Aberle, ed., *Boundaries of Home: Mapping for Local Empowerment* (Gabriola Island, B.C., and Philadelphia: New Society, 1993).

32. Thomas Hubka, "In the Vernacular: Classifying American Folk and Popular Architecture," *The Forum* (Society of Architectural Historians) 7 (December 1985): 1.

33. Barbara Wyatt, "The Challenge of Addressing Vernacular Architecture in a State Historic Preservation Survey Program," in Camille Wells, ed., *Perspectives in Vernacular Architecture II* (Columbia: University of Missouri Press, 1986), 37–43.

34. Camille Wells, "Old Claims and New Demands," in Wells, *Perspectives,* 9–10. Even the medium through which this analysis is presented can reflect these power struggles. Wells refers to the potential conflict between vernacular scholarship and interpretation for a museum audience. The study of ordinary buildings and neighborhoods offers a bridge between academics (in the fields of history and history of architecture) and practitioners (in public history and historic preservation planning), but those in the latter group, such as museum curators and preservationists, may be under pressure to serve certain audiences and funders, and may be asked to avoid conflict and exploitation as themes of research. This is also frequently a problem for architectural journalists.

35. Sam Bass Warner, Jr. pioneered the use of evidence based on buildings, in his *Streetcar Suburbs: The Process of Growth in Boston, 1870–1900* (Cambridge: Harvard University Press, 1962). Warner's *The Urban Wilderness, the Private City: Philadelphia in Three Stages of Its Growth,* and *To Dwell Is to Garden* are classics of urban history that use the built environment well. Other examples include James Borchert, *Alley Life in Washington: Family, Community, Religion and Folklife in the City, 1850–1870* (Champaign: University of Illinois Press, 1980) and Elizabeth Blackmar, *Manhattan for Rent, 1785–1850* (Ithaca: Cornell University Press, 1989).

36. Dolores Hayden, *Seven American Utopias: The Architecture of Communitarian Socialism, 1790–1975* (Cambridge: MIT Press, 1976); Crawford, *Building the Workingman's Paradise;* Wright, *Politics of Design.*

37. One recent example of a study of community space is Gerald L. Pocius, *A Place to Belong: Community Order and Everyday Space in Calvert, Newfoundland* (Athens: University of Georgia Press, 1991). *Perspectives in Vernacular Architecture I, II, III, IV* (Columbia: University of Missouri Press, 1982–1989) gives a selection of work by members of the Vernacular Architecture Forum. On the importance of process to vernacular building studies, see Dell Upton, "Vernacular Buildings," in Diane Maddex, ed., *Built in the USA: American Buildings from Airports to Zoos* (Washington: Preservation Press, 1985), 167–68. Upton has also made a plea for architectural historians to turn away from studying single buildings by master designers (thus serving as the architectural profession's press agents) in favor of looking at landscape history: "Architectural History or Landscape History?" *Journal of Architectural Education* 44 (August 1991): 195–99.

38. Daniel Bluestone, *Constructing Chicago* (New Haven: Yale University Press, 1991); Abigail Van Slyck, *Free to All: Carnegie Libraries and American Culture* (Chicago: University of Chicago Press, 1995). Paul Groth's choice of the single-room-occupancy hotel as a vernacular building type of great importance in analyzing both urban renewal and homelessness (see "'Marketplace' Vernacular Design: The Case of Downtown Rooming Houses," in Wells, ed., *Perspectives,* 179–91) is an example of the new kinds of work possible using these older methods. Also see Paul Groth, *Living Downtown: The History of Residential Hotel Life in the United States* (Berkeley: University of California Press, 1994). For an extended bibliography on vernacular architecture, with a section on housing for persons of moderate incomes, see John Michael Vlach and Richard Longstreth, "Teaching Vernacular Architecture at George Washington University," *ASA News* (newsletter of the American Studies Association) (Fall 1993): 11–14. Also see Gwendolyn Wright, *Building the Dream: A Social History of Housing* (New York: Pantheon, 1981) for an overview of thirteen housing types.

39. Jules David Prown, "Mind in Matter: An Introduction to Material Culture Theory and Method," in Robert Blair St. George, ed., *Material Life in America, 1600–1860* (Boston: Northeastern University Press, 1988), 17–34. Also see essays by Thomas J. Schlereth, *Cultural History and Material Culture: Everyday Life, Landscapes, Museums* (Ann Arbor: UMI Research Press, 1990) and by Dell Upton, "The City as Material Culture," in Anne Yentsch and Mary Beaudry, *The Art and Mystery of Historical Archaeology* (Boca Raton: CRC Press, 1992), 51–74; and "Another City: The Urban Cultural Landscape in the Early Republic," in Catherine Hutchins, ed., *Everyday Life in the Early Republic, 1789–1828* (Wilmington: Winterthur Museum, 1995).

40. Anthony Jackson, *A Place Called Home: A History of Low-Cost Housing in Manhattan* (Cambridge: MIT Press, 1976), 1–29, outlines the issue but does not run the numbers.

41. Other housing types might also lead to larger social analyses. For example, on the suburban house, see Dolores Hayden, *Redesigning the American Dream: The Future of Housing, Work, and Family Life* (New York: Norton, 1984); and Gwendolyn Wright, *Moralism and Model Home: Domestic Architecture and Cultural Conflict in Chicago, 1873–1913* (Chicago: University of Chicago Press, 1980).

42. The old storefronts in the Lower East Side Tenement Museum and some of the dwelling units are open to the public (the entire building has been included in the National Register of Historic Places for its social importance). Similarly, the National Trust for Scotland has a tenement apartment in Glasgow, formerly home to a milliner and dressmaker, open to the public. It is one of their most popular attractions.

43. Christine Stansell, *City of Women: Sex and Class in New York City, 1789–1860* (New York: Knopf, 1986) explores these issues.

44. Upton, *America's Architectural Roots*, 14.

45. For an excellent study of this kind in a rural context, see Richard Westmacott, "Pattern and Practice in Traditional African-American Gardens in Rural Georgia," *Landscape Journal* 10 (Fall 1991): 87–104, and his *African American Gardens and Yards in the Rural South* (Knoxville: University of Tennessee Press, 1992). A new documentation of the gardens of the homeless in New York is Diana Balmori and Margaret Morton, *Transitory Gardens, Uprooted Lives* (New Haven: Yale University Press, 1993). Because many of the homeless they document are African-American, there may be some patterns that recall Westmacott's rural gardens. Morton also has an independent project on homeless dwellings, "The Architecture of Despair," forthcoming. Also see Joseph Sciorra, "Yard Shrines and Sidewalk Altars of New York's Italian Americans," *Perspectives in American Architecture* 3, ed. Thomas Carter and Bernard L. Herman (Columbia: University of Missouri Press, 1989), 185–98.

46. James T. Rojas, "The Enacted Environment of East Los Angeles," *Places* 8:3 (Spring 1993): 42–53.

47. See Gail Lee Dubrow, "Property Types Associated with Asian/Pacific American Settlement in Washington State," in Gail Lee Dubrow, Gail Nomura, et al., *The Historic Context for the Protection of Asian/Pacific American Resources in Washington State* (Olympia, Wash.: Department of Community Development, forthcoming); Gail Lee Dubrow, "Asian Pacific Imprints on the Western Landscape," in Arnold R. Alanen and Robert Z. Melnick, eds., *Preserving Cultural Landscapes in America* (Baltimore: Johns Hopkins University Press, forthcoming); David Chuenyan Lai, *Chinatowns: Towns Within Cities in Canada* (Vancouver: University of British Columbia Press, 1988); "Plaza, Parque, Calle," a special issue of the journal *Places* about Latino spaces (*Places* 8:3 [Spring 1993]); Kay J. Anderson, *Vancouver's Chinatown: Racial Discourse in Canada, 1875–1980* (Montréal and London: McGill-Queen's University Press, 1991); and Borchert, *Alley Life*.

48. Joseph Sciorra, "'I Feel Like I'm in My Country': Puerto Rican Casitas in New York City," photographs by Martha Cooper, *Drama Review* 34 (Winter 1990): 156–68. Also see Geneviève Fabre, forthcoming work on ethnic celebrations in the United States.

49. Dorothy Noyes, *Uses of Tradition: Arts of Italian Americans in Philadelphia* (Philadelphia: Samuel S. Fleisher Art Memorial, 1989).

50. Joseph Sciorra, "Religious Processions in Italian Williamsburg," *Drama Review* 29 (Fall 1985): 65–81.

51. Susan Davis, *Parades and Power: Street Theater in Nineteenth-Century Philadelphia* (Berkeley: University of California Press, 1986); David Glassberg, *American Historical Pageantry: The Uses of Tradition in the Early Twentieth Century* (Chapel Hill: University of North Carolina Press, 1990).

52. Temma Kaplan, "Making Spectacles of Themselves," an essay drawn from her work in progress on women's use of public space as a part of political protest, develops this point.

53. William Serrin, "Shifts in Work Put White Men in the Minority," *New York Times*, 31 July 1984: 1. In 1954, white men comprised 62.5 percent of the paid labor force.

54. Dolores Hayden, *Redesigning the American Dream;* Sam Bass Warner, Jr., "When Suburbs Are the City" (paper delivered at the symposium "The Car and the City," University of California, Los Angeles, 1988); Kenneth T. Jackson, *Crabgrass Frontier: The Suburbanization of the United States* (Oxford and New York: Oxford University Press, 1985).

55. For example, Ricardo Romo, *East Los Angeles: The History of a Barrio* (Austin: University of Texas Press, 1983). Or, for a historical geographer's perspective, see Kay J. Anderson, "The Idea of Chinatown: The Power of Place and Institutional Practice in the Making of a Racial Category," *Annals of the Association of American Geographers* 77 (December 1987): 580–98. Forthcoming work by Robin D. G. Kelley will look at African-American cities across the country.

"Ethnic" is perhaps the hardest of all words to use consistently. Although "ethnic" in its linguistic roots suggests "the people," it is often used in the United States to suggest an outsider, specifically an outsider to the English, white Protestant immigrants of seventeenth- and eighteenth-century New England and the eastern seaboard. (Rarely has anyone of that tradition been described as ethnic, and as a result some community groups think the word *ethnic* is a coded way to imply nonwhite or working-class people.) However, "ethnic" will be used here to indicate a shared cultural tradition, whether that of an indigenous Native American tribe or of an immigrant group—English, African, Irish, Mexican, German, Japanese, Chinese, or Polish, to name a few possibilities.

"Ethnic minority" is a term always defined by time and place that often outlives its accuracy. Sometimes "ethnic minorities" has been used to describe all of the nonwhite groups in a population; in this case, the terms "multicultural" or "multiethnic" will be used instead to refer to a diverse population. See Stephan Thernstrom, Ann Orlov, and Oscar Handlin, eds., *Harvard Encyclopedia of American Ethnic Groups* (Cambridge: Harvard University Press, 1980) and Werner Sollars, *Beyond Ethnicity: Consent and Descent in American Culture* (New York: Oxford University Press, 1986). For a debate on these terms and their uses, see Wilbur Zelinsky, "Seeing Beyond the Dominant Culture," *Places* 7:1 (Fall 1990): 32–34, and rebuttals by Rina Swentzell, David Chuenyan Lai, and Dolores Hayden, 35–37.

56. Toni Morrison, *Playing in the Dark: Whiteness and the American Literary Imagination* (New York: Vintage, 1990), 6.

57. A new, synthetic text is American Social History Project, *Who Built America?* 2 vols. (New York: Pantheon, 1992).

58. Gloria T. Hull, Patricia Bell Scott, and Barbara Smith, *All the Women Are White, All the Blacks Are Men, but Some of Us Are Brave: Black Women's Studies* (Old Westbury, N.Y.: Feminist Press, 1981).

59. For example, Elizabeth Higginbotham, "Laid Bare by the System: Work and Survival for Black and Hispanic Women," in Amy Swerdlow and Hanna Lessinger, eds., *Class, Race and Sex: The Dynamics of Control* (Boston: G. K. Hall, 1983); also see Higginbotham's excellent *Selected Bibliography of Social Science Readings on Women of Color in the United States* (Memphis: Center for Research on Women, Memphis State University, 1989).

60. William Cronon, *Nature's Metropolis: Chicago and the Great West* (New York: Norton, 1991).

61. Lefebvre, *Production of Space*, 286.

62. David Brodsly, *LA Freeway: An Appreciative Essay* (Berkeley: University of California Press, 1981) and Mark Rose, *Interstate: Express Highway Politics, 1939–1989*, rev. ed. (Knoxville: University of Tennessee Press, 1990). Also see Martin Wachs and Margaret Crawford, eds., *The Car and the City: The Automobile, the Built Environment, and Daily Urban Life* (Ann Arbor: University of Michigan Press, 1992) and Virginia Scharff, *Taking the Wheel: Women and the Coming of the Motor Age* (New York: Free Press, 1991).

63. Manuel Castells, *The City and the Grassroots*, 314.

64. David Harvey, "From Space to Place and Back Again: Reflections on the Condition of Postmodernity," paper delivered at University of California, Los Angeles, Graduate School of Architecture and Urban Planning Colloquium, May 13, 1991, 39.

65. Ibid.

CHAPTER TEN

1. *The Compact Edition of the Oxford English Dictionary* (Oxford: 1980).

2. Ibid.

3. Johannes Fabian, *Time and the Other: How Anthropology Makes Its Object* (New York: Columbia University Press, 1983), 106.

4. Or, as I have reservations about using this totalizing expression as an analytic category, at least some aspects of it.

5. James Clifford, "Introduction: Partial Truths," in James Clifford and George E. Marcus, *Writing Culture: The Poetics and Politics of Ethnography* (Berkeley: University of California Press, 1986), 11.

6. Fabian, *Time and the Other,* 105–23.

7. Ira Jacknis, "Franz Boas and Photography," *Studies in Visual Communication* 10 (Winter 1984).

8. Timothy Mitchell, *Colonizing Egypt* (Cambridge: Middle East Library, Cambridge University Press, 1988). The coincidence of the beginnings of cinema with "heights of the imperial project" is discussed in Ella Shohat and Robert Stam, "Media Spectatorship in the Age of Globalization," in Rob Wilson and Wimal Dissanayake, eds., *Global/Local Cultural Production and the Transnational Imaginary* (Durham: Duke University Press, 1996), 145–72.

9. Henri Lefebvre and Donald Nicholson-Smith, trans., *The Production of Space* (Oxford: Blackwell, 1991), 198.

10. Arjun Appadurai, ed., *The Social Life of Things: Commodities in Cultural Perspective* (Cambridge: Cambridge University Press, 1988); M. Csikszentmihalyi and E. Roshberg-Halton, *The Meaning of Things: Domestic Symbols and the Self* (Cambridge: Cambridge University Press, 1981).

11. John Agnew, John Mercer, and David Sopher, eds., *The City in Cultural Context* (Boston: Allen and Unwin, 1984). The essay by Janet Abu-Lughod, "Culture, 'Modes of Production,' and the Changing Nature of Cities in the Arab World" (pp. 44–117) is an exception to my comments.

12. Susan Fainstein, Norman Fainstein, Richard C. Hill, Dennis Judd, and Michael Peter Smith, *Restructuring the City: The Political Economy of Urban Redevelopment* (New York: Longman, 1983); Manuel Castells, *The Urban Question* (London: Edward Arnold, 1977); David Harvey, *Social Justice and the City* (London: Edward Arnold, 1973).

13. This topic is addressed by Abu-Lughod in "Culture, 'Modes of Production,' and the Changing Nature of Cities in the Arab World."

14. Peter Jackson, *Maps of Meaning: An Introduction to Cultural Geography* (London: Unwin Hyman, 1989), 23 and passim. In this context see also Nicholas B. Dirks, Geoff Eley, and Sherry Ortner, eds. *Culture/Power/History: A Reader in Contemporary Social Theory* (Princeton: Princeton University Press, 1993).

15. Jackson cites Carl Sauer and Wilbur Zelinsky as representative of this approach.

16. Michel Foucault, *Power-Knowledge: Selected Interviews and Other Writings* (New York: Pantheon, 1980).

17. Talal Asad, ed., *Anthropology and the Colonial Encounter* (London: Ithaca Press, 1973).

18. Edward B. Tylor, in a book significantly entitled *Primitive Culture*, described culture as "that complex whole which includes knowledge, belief, art, morals, law, custom, and any other capabilities acquired by man as a member of society" (quoted in Charlotte Seymour-Smith, *Macmillan Dictionary of Anthropology* [New York: Macmillan, 1986], 65). According

to Raymond Williams, *Keywords: A Vocabulary of Culture and Society* (London: Fontana, 1984), 20.

19. George Marcus and Michael Fischer, *Anthropology as Cultural Critique* (Chicago: University of Chicago Press, 1986).

20. Roland Robertson, "The Sociological Significance of Culture: Some General Considerations," in *Theory, Culture and Society* 5 (1988): 3–24.

21. Stuart Hall, "Cultural Studies: Two Paradigms," in Tony Bennet et al., Graham Martin, Colin Mercer, and Janet Wollacott, eds., *Culture, Ideology and Social Process* (London: Batsford, 1987), 19–38.

22. Jackson, *Maps of Meaning,* 16–17.

23. See *Public Culture: Bulletin for the Center of Transnational Cultural Studies* (Philadelphia: University Museum, University of Pennsylvania, 1988–1993; Chicago: University of Chicago Press, 1993–).

24. Nicholas Abercrombie, Stephen Hill, and Bryan S. Turner, eds., *The Penguin Dictionary of Sociology* (London: Penguin, 1988), under "ethnic group," 90.

25. Seymour-Smith, *Macmillan Dictionary of Anthropology,* 95 (under "ethnic group"); *Compact Oxford English Dictionary,* under "ethnic."

26. Seymour-Smith, *Macmillan Dictionary of Anthropology,* 95.

27. Immanuel Wallerstein, "The Construction of Peoplehood: Racism, Nationalism and Ethnicity," *Sociological Forum* 2:2 (1987): 373–86, 385.

28. Dell Upton, ed., *America's Architectural Roots: Ethnic Groups That Built America* (Washington, D.C.: Preservation Press, 1986).

29. Stuart Hall, "The Local and the Global; Globalization and Ethnicity," in Anthony D. King, ed., *Culture, Globalization, and the World-System: Contemporary Conditions for the Representation of Identity* (Minneapolis: University of Minnesota Press, 1997).

30. See Anthony D. King, "Identity and Difference: The Internationalization of Capital and the Globalization of Culture," in Paul Knox, ed., *The Restless Urban Landscape* (Englewood Cliffs, N.J.: Prentice Hall, 1992), in which I refer to five such approaches: world-systems, globalization, postmodernism, postcolonialism, and postimperialism. See also Preface to the revised edition of King, *Culture, Globalization, and the World-System* and Peter J. Taylor, "On the Nation-State, the Global, and Social Science," *Environment and Planning A* 28 (1996), with commentaries by fourteen scholars currently writing on issues of globalization.

31. Anthony D. King, *Global Cities: Post-Imperialism and the Internationalization of London* (London and New York: Routledge, Chapman, and Hall, 1990); Saskia Sassen, *The Global City: New York, London, Tokyo* (Princeton: Princeton University Press, 1991).

32. Anthony D. King, "Worlds in the City: Manhattan Transfer and the Rise of Spectacular Space," *Planning Perspectives* 11 (1996): 97–114.

33. I owe this insight to Immanuel Wallerstein.

CHAPTER ELEVEN

1. An excellent discussion of how this has happened and how vernacular activity has transformed many streets is Mike Helm and George Tukel, "Restoring Cities from the Bottom Up: A Bi-Coastal View from the Street," *The Whole Earth* (Spring 1990).

CHAPTER THIRTEEN

My thanks to Paul Groth for inviting me to participate in the *Vision, Culture, and Landscape* conference, to T. J. Clark for correcting my most egregious errors in art history, and to Todd W. Bressi for close editing.

1. The great exception to this blinkered attitude was Clarence Glacken, a marvelous and gentle man who warmly accepted this newcomer into the fold and who guided me to many valuable texts in cultural studies.

2. See, for example, Allan Pred and Michael Watts, *Reworking Modernity: Capitalisms*

and Symbolic Discontent (New Brunswick: Rutgers University Press, 1992); Roderick Neumann, "The Social Origins of Natural Resource Conflict in Arusha National Park, Tanzania" (Ph.D. diss., University of California, Berkeley, Department of Geography, 1992); George Henderson, "Regions and Realism: Social Spaces, Regional Transformation, and the Novel in California, 1882–1924" (Ph.D. diss., University of California, Berkeley, Department of Geography, 1992).

3. See, for example, Denis Cosgrove, "Towards a Radical Cultural Geography" *Antipode* 15 (1983):1–11; Denis Cosgrove and Stephen Daniels, eds., *The Iconography of Landscape* (Cambridge: Cambridge University Press, 1987); Denis Cosgrove and Peter Jackson, "New Directions in Cultural Geography," *Area* 19:2 (1987): 95–101; Peter Jackson, *Maps of Meaning: An Introduction to Cultural Geography* (London: Unwin Hyman, 1989); Deryck W. Holdsworth, "Evolving Urban Landscapes," in Larry Bourne and David Ley, eds., *The Changing Social Geography of Canadian Cities* (Montréal: McGill-Queen's University Press, 1993), 33–51.

4. For example, David Harvey, *Consciousness and the Urban Experience* (Baltimore: Johns Hopkins University Press, 1985); Edward Soja, *Post-Modern Geographies* (London: Verso, 1989); Mike Davis, *City of Quartz: Excavating the Future in Los Angeles* (London: Verso, 1990); Elizabeth Wilson, *The Sphinx and the City* (Berkeley: University of California Press, 1991); Michael Sorkin, ed., *Variations on a Theme Park: The New American City and the End of Public Space* (New York: Hill and Wang/Noonday Press, 1992).

5. Denis Cosgrove, *Social Formation and Symbolic Landscape* (London: Croom Helm, 1984); David Harvey, *The Condition of Postmodernity* (Oxford: Blackwell, 1989)

6. John Brinckerhoff Jackson "Landscape as Theater," *Landscape* 23:1 (1979); Jean-Christophe Agnew, *Worlds Apart: The Market and the Theatre in Anglo-American Thought, 1550–1750* (New York: Cambridge University Press, 1986).

7. Edward Soja, "Inside Exopolis: Scenes from Orange County," in Sorkin, *Variations on a Theme Park,* 94–122.

8. Guy Debord, *Society of the Spectacle* (Detroit: Black and Red Books, 1983)

9. For example, John Brinckerhoff Jackson, *American Space, The Centennial Years: 1865–76* (New York: Norton, 1972); John Brinckerhoff Jackson, *Discovering the Vernacular Landscape* (New Haven: Yale University Press, 1984); Thomas R. Vale and Geraldine R. Vale, *U.S. 40 Today: Thirty Years of Landscape Change in America* (Madison: University of Wisconsin Press, 1983). A personal favorite is Phil Patton, *Open Road: A Celebration of the American Highway* (New York: Simon and Schuster, 1986).

10. Peter Jackson, *Maps of Meaning;* Paul Groth, *Living Downtown: The History of Residential Hotels in the United States* (Berkeley: University of California Press, 1994).

11. Raymond Williams, *The Country and the City* (London: Chatto and Windus, 1973). Also, Peter Schmitt, *Back to Nature: The Arcadian Myth in Urban America* (New York: Oxford University Press, 1969).

12. For an attempt at a balanced assessment, see Edward Relph, *The Modern Urban Landscape* (London: Croom Helm, 1987).

13. Harvey, *Postmodernity,* 42.

14. Robert Fishman, *Bourgeois Utopias: The Rise and Fall of Suburbia* (New York: Basic Books, 1987), 3.

15. Michael Heiman, "Production Confronts Consumption: Landscape Perception and Social Conflict in the Hudson Valley," *Society and Space* 7:2 (1989): 165–78. Cf. Raymond Williams, *Culture and Society, 1780–1950* (London: Penguin, 1963); Hugh Prince, "Art and Agrarian Change, 1710–1815," in Cosgrove and Daniels, *Iconography,* 98–118. Davis, in *City of Quartz,* successfully weaves the two themes together.

16. I recall debating Peirce Lewis over the origins of the upright-and-wing house in upstate New York in the age of the Erie Canal, where I insisted on rooting Jeffersonian agrarianism in free-soil and small-town prosperity in the brimming 1830s.

17. Anthony D. King, *The Bungalow: The Production of a Global Culture* (London: Routledge and Kegan Paul, 1984); Anthony D. King, ed., *Buildings and Society: Essays on the Social Development of the Built Environment* (London: Routledge and Kegan Paul, 1980); Michael Doucet and John Weaver, *Housing the North American City* (Montréal: Queens-McGill University Press, 1991); Deryck W. Holdsworth, "House and Home in Vancouver: Images of West Coast Urbanism, 1886–1929," in G. Stelter and A. Artibise, eds., *The Canadian City* (Toronto: McClelland and Stewart, 1984), 187–209.

18. As treated by Richard Walker, "A Theory of Suburbanization: Capitalism and the Construction of Urban Space in the United States," in Michael Dear and Allen Scott, eds., *Urbanization and Urban Planning in Capitalist Societies* (New York: Methuen, 1981), 383–430; David Harvey, *The Urbanization of Capital* (Oxford: Blackwell, 1985); John Logan and Harvey Molotch, *Urban Fortunes: The Political Economy of Place* (Berkeley: University of California Press, 1986).

19. Deryck W. Holdsworth, "Landscape and Archives as Text," Chap. 3 in this volume.

20. For example, Allen Scott, *Metropolis* (Los Angeles: University of California Press, 1988); Michael Storper and Richard Walker, *The Capitalist Imperative: Territory, Technology and Industrial Growth* (Cambridge, Mass.: Blackwell, 1989).

21. Not to mention a lack of critique of embodiments of patriarchy in the built environment. Cf. Leslie Weisman, *Discrimination by Design: A Feminist Critique of the Man-Made Environment* (Chicago: University of Illinois Press, 1992); Deryck W. Holdsworth, "'I'm a Lumberjack and I'm O.K.: The Built Environment and Varied Masculinities," in Carter Hudgins and Betsy Cromley, eds., *Perspectives in Vernacular Architecture V* (Knoxville: University of Tennessee Press, 1994).

22. There are points at which Harvey, in *Condition of Postmodernity,* slips into a flattened perception of images and their production, but this is not the gist of his contribution. One wonders what Cosgrove makes of his fellow postmodernist cultural geographer James Duncan, who argues that one must read the landscape as text. James Duncan, *The City as Text: The Politics of Landscape Interpretation in the Kandya Kingdom* (New York: Cambridge University Press, 1990).

23. See Cosgrove, *Social Formation,* 27–33, on the "visual bias" in geography. His principal target is a static visualization of landscapes that eliminates social processes at work. For a wider perspective, see Martin Jay, *Downcast Eyes: The Denigration of Vision in Twentieth-Century French Thought* (Berkeley: University of California Press, 1993).

24. Cosgrove, *Social Formation;* see also Harvey, *Postmodernity.*

25. Cosgrove, *Social Formation,* 15.

26. Compare King's reference, in "The Politics of Vision" (Chap. 10 in this volume), to "the privileging of vision in Western culture" to his allusion to "the scriptocentric West."

27. Svetlana Alpers, *The Art of Describing: Dutch Art in the Seventeenth Century* (Chicago: University of Chicago Press, 1983).

28. Norman Bryson, *Vision and Painting: The Logic of the Gaze* (New Haven: Yale University Press, 1983). Catherine Howett, in "Where the One-Eyed Man Is King" (Chap. 7 in this volume), speaks of "increasing delight in the manipulation of perspectival vistas" during "the great age of Baroque architecture and urban design" without any sense of contradiction with her notion of a rigid perspectival order.

29. John Barrell, *The Idea of Landscape and the Sense of Place, 1730–1840: An Approach to the Poetry of John Clare* (Cambridge: Cambridge University Press, 1972), chap. 1.

30. T. J. Clark, *The Painting of Modern Life* (New York: Knopf, 1985); Robert Herbert, *Impressionism: Art, Leisure and Parisian Society* (New Haven: Yale University Press, 1988); Stephen Kern, *The Culture of Time and Space, 1880–1918* (Cambridge: Harvard University Press, 1983). There is considerable irony in the way Haussmann's linear boulevards and theatrical vistas bred a generation of painters who undermined such ways of seeing on canvas, and

how the ability to command space by modern means of transportation and communication influenced the dismantling of pictorial forms by the cubists.

31. Harvey, *Postmodernity*, esp. chap. 4. Cf. Davis, *City of Quartz*. This point is missed by Harvey's critics, such as Rosalind Deutsch, "Boy's Town," *Society and Space* 9:1 (1991): 5–30. What Harvey argues of postmodernist architecture is true with regard to all ideology: it is not a coherent and imposed discourse but fragmented and riven with contradiction. Ideology is "scarred and disarticulated by its relational character; by the conflicting interests among which it must ceaselessly negotiate"; it is not "the founding principle of social unity, but rather strives in the teeth of political resistance to reconstitute that unity at an imaginary level." Terry Eagleton, *Ideology: An Introduction* (London: Verso, 1991), 222.

32. This suggests more contiguity than opposition between Cosgrove, who hints at "an old debate whose connections with the Modern are complex and historically deep" ("Spectacle and Society: Landscape as Theater in Premodern and Postmodern Cities," Chap. 8 in this volume) and Harvey, who is at pains to argue that "there is much more continuity than difference between the broad history of modernism and the movement called postmodernism." Harvey sees that latter as a "particular kind of crisis within the former, one that emphasizes the fragmentary, the ephemeral and the chaotic." Harvey, *Postmodernity*, 116. Certainly, the critique of the landscapes of high modernism, Stalinism, and fascism did not wait for the declaration of postmodernism in the 1970s.

33. Cosgrove, *Social Formation*, 38, quote at 26. Cf. Williams, *Country and the City*, and Barrell, *Idea of Landscape*. Oddly enough, Cosgrove goes on to say that landscape no longer carries the "moral significance attached to it during the time of its most active cultural evolution" (*Social Formation*, 2). This is almost certainly false, as the contemporary iconography of national parks illustrates; see Neumann, *Social Origins*.

34. Eagleton, *Ideology*. There is a discordance between the introductory section of Cosgrove's "Spectacle and Society," which discusses image and text, and the subsequent discussion of portrayals of Venice, in which Cosgrove uses the term *ideology* quite freely. See my comments below on his postmodernist drift.

35. Barrell, *Idea of Landscape*. Cf. Clark, *Painting of Modern Life*, for another good example of art criticism, applied to urban landscapes of nineteenth-century Paris.

36. Cf. Peter Jackson, *Maps of Meaning*, for such a critical program for geographers.

37. Holdsworth, "Landscape and Archives as Text."

38. Cf. Holdsworth's comment that, in understanding the construction of the built environment, "the Marxist critique has sharpened the scholarly agenda," ibid.

39. His book, *Social Formation*, by contrast, is an eloquent brief for the explanatory power of the Marxian sequence of feudalism to capitalism. His commitment to political economy has diminished over the conservative decade of the 1980s.

40. Cf. Bryson, *Vision and Painting*.

41. Cosgrove, "Spectacle and Society"; also *Social Formation*, 87–98 and 111–12.

42. On the play of social position and prestige in the "panoramic pictures," see Patricia Brown, *Venetian Narrative Painting in the Age of Carpaccio* (New Haven: Yale University Press, 1988).

43. Cosgrove, *Social Formation*, 80–82.

44. Rather, there was a refeudalization of the countryside and greater hold of the countryside over the once supreme city, comparable in consequence to the Second Feudalism of Central and Eastern Europe around the same time. Cosgrove, *Social Formation*, 155–60. Robert Brenner, "The Agrarian Roots of European Capitalism," *Past and Present* 97 (1982): 16–113.

45. Cosgrove, *Social Formation*, 82–83.

46. On the dynamism of Europe before this time, see Michael Mann, *States, War and Capitalism: The Sources of Social Power* (New York: Cambridge University Press, 1986)

47. Cosgrove, *Social Formation*, 114–15. Yet within renaissance Venice, the architectural

handling of the different morphological areas of the city is striking: St. Mark's Square and the Doge's Palace were made over in Roman revival style around 1500, while the commercial heart of the city, the Rialto, was never rebuilt, despite plans by Palladio and Fra Giocondo after the Fire of 1514; the Arsenal, in fine absolutist military style, was encircled by a blind wall. Cosgrove, *Social Formation,* 114–17. See also Manfredo Tafuri, *Venice and the Renaissance* (Cambridge: MIT Press, 1989).

48. Tafuri, *Venice and the Renaissance,* 157–60.

49. On Descartes, see Stephen Toulmin, *Cosmopolis: The Hidden Agenda of Modernity* (New York: Free Press, 1990).

50. Fishman, *Bourgeois Utopias.*

51. As exemplified by some reactions to Harvey's *Condition of Postmodernity;* see Deutsch, "Boys Town" and David Harvey, "Postmodern Morality Plays" *Antipode* 24:4 (1992): 300–326.

52. Cosgrove and Jackson, "New Directions," 98; Cosgrove and Daniels, *Iconography,* 7.

53. Cosgrove and Daniels, *Iconography,* 5. Cf. Williams, *Culture and Society;* Wilson, *Sphinx in the City,* chap. 9.

54. John Berger, *Ways of Seeing* (New York: Viking, 1973); Raymond Williams, *Problems in Materialism and Culture* (London: New Left Books, 1980).

55. Cosgrove and Daniels, *Iconography,* 7–8.

56. King "Politics of Vision."

57. A position shared by conservative cultural geographers, traditional left laborites, and radical cultural nationalists. It shows up in the essays by Howett and King in this volume. Howett follows Kenneth Frampton, "Toward a Critical Regionalism: Six Points for an Architecture of Resistance" in H. Foster, ed., *The Anti-Aesthetic: Essays on Postmodern Culture* (Port Townsend, Wash.: Bay Press, 1983) into the dead-end of lionizing an "architecture of resistance" directed toward "overcoming the 'universalization' that destroys indigenous cultural traditions and regional diversity." (She later contradicts this in her closing quote from McLuhan that "the aspiration of our time [is] for wholeness, empathy and depth of awareness.") King is more adept at catching the interplay of common cultures of large-scale economic systems and more localized, dissimilar common cultures, and calls, most sensibly, for "the historical and empirical charting of universality and difference" (see "The Politics of Vision"). He notes that ethnicities— like subcultures—are very largely constituted in reaction to the hegemonic intrusions of capitalist and Euro-American modes of life. Yet his view of a collision between local and global is almost as bleak as Howett's.

58. For example, Susan Buck-Morss, *The Dialectics of Seeing* (Cambridge: MIT Press, 1989); Sorkin, *Variations;* Peter Jackson, "Social Geography and the Cultural Politics of Consumption," *Nordisk Samhallsgeografisk Tidskrift* 9 (1991): 3–16; Stewart Ewan, *Captains of Consciousness* (New York: McGraw-Hill, 1976); Roger Miller, "Selling Mrs. Consumer: Advertising and the Creation of Suburban Socio-spatial Relations," *Antipode* 23 (1991): 263–306.

59. Jackson, *Maps of Meaning;* Paul Willis, *Common Cultures* (Boulder, Colo., and San Francisco: Westview, 1990).

60. Cf. King's remark on the two faces of culture, in "The Politics of Vision."

61. Jackson, *Maps of Meaning,* 19.

62. Although, as Holdsworth observes, there is often too little evidence in the landscape of the lives of common people, whose humble edifices disappear all too quickly, while those of the rich and powerful continue to haunt the present.

63. Daniel Miller, *Material Culture and Mass Consumption* (Oxford: Blackwell, 1987).

64. The principal blame no doubt lies with the Cartesian philosophers, including Kant and the Enlightenment philosophers, and carrying right down to the twentieth-century logical positivists, who have made quite outrageous claims for a denatured rationality, of human minds operating like analytic machines. See Toulmin, *Cosmopolis.*

65. George Lakoff, *Women, Fire and Dangerous Things* (Chicago: University of Chicago Press, 1987).

CHAPTER FOURTEEN

1. If vision is indeed so privileged, then scholars are lamentably incompetent in making use of it. Vision's great power to frame and to define seems to be lost between eye and pen. Consequently, scholarly analysis of visual evidence remains curiously descriptive and inarticulate.

2. Anthony D. King, "The Politics of Vision," in *Vision, Culture and Landscape: Working Papers from the Berkeley Symposium on Cultural Landscape Interpretation* (Berkeley: University of California, Berkeley, Center for Environmental Design Research, 1990).

3. Kirk Eugene Savage, "Blood and Stone: The Memorialization of Two American Nations in Washington, D.C., and Richmond, Virginia" (Ph.D. diss., University of California, Berkeley, 1991); Catherine W. Bishir, "Landmarks of Power: Building a Southern Past, 1885–1915," *Southern Cultures* (1993): 5–45.

CHAPTER FIFTEEN

1. Pierre Nora, "L'ère de la commemoration," in Nora, ed., *Les lieux de mémoire, Les France,* vol. 3: *De l'archive à l'emblème* (Paris: Gallimard, 1992).

2. Joanna Morland, *New Milestones: Sculpture, Community and the Land* (London: Common Ground, 1988); Sue Clifford and Angela King, eds., *Local Distinctiveness: Place, Particularity and Identity* (London: Common Ground, 1993); Sue Clifford and Angela King, eds., *From Place to PLACE: Maps and Parish Maps* (London: Common Ground).

3. Rachel Carson, *Silent Spring* (Harmondsworth: Penguin, 1962); David Lowenthal, "Awareness of Human Impacts: Changing Attitudes and Emphases," in B. L. Turner II, et al., *The Earth as Transformed by Human Action* (New York: Cambridge University Press, 1990), 121–35.

4. Joshua Fishman, "Nationality-Nationalism and Nation-Nationalism," in Joshua Fishman, Charles A. Ferguson, and J. D. Gupta, eds., *Language Problems of Developing Nations* (New York: Wiley, 1968), 41.

5. Simon Riser, quoted in David Toop, "Going down to Eavis's Farm," *The Times* (London), 25 June 1993: 37.

6. Quoted in Sally Brompton, "Seeing Red across the Village Green," *The Times* (London), 29 Aug. 1990: 16.

7. British Rail advertisement for a first-class seat from London to Bristol; John Hopkinson, director, British Field Sports Society, quoted in John Young, "Green Policies May Harm Wildlife," *The Times* (London), 18 Aug. 1990: 7.

8. Howard Newby, "Revitalizing the Countryside: The Opportunities and Pitfalls of Counter-urban Trends," *Royal Society of Arts Journal* 138 (1990): 630–36.

9. Stanley Baldwin, "The Classics" (1926), in his *On England* (London: Philip Allan, 1926), 101.

10. Quoted in Hunter Davies, "After the Banknote, Where's the Book?" *Independent on Sunday* (London), 29 Sept. 1991: 23.

11. Timothy Hornsby, introductory speech, Royal Society of Arts, Future Countryside Programme, Seminar 1: "A Stake in the Country" (29 Sept. 1989).

12. Pierre-Jakez Hélias, *The Horse of Pride: Life in a Breton Village* (New Haven: Yale University Press, 1978), 335–36.

13. William Cronon, *Nature's Metropolis: Chicago and the Great West* (New York: Norton, 1991).

CHAPTER SIXTEEN

1. The Institute of British Geographers, for example, now has no less than seventeen study groups. It holds an annual conference at which these groups conduct their own concurrent

group meetings. Some members still move from one group to another, but many assume that the only part of the program that is for them is that which falls within their own study group.

The Association of American Geographers came rather later to the point of introducing specialty groups of this kind, but soon made up for lost time. In 1978 there was merely a recommendation to have such specialty groups, but by 1986 they numbered no less than 37. See Michael F. Goodchild and Donald G. Janelle, "Specialization in the Structure and Organization of Geography," *Annals of the Association of American Geographers* 78 (March 1988): 1.

I am not denigrating the existence of these study groups, which collectively have produced some excellent work. I am merely drawing attention to the fact that the image of academic geography, as an integrated entity, has inevitably suffered, and the confused public is once again asking whether it is not just a scrapbook of bits and pieces culled from other people's patches.

2. Jay Appleton, *Landscape in the Arts and Sciences* (Hull: University of Hull Press, 1980); also "The Role of the Arts in Landscape Research" in E. C. Penning-Rowsell and David Lowenthal, *Landscape Meanings and Values* (London: Allen and Unwin, 1986), 26–47.

3. Notably by Peter Howard in *Landscapes: The Artists' Vision* (London and New York: Routledge, 1991).

4. If we were to look at other sciences, we would find that their literature often includes a fair sprinkling of the idiographic among the nomothetic. If you were to take almost any psychological disorder, for example, you would find that the literature on the subject contains not only works dealing with the general principles involved but also published individual case studies, because it is recognized that the phenomenon itself is always an irregularity within the whole personality of the patient. If the psychologists were to abstract from, say, a hundred patients only such information as could be expressed in laws of universal application and to dismiss as irrelevant all the other circumstances that characterized the patient as an individual, they would have much less understanding of what they were purporting to study.

5. I myself have made a modest move in this direction. See Jay Appleton, *How I Made the World: Shaping a View of Landscape* (Hull: University of Hull Press, 1994).

6. Maurice W. Beresford, *The Lost Villages of England* (London: Butterworth, 1954), 79–80, 392–93.

7. Ronald Paulson, *Literary Landscapes: Turner and Constable* (New Haven: Yale University Press, 1982), chap. 17.

CHAPTER SEVENTEEN

1. For a rare example of specialized landscape inquiry placed within an explicit such framework, see Joachim Wohlwill, "The Concept of Nature: A Psychologist's View," in Irwin Altman and Joachim F. Wohlwill, eds., *Behavior and the Natural Environment* (New York: Plenum, 1983), 5–34.

2. On affect and cognition, see R. B. Zajonc, "On the Primacy of Affect" and Richard S. Lazarus, "On the Primacy of Cognition," *American Psychologist* 34:2 (117–29), which provide closing arguments in a lengthy debate on this subject. On vision as a source of landscape experience, see the works of Rachel and Stephen Kaplan, particularly *The Experience of Nature: A Psychological Perspective* (New York: Cambridge University Press, 1989) and Roger Ulrich, particularly, "Visual Landscapes and Psychological Well Being," *Landscape Research* 4:1 (17–34). On landscapes in childhood, see Roger Hart, *Children's Experience of Place* (New York: Irvington, 1979)

3. Among the earliest examples of the visual assessment tradition are R. Burton Litton, Jr., *Forest Landscape Description and Inventories* (Berkeley: Pacific Southwest Forest and Range Experiment Station, 1968), and Kenneth H. Craik, "The Comprehension of the Everyday Physical Environment," *Journal of the American Institute of Planning* 34:2: 29–37. On the humanistic tradition, Yi-Fu Tuan, *Topophilia* (Englewood Cliffs, N.J.: Prentice-Hall, 1974), and John Brinckerhoff Jackson, *Landscapes* (Amherst: University of Massachusetts Press, 1970) are

mature expressions of these authors' early work. The Jackson collection includes essays written over the previous fifteen years.

4. John Brinckerhoff Jackson, "The Word Itself," in *Discovering the Vernacular Landscape* (New Haven: Yale University Press, 1984), 1–8. Denis Cosgrove, "The Idea of Landscape," in *Social Formation and Symbolic Landscape* (London: Croom Helm, 1984), 13–38.

5. The broadest, although not necessarily the most scholarly, sampling of this vast literature remains the magazine *Landscape*.

6. David Lowenthal, "The American Scene," *Geographical Review* 58: 61–88, quotes William James on the insider-outsider landscape and applies the distinction to American attitudes. Edward Relph, *Place and Placelessness* (London: Pion, 1976) subsumes that distinction in a lengthy discussion of conceptual landscapes, in which he proposes an "authentic-unauthentic" dichotomy.

7. Some of the best nonacademic writing on this subject focuses on regional landscapes of the American West. See Joan Didion, *Slouching toward Bethlehem* (New York: Farrar, Straus, and Giroux, 1968) and *The White Album* (New York: Simon and Schuster, 1979), Louise Erdrich, *The Beet Queen* (New York: Holt, 1986), William Least Heat-Moon, *PrairyErth (A Deep Map)* (Boston: Houghton Mifflin, 1991), and almost anything by Wallace Stegner.

8. Marcel Proust, *Remembrance of Things Past,* trans. K. C. Scott Moncrief, (New York: Random House, 1934); James Agee, *A Death in the Family* (New York: McDowell, Obolensky, 1957).

9. Wallace Stegner, *Wolf Willow* (New York: Viking, 1962), 18.

10. Marshall McLuhan, *The Medium Is the Massage* (New York: Bantam, 1969).

PAUL GROTH

Bibliography: Basic Works in Cultural Landscape Studies

The literature of cultural landscape studies, like the enterprise itself, has a core of central subjects and texts, but highly negotiable borders with related fields—most notably geography, history, architecture history, American studies, sociology, and planning. The following lists emphasize works that are introductory, classic, or provocative—or all three. For inclusion here, works had to exhibit the following characteristics: (a) strong interest in the interaction of people and their surroundings; (b) spatially specific analysis that includes details of buildings, open spaces, or settlements; and (c) concern for the cultural meanings of space rather than mere image, form, provenance, or economic location. The underlying questions of the works are usually about people and human relations, rather than simply about objects. The settings studied are typically generic structures rather than authored spaces of high-style design.

The bibliography is grouped into four sections: (1) general works, (2) dwellings and their yards, (3) rural and small-town landscapes, and (4) urban and suburban landscapes.

These lists sample primarily academic works. A cultural landscape bibliography that focused more on particular places would certainly include more primary source documents—essays, guidebooks, novels, and journalistic accounts. Even within the academic literature, these lists are not exhaustive; they suggest the range and intersections of literatures that inform the field, as well as some of its notable gaps. For instance, Native American landscapes (in fact, most racial and ethnic minority landscapes) and the post–World War II suburb and interstate highway are underrepresented in spite of their importance. Although novels are absent, included is one of several guides to landscape in literature (Kazen, listed in part 1). Where available and useful, article summaries (or excerpts) of books are given as well as the longer works. The following lists do not include all of the sources cited in the footnotes of this book, and focus primarily on North American topics, leaving out the substantial literature in English that concerns cultural landscapes on other continents.

Six senior authors—John Brinckerhoff Jackson, Peirce Lewis, Donald W. Meinig,

Wilbur Zelinsky, David Lowenthal, and Michael P. Conzen—have contributed most to the center of the literature in the United States. Because Jackson is so central, these lists give him more prominence but by no means a complete listing. All of Jackson's collections of essays are listed in part 1. Where Jackson has published his own essays first in *Landscape* magazine, that citation is given first, so readers can find Jackson's original illustrations (usually omitted in reprints). Important individual articles from Jackson's later collections are also listed separately. Helen Horowitz's anthology of Jackson's work, *Landscape in Sight* (1997), draws from his entire output. In addition to an excellent introductory essay, she provides a complete bibliography of Jackson's writings, including the work in *Landscape* magazine that he wrote under several pseudonyms.

Next to Jackson's own works, the contents of *Landscape* magazine rank as an effective exposition of work in the field. The first seventeen years of *Landscape* have typescript indexes, available in most libraries. However, the volumes before 1980 have not yet been indexed in national reference guides. Other journals that frequently publish cultural landscape works include *Landscape Journal, Winterthur Portfolio, Places* and *Perspectives in Vernacular Architecture* (whose volumes are usually catalogued not as a serial but as separate books, identified by the names of their editors).

Throughout the bibliography, the following abbreviations are also used:

  °° = a core work
  °°° = a classic work and important starting point
   S = especially useful for learning to see spatial aspects of the landscape

Where the title of an article does not make its subject clear, an annotation is added.

1. GENERAL WORKS: METHODS, REGIONAL STUDIES, AND NATIONAL ISSUES

These works bridge the fertile terrain between theory and description, and between regional (or national) trends and local landscapes. For geographers, especially, the landscape elements of the nation and region have posed important questions. For works at the national scale, Wilbur Zelinsky's *Cultural Geography of the United States* is a basic reference. Donald W. Meinig's regional studies look to processes and structures of the region; John Fraser Hart examines the internal cohesion of a region. Grounding concerns in the field are ideas about the abstract relationships between humans and nature. The ultimate reference is Clarence Glacken's finely distilled reference work on the history of three ideas—teleology, environmental determinism, and human agency; Carolyn Merchant and William Cronon have extended the discussion to modern situations. Edgar Anderson and Mae Theilgaard Watts see plants as cultural texts as well as ecological markers.

Recreation, as a subject, cuts across all types of landscapes, and hence is included with general works; J. B. Jackson's "Abstract World of the Hot-Rodder" examines recreation as a modern substitute for religion, and also is an illuminating glimpse of Jackson's phenomenological bent.

On the history of cultural landscape studies, see Donald W. Meinig's "Reading the Landscape," Helaine Caplan Prentice, and Peirce Lewis's "Learning from Looking."

Two public television productions are also available about Jackson and, more generally, about cultural landscape studies: Bob Calo, producer, *J. B. Jackson and the Love of Everyday Places*, 1989 (distributed by KQED, 2601 Mariposa, San Francisco, Calif. 04107); and Janet Mendelsohn and Claire Marino, *Figure in a Landscape: A Conversation with J. B. Jackson,* 1988 (distributed by Direct Cinema Limited, P.O. Box 69799, Los Angeles, Calif. 90069).

Agnew, John A., and James S. Duncan, eds. *The Power of Place: Bringing Together Geographical and Sociological Imaginations.* Boston: Unwin Hyman, 1989.
Anderson, Edgar. "The City Watcher." *Landscape* 8:2 (Winter 1958–59): 7–8.
———. *Plants, Man and Life.* Boston: Little, Brown, 1952; rpt., Berkeley: University of California Press, 1967.
———. *Landscape Papers.* Berkeley: Turtle Island Foundation, 1976.
Borchert, John R. *America's Northern Heartland: An Economic and Historical Geography of the Upper Midwest.* Minneapolis: University of Minnesota Press, 1987.
Carson, Cary. "Doing History with Material Culture." In *Material Culture and the Study of American Life,* ed. Ian M. G. Quimby. New York: Norton, 1978.
Conzen, Michael P., ed. *The Making of the American Landscape.* Boston: Unwin Hyman, 1990. °°°
Conzen, Michael P., Thomas A. Rumney, and Graeme Wynn, eds. *A Scholar's Guide to Geographical Writing on the American and Canadian Past.* Geography Research Paper 235. Chicago: University of Chicago Press, 1993.
Cosgrove, Denis. *Social Formation and Symbolic Landscape.* Totowa, N.J.: Barnes and Noble Books, 1984.
Cronon, William. *Nature's Metropolis: Chicago and the Great West.* New York: Norton, 1991.
Davis, Tim. "Photography and Landscape Studies." *Landscape Journal* 8:1 (1989): 1–12.
de Certeau, Michel. *The Practice of Everyday Life.* Berkeley: University of California Press, 1984; first published in 1980.
Deetz, James. *Invitation to Archaeology.* Garden City, N.Y.: Natural History Press, 1967. °° S
———. *In Small Things Forgotten.* Garden City, N.Y.: Doubleday, 1977. °° S
Duncan, James, and David Ley, eds. *Place/Culture/Representation.* London: Routledge, 1993.
Drucker, Johanna. "Language in the Landscape." *Landscape* 28:1 (1984): 7–13. S
Eliade, Mircea. *The Sacred and the Profane: The Nature of Religion: The Significance of Religious Myth, Symbolism, and Ritual within Life and Culture.* New York: Harper, 1959.
Foote, Kenneth E., Peter J. Hugill, Kent Mathewson, and Jonathan M. Smith, eds. *Re-Reading Cultural Geography.* Austin: University of Texas Press, 1994.
Foucault, Michel. *The Order of Things: An Archeology of the Human Sciences.* New York: Pantheon, 1971; first published in French in 1966.
Geertz, Clifford. "Thick Description: Toward an Interpretive Theory of Culture." In *The Interpretation of Cultures: Selected Essays,* 3–30. New York: Basic Books, 1973.
Glacken, Clarence. *Traces on the Rhodian Shore: Nature and Culture in Western Thought from Ancient Times to the End of the Eighteenth Century.* Berkeley: University of California Press, 1967. °°
Glassie, Henry. *Folk Housing in Middle Virginia: A Structural Analysis of Historic Artifacts.* Knoxville: University of Tennessee Press, 1975. S
Hall, Edward T. *The Hidden Dimension.* New York: Doubleday, 1966.
Harris, Cole. "Power, Modernity, and Historical Geography." *Journal of the Association of*

American Geographers 81:4 (1991): 671–83. An elegant introduction to the links between human geography and recent social theory.°°

Hart, John Fraser, "The Middle West." *Annals of the Association of American Geographers* 62 (1972): 258–82. °°

Hart, John Fraser, ed. *Regions of America*. New York: Harper and Row, 1972. Republished from a special issue of the *Annals of the Association of the American Geographers* 62:2 (June 1972). °°

Helen Lefkowitz Horowitz, "J. B. Jackson and the Discovery of the American Landscape." In John Brinckerfhoff Jackson, *Landscape in Sight: Looking at America*. New Haven: Yale University Press, 1997.

Huzinga, Johan. *Homo Ludens: A Study of the Play Element in Culture*. Boston: Beacon Press, 1933.

Jackson, John Brinckerhoff (books)

———. *American Space: The Centennial Years, 1865–1876*. New York: Norton, 1972. °°

———. *Discovering the Vernacular Landscape*. New Haven: Yale University Press, 1984.

———. *The Essential Landscape: The New Mexico Photographic Survey*. Albuquerque: University of New Mexico Press, 1985.

———. *Landscape in Sight: Looking at America*. Helen Lefkowitz Horowitz, ed. New Haven: Yale University Press, 1997.

———. *Landscapes: Collected Writings of John Brinckerhoff Jackson*. Erwin H. Zube, ed. Amherst: University of Massachusetts Press, 1975. °°°

———. *The Necessity for Ruins and other Essays*. Amherst: University of Massachusetts Press, 1980. °°°

———. *A Sense of Place, a Sense of Time*. New Haven: Yale University Press, 1994. °°° S

———. *The Southern Landscape Tradition in Texas*. Fort Worth: Amon Carter Museum, 1980. A three-chapter monograph, drawn in part from Jackson's teaching lectures. °° S

Jackson, John Brinckerhoff (articles)

———. "The Abstract World of the Hot-Rodder," *Landscape* 7:2 (1957–58): 22–27. Reprinted in *Changing Rural Landscapes* and *Landscape in Sight*. °°° S

———. "Beyond Wilderness." In *A Sense of Place, a Sense of Time*, 71–91. Jackson compares the Sierra Club and vernacular, urban perceptions of nature. °°

———. "By Way of Conclusion: How to Study the Landscape." In *The Necessity for Ruins and Other Essays*, 113–26. Reprinted in *Landscape in Sight*. Jackson describes his Berkeley and Harvard survey courses. °° S

———. "Concluding with Landscapes." In *Discovering the Vernacular Landscape*, 145–57. °°

———. "Goodbye to Evolution." *Landscape* 13:2 (Winter 1963–64): 1–2. Reprinted in *The Essential Landscape* and *Landscape in Sight*. °°°

———. "Human, All Too Human, Geography." *Landscape* 2:2 (Autumn 1952): 2–7. Reprinted in *Landscape in Sight*.°°

———. "Learning about Landscapes." In *The Necessity for Ruins and Other Topics*, 1–18. °°

———. "Looking into Automobiles." In *A Sense of Place, a Sense of Time*, 165–69.

———. "Notes and Comments: Tenth Anniversary Issue." *Landscape* 10:1 (Fall 1960): 1–2. Reprinted in *Landscape in Sight*.

———. "Once More: Man and Nature." *Landscape* 13:1 (Autumn 1963): 1–3. Reprinted in *Landscape in Sight*. °°

———. "The Word Itself." In *Discovering the Vernacular Landscape*, 1–8. Reprinted in *Landscape in Sight.* ° °

Jackson, Peter. *Maps of Meaning: An Introduction to Cultural Geography*. London: Unwin Hyman, 1989.

Kazin, Alfred. *A Writer's America: Landscape in Literature*. New York: Knopf, 1988.

Kostof, Spiro. *America by Design*. New York: Oxford University Press, 1987.

Layton, Edwin T. *The Revolt of the Engineers: Social Responsibility and the American Engineering Profession*. Cleveland: The Press of Case Western University, 1971.

Lefebvre, Henri. *The Production of Space*. London: Blackwell, 1991; first published in 1974.

Lewis, Peirce. "Axioms for Reading the Landscape: Some Guides to the American Scene." In *The Interpretation of Ordinary Landscapes: Geographical Essays*, 11–32 (see Meinig, Donald W., ed.) ° ° ° S

———. "Common Landscapes as Historic Documents." In *History from Things: Essays on Material Culture,* Steven Lubar and W. David Kingery, eds., 115–39. Washington, D.C.: Smithsonian Institution Press, 1993. ° °

———. "Learning from Looking: Geographic and Other Writing about the American Cultural Landscape." *American Quarterly* 35:3 (1983): 242–61. ° ° °

Lowenthal, David. "The American Scene." *Geographical Review* 58 (1968): 61–88. ° °

———. "The American Way of History." *Columbia University Forum* 9 (1966): 27–32. ° ° °

Lowenthal, David, and Martyn Bowden, eds. *Geographies of the Mind: Essays in Historical Geosophy in Honor of John Kirtland Wright*. New York: Oxford University Press, 1976. Useful on individual and social perception of landscape. ° °

Lynch, Kevin. *What Time Is This Place?* Cambridge: MIT Press, 1972.

MacCannell, Dean. *The Tourist: A New Theory of the Leisure Class*. New York: Schocken, 1989; first published in 1976.

McMurry, Sally. "Women in the American Vernacular Landscape." *Material Culture* 20:1 (1989): 33–49.

Meinig, Donald W. "American Wests: Preface to a Geographical Interpretation." In *Regions of the United States,* ed. John Fraser Hart, 159–84.

———. "The Beholding Eye: Ten Versions of the Same Scene." In *The Interpretation of Ordinary Landscapes* (see Meinig, Donald W., ed.), 33–48.

———. "Environmental Appreciation: Localities as Humane Art." *The Western Humanities Review* 25 (1971): 1–11. ° °

———. *Imperial Texas: An Interpretive Essay in Cultural Geography*. Austin: University of Texas Press, 1969. ° °

———. "Reading the Landscape: An Appreciation of W. G. Hoskins and J. B. Jackson." In *The Interpretation of Ordinary Landscapes*, 195–244 (see Meinig, Donald W., ed.). ° ° °

———. "The Mormon Culture Region: Strategies and Patterns in the Geography of the American West, 1847–1964." *Annals of the Association of American Geographers* 55 (1965): 191–220. ° °

Meinig, Donald W., ed. *The Interpretation of Ordinary Landscapes: Geographical Essays*. New York: Oxford University Press, 1979. ° ° °

Merchant, Carolyn. *The Death of Nature: Women, Ecology, and the Scientific Revolution*. San Francisco: Harper and Row, 1980.

Norton, William. *Explorations in the Understanding of Landscape: A Cultural Geography*. New York: Greenwood, 1989.

Penning-Rowsell, Edmund C., and David Lowenthal. *Landscape Meanings and Values*. London: Allen and Unwin, 1986.

Prentice, Helaine Kaplan. "John Brinckerhoff Jackson." *Landscape Architecture* 71 (1981): 740–45. °°

Relph, Edward. *Place and Placelessness*. London: Pion, 1976.

Riley, Robert B. "Speculations on the New American Landscapes," *Landscape* 24:3 (1980): 1–9. °°

Sack, Robert David. *Human Territoriality: Its Theory and History*. New York: Cambridge University Press, 1986

Sauer, Carl Ortwin. "The Education of a Geographer." In *Land and Life: A Selection from the Writings of Carl Ortwin Sauer*, ed. by John Leighly, 389–404. Berkeley: University of California Press, 1963.

———. "The Morphology of Landscape." In *Land and Life: A Selection from the Writings of Carl Ortwin Sauer*, ed. John Leighly, 315–350. Berkeley: University of California Press, 1963.

Schlereth, Thomas J. *Artifacts and the American Past*. Nashville, Tenn.: American Association for State and Local History, 1980.

Sobel, Mechal. *The World They Made Together: Black and White Values in Eighteenth-Century Virginia*. Princeton: Princeton University Press, 1987.

Stewart, George R. *U.S. 40: Cross Section of the United States of America*. Boston: Houghton Mifflin, 1953; rpt. Westport, Conn: Greenwood, 1973. °° S

Stilgoe, John R. *Common Landscape of America, 1580 to 1845*. New Haven: Yale University Press, 1982. °°°

———. *Metropolitan Corridor: Railroads and the American Scene*. New Haven: Yale University Press, 1983. °°

Thompson, George F., ed. *Landscape in America*. Austin: University of Texas Press, 1995.

Tuan, Yi-Fu. *Space and Place: The Perspective of Experience*. Minneapolis: University of Minnesota Press, 1977.

———. *Topophilia: A Study of Environmental Perception, Attitudes, and Values*. Englewood Cliffs, N.J.: Prentice Hall, 1974.

Upton, Dell. "Architectural History or Landscape History?" *Journal of Architecture Education* 44:4 (August 1991): 195–99.

———. "The Power of Things: Recent Studies in American Vernacular Architecture." *American Quarterly* 35:3 (1983): 262–80.

Watts, May Thielgaard. *Reading the Landscape: An Adventure in Ecology*. New York: Macmillan, 1957. S

Williams, Raymond. *The Country and the City*. New York: Oxford University Press, 1973.

———. *Culture*. Cambridge: Fontana, 1981.

Zelinsky, Wilbur. *The Cultural Geography of the United States*, rev. ed. Englewood Cliffs, N.J.: Prentice Hall, 1992; first published in 1973. °°°

Zelinsky, Wilbur. *Exploring the Beloved Country: Geographic Forays into American Society and Culture*. Iowa City: University of Iowa Press, 1994. A collection of Zelinsky's articles on wide-ranging topics, including cultural landscape studies.

Zube, Erwin H., and Margaret Zube, eds. *Changing Rural Landscapes*. Amherst: University of Massachusetts Press, 1970. Contains essays by J. B. Jackson and several other *Landscape* magazine authors.

Zube, Erwin H., ed. *Landscapes: Collected Writings of John Brinckerhoff Jackson* (see listing under "Jackson [books]").

2. DWELLINGS AND THEIR YARDS, BOTH URBAN AND RURAL

Dwellings—whether houses, apartments, trailers, or farmhouses—are the most pervasive built elements of the landscape, and they are typically the center of individual and household experience. As the urban geographer James Vance reminds us, they also represent the most intensely cultural of landscape artifacts. When people assume that ideas about homes are driven solely by economics or practical concerns, they forget to what degree decisions about dwellings are often highly irrational and arbitrary, as well.

Cultural landscape writers have consistently emphasized all sizes and types of single-family houses and yards. More recent writers have begun to study the landscapes of apartment renters and tenement dwellers. Related, too, are the landscapes of those without a typical home—residential hotels and rooming houses (see especially Arnold Rose), and of the homeless (see Kenneth Allsop and Rick Beard). For studies that particularly examine the interior spaces of dwellings, see Lizabeth A. Cohen, Elizabeth Cromley, Paul Groth, Dolores Hayden, Bernard L. Herman, Sally Ann McMurry, Albert Eide Paar, Dell Upton ("Vernacular Domestic Architecture"), John Michael Vlach, Chris Wilson, and Gwendolyn Wright (*Moralism and the Model Home*). Strangely, no serious, authoritative work yet exists on the most common housetype of all, the post–World War II suburban ranch house.

Arreola, Daniel D. "Fences as Landscape Taste: Tucson's Barrios." *Journal of Cultural Geography* 2 (1981): 96–105.

Allsop, Kenneth. *Hard Travellin': The Hobo and His History*. New York: New American Library, 1967.

Barrows, Robert G. "Beyond the Tenement: Patterns of American Urban Housing." *Journal of Urban History* 9 (1983): 395–420. The small house or worker's cottage.

Beard, Rick, ed. *On Being Homeless: Historical Perspectives*. New York: Museum of the City of New York, 1987. °°

Bushman, Richard. *The Refinement of America: Persons, Houses, Cities*. New York: Knopf, 1992. See especially the chapters entitled "Houses and Gardens" and "The Comforts of Home."

Chappell, Edward. "Acculturation in the Shenandoah Valley: Rhenish Houses of the Massanutten Settlement." In *Common Places,* ed. Dell Upton and John Michael Vlach, 27–57. S

Cohen, Lizabeth A. "Embellishing a Life of Labor: An Interpretation of the Material Culture of American Working-Class Homes, 1885–1915." *Journal of American Culture* 3 (1980): 752–75. On the interiors of small dwellings. °°

Cromley, Elizabeth. *Alone Together: A History of New York's Early Apartments*. Ithaca: Cornell University Press, 1990. S

———. "A History of American Beds and Bedrooms, 1890–1930." In *Perspectives in Vernacular Architecture* 4, ed. Thomas Carter and Bernard L. Herman, 177–86. Columbia: University of Missouri Press, 1991.

Cummings, Abbott Lowell. *The Framed Houses of Massachusetts Bay, 1625–1725*. Cambridge: Harvard University Press, 1979.

Duncan, James. "Landscape Taste as a Symbol of Group Identity: A Westchester County Village." *Geographical Review* 63 (1973): 334–55. S

Edwards, Jay. "The Evolution of a Vernacular Tradition." In *Perspectives in Vernacular Architecture* 4, ed. Thomas Carter and Bernard L. Herman, 75–86. Columbia: University of Missouri Press, 1991.

Foy, Jessica, and Thomas J. Schlereth, eds. *American Home Life, 1880–1930: A Social History of Spaces and Services.* Knoxville: University of Tennessee Press, 1992. °°

Gowans, Alan. *The Comfortable House: North American Suburban Architecture, 1890–1930.* Cambridge: MIT Press, 1986.

Grampp, Christopher. "Gardens for California Living." *Landscape* 28:3 (1985): 40–47.

Groth, Paul. *Living Downtown: The History of Residential Hotel Life in the United States.* Berkeley: University of California Press, 1994. °° S

———. "Lot, Yard, and Garden: American Distinctions," *Landscape* 30:3 (1990): 29–35.

———. "Nonpeople: A Case Study of Public Architects and Impaired Social Vision." In *Architects' People,* ed. Russell Ellis and Dana Cuff, 213–37. New York: Oxford University Press, 1989. On attitudes toward single-room housing.

Hancock, John. "The Apartment House in Urban America." In *Buildings and Society,* ed. Anthony D. King, 151–89. London: Routledge and Kegan Paul, 1980.

Hayden, Dolores. *The Grand Domestic Revolution: A History of Feminist Designs for American Homes, Neighborhoods, and Cities.* Cambridge: MIT Press, 1981.

Hecht, Melvin. "The Decline of the Grass Lawn Tradition in Tucson." *Landscape* 19:3 (1975): 3–10.

Herman, Bernard L. "Multiple Materials, Multiple Meanings: The Fortunes of Thomas Mendenhall." *Winterthur Portfolio* 19:1 (Spring 1984): 67–86.

Jackson, John Brinckerhoff. "The Domestication of the Garage." *Landscape* 20:2 (Winter 1976): 10–19. Reprinted in *The Necessity for Ruins* and *Landscape in Sight.* °°

———. "First Comes the House." *Landscape* 9:2 (Winter 1959–60): 26–32. Reprinted in *The Essential Landscape.*

———. "Ghosts at the Door." *Landscape* 1:2 (Autumn 1951): 2–9. Reprinted in *Changing Rural Landscapes* and *Landscape in Sight.* About the house yard. °°

———. "The Mobile Home on the Range." In *A Sense of Place, a Sense of Time,* 51–70. New Mexico dwellings of the rural poor. °°

———. "Nearer than Eden." In *The Necessity for Ruins,* 19–35. About relationships of yard, garden, and field. °°°

———. "Pueblo Dwellings and Our Own." *Landscape* 3:2 (Winter 1953–54): 20–25. Reprinted in *A Sense of Place, a Sense of Time.*

———. "Vernacular Gardens." In *A Sense of Place, a Sense of Time,* 119–33.

———. "The Westward Moving House." *Landscape* 2:3 (Spring 1953): 8–21. Reprinted in *Landscapes* and *Landscape in Sight.* °°°

———. "Working at Home." In *A Sense of Place, a Sense of Time,* 135–45. °°

Jenkins, Virginia Scott. *The Lawn: A History of an American Obsession.* Washington, D.C.: Smithsonian Institution Press, 1994.

King, Anthony D. *The Bungalow: The Production of a Global Culture.* London: Routledge and Kegan Paul, 1984. °°

Kniffen, Fred B. "Folk Housing: Key to Diffusion." *Annals of the Association of American Geographers* 55 (1965): 549–77. °°

————. "Louisiana House Types." *Annals of the Association of American Geographers* 26 (1936): 173–93.

Kniffen, Fred B. and Henry Glassie. "Building in Wood in the Eastern United States: A Time-Place Perspective." *Geographical Review* 56 (1966): 40–66. Excellent summary of eastern log building.

Landcaster, Clay. "The American Bungalow." *Art Bulletin* 40 (September 1958): 239–53.

Lewis, Peirce, "Common Houses, Cultural Spoor." *Landscape* 19 (1975): 1–22. ° ° ° S

Lubove, Roy. *The Progressives and the Slums: Tenement House Reform in New York City, 1890–1917.* Pittsburgh: University of Pittsburgh Press, 1962.

McDannell, Colleen. *The Christian Home in Victorian America, 1840–1900.* Bloomington: Indiana University Press, 1986.

McMurry, Sally Ann. *Families and Farmhouses in Nineteenth-Century America: Vernacular Design and Social Change.* New York: Oxford University Press, 1988.

Martin, Christopher. "'Hope Deferred': The Origin and Development of Alexandria's Flounder House." In *Perspectives in Vernacular Architecture* 2, ed. Camille Wells, 111–19. Columbia: University of Missouri Press, 1986.

Mindeleff, Victor. *A Study of Pueblo Architecture in Tusayan and Cibola.* Introduction by Peter Nabokov. Washington, D.C.: Smithsonian Institution Press, 1989; first published in 1891.

Modell, John, and Tamara K. Hareven. "Urbanization and the Malleable Household: An Examination of Boarding and Lodging in American Families." *Journal of Marriage and the Family* 35 (1975): 467–79.

Nabokov, Peter, and Robert Easton. *Native American Architecture.* New York: Oxford University Press, 1989.

Paar, Albert Eide. "Heating, Lighting, Plumbing, and Human Relations." *Landscape* 19:1 (Winter 1970): 28–29. A short essay packed with insights about family life and interior space. ° ° °

Peel, Mark. "On the Margins: Lodgers and Boarders in Boston, 1860–1900." *The Journal of American History* 72:4 (1986): 813–34.

Peterson, Fred W. *Homes in the Heartland: Balloon Frame Farmhouses of the Upper Midwest, 1850–1920.* Lawrence: University Press of Kansas, 1992. S

Plunz, Richard. *A History of Housing in New York City: Dwelling Type and Social Change in the American Metropolis.* New York: Columbia University Press, 1990.

Rose, Arnold M. "Living Arrangements of Unattached Persons." *American Sociological Review* 12 (1947): 429–35.

Sandweiss, Eric. "Building for Downtown Living: The Residential Architecture of San Francisco's Tenderloin." In *Perspectives in Vernacular Architecture* 3, ed. Thomas Carter and Bernard L. Herman, 160–175. Columbia: University of Missouri Press, 1989. S

Simpson, Pamela H. "Cheap, Quick, and Easy: The Early History of Rockfaced Concrete Block Building." In *Perspectives in Vernacular Architecture* 3, ed. Thomas Carter and Bernard L. Herman, 108–19. Columbia: University of Missouri Press, 1989.

Stewart, Janet Ann. *Arizona Ranch Houses: Southern Territorial Styles, 1867–1900.* Tucson: Arizona Historical Society, 1974.

Upton, Dell. "Vernacular Domestic Architecture in Eighteenth-Century Virginia." *Winterthur Portfolio* 17:2–3 (Summer–Autumn 1982): 220–44. Upton compares the three-room "molecule" of room uses and names to a four-room structural challenge. ° °

————. "Outside the Academy: A Century of Vernacular Architecture Studies, 1890–1990." In *The Architectural Historian in America: Studies in the History of Art* 33, ed. Elizabeth Blair MacDougall, 199–213. Washington, D.C.: National Gallery of Art, 1990.

Upton, Dell, and John Michael Vlach, eds. *Common Places: Readings in American Vernacular Architecture*. Athens, Ga.: University of Georgia Press, 1986. ° ° °

Vlach, John Michael. "The Shotgun House: An African Architectural Legacy." *Pioneer America: Journal of Historic American Material Culture* 8 (January–July 1976): 47–70. ° ° °

Watts, May Thielgaard. "The Stylish Yard." In *Reading the Landscape*. ° ° S

West, Pamela. "The Rise and Fall of the American Porch." *Landscape* 20:3 (Spring 1976): 42–47.

Westmacott, Richard. "Pattern and Practice in Traditional African-American Gardens in Rural Georgia." *Landscape Journal* 10:2 (Fall 1991): 87–104. ° ° S

Westmacott, Richard. *African American Gardens and Yards in the Rural South*. Knoxville: University of Tennessee Press, 1992. ° ° S

Williams, Michael Ann. *Homeplace: The Social Use and Meaning of the Folk Dwelling in Southwestern North Carolina*. Athens: University of Georgia Press, 1991.

Wilson, Chris. "When a Room Is the Hall." *Mass* 2 (Summer 1984): 17–23. ° ° S

Wright, Gwendolyn. *Building the Dream: The Social History of Housing in America*. New York: Pantheon, 1982.

Wright, Gwendolyn. *Moralism and the Model Home: Domestic Architecture and Cultural Conflict in Chicago, 1873–1913*. Chicago: University of Chicago Press, 1980. ° °

3. RURAL AND SMALL-TOWN LANDSCAPES: ELEMENTS OTHER THAN DWELLINGS

If dwellings are the most common landscape element, then the fields, rural roads or highways, and isolated farmsteads are the most pervasive cultural landscape elements. Similarly pervasive are the markers of rural social institutions such as churches, crossroads stores, fairgrounds, and the thousands of small farm-service towns and county seats in America. They form several interlocking regional and national landscapes visible to those who have learned to interpret them.

J. B. Jackson's "Almost Perfect Town" provides a masterful analytical description of the typical county-seat town on the southern Great Plains. Along with the urban "Stranger's Path," this is one of Jackson's most famous essays. Tom Harvey and John Hudson offer views of a different type of place, the railroad town of the northern Great Plains. Again, for their pervasive importance, the road, factory, and communications works of engineers are essential (and still too little researched) within cultural landscape studies; see Margaret Purser, Albert C. Rose, and a primary source, David Stevenson.

The most accessible introduction to the farm-owner's rural landscape and the business of farming is John Fraser Hart's *Look of the Land*. There is no similar introduction to the landscape of hired farm workers, in town or on the farm, although Carol Bly's essay gives a vivid sense of the occasional laborer's sense of working atop a tractor in a huge Minnesota field. Much of the rural literature, for better or worse, is organized around the folklorist's and geographer's fascination with the imprint of ethnic and racial minority land owners in ordinary farmstead architecture; see Dell Upton's bibliographical survey and short guidebook to ethnic architecture. One revisionist work, emphasizing temporary colonial building, is the piece by Cary Carson et al. Note that works about farmhouses, alone, are listed above in section 2, on dwellings. Works that include both farmhouses and barns (or other outbuildings or fields) are listed here. See also the regional works listed in section 1.

Blackmar, Betsy. "Going to the Mountains: A Social History." In *Resorts of the Catskills,* ed. Alf Evers, Elizabeth Cromley, Betsy Blackmar, and Neil Harris, 71–98. New York: St. Martin's, 1979.

Bly, Carol. "Getting Tired." In *Letters from the Country,* 8–13. New York: Penguin, 1981.

Brody, Hugh. *Maps and Dreams.* New York: Pantheon, 1981. About recent Native American hunters in Canada and their sense of time, space, and hunting grounds.

Brown, Mary Ann. "Vanished Black Rural Communities in Western Ohio." In *Perspectives in Vernacular Architecture* 1, ed. Camille Wells, 97–113. Columbia: University of Missouri Press, 1982.

Campanella, Thomas J. "Sanctuary in the Wilderness: Deborah Moody and the Town Plan of Colonial Gravesend." *Landscape Journal* 12:2 (Fall 1983): 107–30. The street plan of a colonial agricultural village on Long Island, followed to its present-day suburban state. S

Carson, Cary, Norman F. Barka, William M. Kelso, Garry Wheeler Stone, and Dell Upton. "Impermanent Architecture in the Southern American Colonies," *Winterthur Portfolio* 16 (1981). °° S

Daniel, Pete. *Breaking the Land: The Transformation of Cotton, Tobacco, and Rice Cultures since 1880.* Urbana: University of Illinois Press, 1985.

Cronon, William. *Changes in the Land: Indians, Colonists, and the Ecology of New England.* New York: Hill and Wang, 1983.

Darnell, M. J. "The American Cemetery as Picturesque Landscape." *Winterthur Portfolio* 18:4 (Winter 1983): 249–69.

Ellis, Cliff. "Visions of Urban Freeways, 1930–1970." Ph.D. diss., Department of City and Regional Planning, University of California, Berkeley, 1990.

Fite, Gilbert C. *The Farmers' Frontier, 1865–1900.* Norman: University of Oklahoma Press, 1966.

Francaviglia, Richard V. "The Cemetery as Evolving Cultural Landscape." *Annals of the Association of American Geographers* 61:3 (September 1971): 501–9. S

Gallatin, Albert. "Report on Roads and Canals." In *Writings,* 3 vols., ed. Henry Adams. New York: Antiquarian Press, 1960.

Glassie, Henry. "Eighteenth-Century Cultural Process in Delaware Valley Folk Building." *Winterthur Portfolio* 7 (1972): 29–57. S

———. *Pattern in the Material Folk Culture of the Eastern United States.* Philadelphia: University of Pennsylvania Press, 1968. °°

Goldschmidt, Walter. *As You Sow: Three Studies in the Social Consequences of Agribusiness.* Montclair, N.J.: Allanheld, Osmun, 1978. On the connection to Main Street commercial life.

Hart, John Fraser. *The Look of the Land.* Englewood Cliffs, N.J.: Prentice Hall, 1973. °°°

Hart, John Fraser. "Field Patterns in Indiana," *Geographical Review* 58 (1968): 450–71.

Harvey, Thomas. "Railroad Towns: Urban Form on the Prairie," *Landscape* 27:3 (1983): 26–34. S

Heath, Kingston. "False-Front Architecture on Montana's Urban Frontier." In *Perspectives in Vernacular Architecture* 3, ed. Thomas Carter and Bernard L. Herman, 199–213. Columbia: University of Missouri Press, 1989. S

Helphand, Kenneth I., and Ellen Manchester. *Colorado: Visions of an American Landscape*. Niwot, Colo.: Roberts Rinehart, 1991. S

Herman, Bernard L. *The Stolen House*. Charlottesville: University Press of Virginia, 1992. °°

Hill, Forest. *Roads, Railways, and Waterways: The Army Engineers and Early Transportation*. Norman: University of Oklahoma Press, 1957.

Hilliard, Sam B. "Headright Grants and Surveying in Northeastern Georgia," *Geographical Review* 82 (1982): 416–26.

Hubka, Thomas C. *Big House, Little House, Back House, Barn: The Connected Farm Buildings of New England*. Hanover, N.H.: University Press of New England, 1984.

Hudson, John C. *Plains Country Towns*. Minneapolis: University of Minnesota Press, 1985.

Interrante, Joseph. "You Can't Go to Town in a Bathtub: Automobile Movement and the Reorganization of American Rural Space, 1900–1930," *Radical History Review* 21 (Fall 1979): 151–68.

Issac, Rhys. *The Transformation of Virginia, 1740–1790*. Chapel Hill: University of North Carolina Press, 1982. See esp. pp. 43–87. °°° S

Jackson, John Brinckerhoff. "The Almost Perfect Town." *Landscape* 2:1 (1952): 2–8. Reprinted in *Landscapes* and *Landscape in Sight*. °°° S

———. "Design for Travel." *Landscape* 11:3 (Spring 1962): 6–8. Phases of motel designs. S

———. "The New American Countryside: An Engineered Environment." *Landscape* 16:1 (Autumn 1966): 16–20. Reprinted in *Landscape in Sight* and *Changing Rural Landscapes* (see Zube, Erwin H. and Margaret). °°° S

———. "The Four Corners Country." *Landscape* 10:1 (Fall 1960): 20–25. Reprinted in *Changing Rural Landscapes* (see Zube, Erwin H. and Margaret). Boom landscapes, mobility, and trailers.

———. "From Monument to Place." *Landscape* 17:2 (Winter 1967–68): 22–26. About cemeteries.

———. "A New Kind of Space." *Landscape* 18 (Winter 1968–69): 33–35. Reprinted in *Changing Rural Landscapes* (see Zube, Erwin H. and Margaret). °°° S

———. "The Nineteenth-Century Rural Landscape: The Courthouse, the Small College, the Mineral Spring, and the Country Store." In *The Southern Landscape Tradition in Texas*, 13–24. Reprinted in *Landscape in Sight*. °°

———. "The Sacred Grove in America." In *The Necessity for Ruins*, 77–88. °°

———. "The Virginian Heritage: Fencing, Farming, and Cattle Raising." In *The Southern Landscape Tradition in Texas*, 1–13. Reprinted in *Landscape in Sight*.

Jakle, John. *The American Small Town*. Hamden, Conn.: Archon, 1982. S

Johnson, Hildegard Binder. *Order upon the Land: The U.S. Rectangular Land Survey and the Upper Mississippi Country*. New York: Oxford University Press, 1976. S

Johnson, Hildegard Binder, and Gerald R. Pitzl. "Viewing and Perceiving the Rural Scene: Visualization in Human Geography." *Progress in Human Geography* 5 (1981): 211–33. S

Jordan, Terry. "The Imprint of the Upper and Lower South on Mid-Nineteenth Century Texas," *Annals of the Association of American Geographers* 57 (1967): 667–90.

———. *Texas Log Buildings: A Folk Architecture*. Austin: University of Texas Press, 1978.

Kemp, Louis Ward. "Aesthetes and Engineers: The Occupational Ideology of Highway Design." *Technology and Culture* 27:4 (October 1886): 759–97.

Kniffen, Fred. "The American Agricultural Fair." *Annals of the Association of American Geographers* 39:4 (1949): 264–82. S

Lemon, James T. *The Best Poor Man's Country: A Geographical Study of Early Southeastern Pennsylvania*. Baltimore: Johns Hopkins University Press, 1972.

———. "Early Americans and Their Social Environment." *Journal of Historical Geography* 6 (1980): 115–31. Lemon rereads his earlier work.

Lounsbury, Carl. "The Structure of Justice: The Courthouses of Colonial Virginia." In *Perspectives in Vernacular Architecture* 3, ed. Thomas Carter and Bernard L. Herman, 214–26. Columbia: University of Missouri Press, 1989. S

Mattson, Richard L. "The Cultural Landscape of a Southern Black Community: East Wilson, North Carolina, 1890 to 1930." *Landscape Journal* 11:2 (Fall 1992): 145–59. S

Newton, Milton B., Jr. "Settlement Patterns as Artifacts of Social Structure." Chap. 14 in *The Human Mirror: Material and Spatial Images of Man*, ed. Miles Richardson. Baton Rouge: Louisiana State University Press, 1974.

Noble, Allen. "The Diffusion of Silos." *Landscape* 25:1 (1981): 11–14. S

Pare, Richard, ed. *Courthouse: A Photographic Document*. New York: Horizon, 1978. An intelligent collection of images and essays, aimed at a popular audience.

Purser, Margaret. "All Roads Lead to Winnemucca: Local Road Systems and Community Material Culture in Nineteenth-Century Nevada." In *Perspectives in Vernacular Architecture* 3, ed. Thomas Carter and Bernard L. Herman, 120–34. Columbia: University of Missouri Press, 1989.

Rose, Albert C. *Historic American Roads: From Frontier Trails to Superhighways*. New York: Crown, 1976. Folksy in format but invaluable in content. °° S

Sauer, Carl. "Homestead and Community on the Middle Border." *Landscape* 20:2 (Winter 1976): 3–7.

Seely, Bruce E. *Building the American Highway System: Engineers as Policy Makers*. Philadelphia: Temple University Press, 1987.

Sobel, Mechal. *The World They Made Together: Black and White Values in Eighteenth-Century Virginia*. Princeton: Princeton University Press, 1987.

Stevenson, David. *Sketch of the Civil Engineering of North America*. London: J. Weale, 1838.

Upton, Dell. "Black and White Landscapes in Eighteenth-Century Virginia," *Places* 2:2 (1985): 59–72. °°

Upton, Dell, ed. *America's Architectural Roots: Ethnic Groups that Built America*. Washington, D.C.: National Trust for Historic Preservation, 1986. An introductory index to the ethnic building literature. S

Wallach, Bret. "The Potato Landscape: Aroostook County, Maine." *Landscape* 23:1 (1979): 15–22.

———. "The West Side Oil Fields of California," *Geographical Review* 70 (1980): 50–59.

Wells, Camille. "The Planter's Prospect: Houses, Outbuildings, and Rural Landscapes in Eighteenth-Century Virginia." *Winterthur Portfolio* 28:1 (1993): 1–31.

Wood, Joseph S. "The New England Village as an American Vernacular Form." In *Perspectives in Vernacular Architecture* 2, ed. Camille Wells, 54–63. Columbia: University of Missouri Press, 1986. S

Worster, Donald. "Transformations of the Earth: Toward an Agroecological Perspective in History." *Journal of American History* 76:4 (1990): 1087–1106.

Wright, Gavin. *The Political Economy of the Cotton South: Households, Markets, and Wealth in the Nineteenth Century*. New York: Norton, 1978.

Wycoff, William. *The Developer's Frontier: The Making of the Western New York Landscape*. New Haven: Yale University Press, 1988. °°

Zelinsky, Wilbur. "The Pennsylvania Town: An Overdue Geographical Account." *Geographical Review* 67 (1977): 127–47. °° S

Zube, Ervin H., and Margaret Zube, eds., *Changing Rural Landscapes*. Amherst: University of Massachusetts Press, 1977. °°

4. CITIES, SUBURBS, AND URBAN REGIONS

Urban landscape analysis is the least developed arena of landscape studies to date. J. B. Jackson's leadership in this field is less complete than his work on rural landscapes; Michael P. Conzen and Peirce Lewis have taken the lead. Lewis's New Orleans monograph, in particular, is one of the best introductions in print to the spatial order and architecture of an American city. Joan Didion's autobiographical "Notes from a Native Daughter," an idea-packed and spatially astute essay, depicts a novelist's sensitivity to the interweaving of wealthy Episcopalians and the meaning of their urban space. Mike Davis, John M. Findlay, and Barbara Rubin provide incisive samples of more recent urban landscapes.

Although several urban historians and historical geographers have tackled the suburbs as a subject, no single work is yet a spatially specific cultural landscape study; the closest might be Michael H. Ebner's eclectic view of both the ordinary and elegant aspects of Chicago's North Shore, backed up by Robert Fishman, Kenneth T. Jackson, Richard Walker, and Marc Weiss. As Bolton's article shows, for students of the official rebuilding and reordering of the American city during the Progressive era, an invaluable introductory source is the journal *American City*.

Although Jackson did not lead in urban landscape analysis, he nonetheless made clear his interest in urbanity and the public landscape of the city. His 1967 essay "To Pity the Plumage but Forget the Dying Bird," calls for work—still undone—on the medium-sized city. His "Stranger's Path" views a generic city of "between twenty and fifty thousand" from the perspective of someone arriving by bus or train or a car parked just outside the downtown area. Jackson published his thoughtful article about the commercial highway strip (see "Other-Directed Houses") well before *Learning from Las Vegas* broadened interest in the subject among architects. Jackson went on to examine the changing nature of public streets and street life (see especially "The Discovery of the Street" and "Truck City").

Averbach, Alvin. "San Francisco's South of Market District, 1850–1950: The Emergence of a Skid Row." *California Historical Quarterly* 52 (1973): 197–223.

Banham, Reyner. *Los Angeles: The Architecture of Four Ecologies*. New York: Harper and Row, 1971. °° S

Barnett, Roger. "The Libertarian Suburb." *Landscape* 22:3 (1978): 44–48. S

Barth, Gunther. *City People: The Rise of Modern City Culture in Nineteenth-Century America*. New York: Oxford University Press, 1980. Includes chapters on apartments, department stores, and sports.

Blackmar, Elizabeth. *Manhattan for Rent, 1789–1850*. Ithaca: Cornell University Press, 1989.

————. "Re-Walking the 'Walking City': Housing and Property Relations in New York City, 1780–1840." *Radical History Review* 21 (Fall 1979): 131–48.

Bluestone, Daniel. *Constructing Chicago.* New Haven: Yale University Press, 1991. S

————. "The Pushcart Evil." In *The Landscape of Modernity: New York City's Built Environment, 1900–1990,* ed. David Ward and Olivier Zunz, 287–312.

Blumin, Stuart M. *The Emergence of the Middle Class: Social Experience in the American City.* New York: Cambridge University Press, 1989.

Bolton, Kate. "The Great Awakening of the Night: Lighting America's Streets." *Landscape* 23:3 (1979): 41–47. °° S

Borchert, James. "Alley Landscapes of Washington." *Landscape* 23:3 (Spring 1979): 3–10.

————. *Alley Life in Washington: Family, Community, Religion, and Folklife in the City, 1850–1970.* Urbana: University of Illinois Press, 1980. °° S

Byington, Margaret F. *Homestead: The Households of a Mills Town.* Pittsburgh: University Center for International Studies, 1974; first published in 1910.

Cybriwsky, Roman A. "Social Aspects of Neighborhood Change." *Annals of the Association of American Geographers* 68:1 (March 1978): 17–33.

Clay, Grady. *Close Up: How to Read the American City.* Chicago: University of Chicago Press, 1980; first published in 1973. °° S

Conzen, Kathleen Neils. "Community Studies, Urban History, and American Local History." In *The Past Before Us,* ed. Michael Kammen, 270–91. Ithaca: Cornell University Press, 1981.

————. *Immigrant Milwaukee, 1836–1860: Accommodation and Community in a Frontier City.* Cambridge: Harvard University Press, 1976.

Conzen, Michael P. "Analytical Approaches to the Urban Landscape." In *Dimensions in Human Geography,* Geography Research Paper 186, ed. Karl W. Butzer, 128–65. Chicago: University of Chicago Press, 1978. °°

————. "Ethnicity on the Land." In *The Making of the American Landscape,* 221–48. Boston: Unwin Hyman, 1990. Surveys both rural and urban ethnic landscapes. S

————. "The Morphology of Nineteenth-Century Cities in the United States." In *Urbanization in the Americas,* ed. Woodrow Borah et al. Ottawa: National Museum of Man, 1980. °° S

Cranz, Galen. "Changing Roles of Urban Parks: From Pleasure Garden to Open Space." *Landscape* 22:3 (Summer 1978): 9–18.

————. *The Politics of Park Design: A History of Urban Parks in America.* Cambridge: MIT Press, 1982.

Cutler, Phoebe. "On Recognizing a WPA Rose Garden or a CCC Privy." *Landscape* 20:2 (Winter 1976): 3–9. °° S

Cutler, Phoebe. *The Public Landscape of the New Deal.* New Haven: Yale University Press, 1985. °° S

Davis, Mike. *City of Quartz, Excavating the Future in Los Angeles.* New York: Vintage, 1990. °°

Didion, Joan. "Notes from a Native Daughter." In *Slouching Towards Bethlehem,* 171–86. New York: Simon and Schuster, 1979. About growing up in Sacramento in the early 1950s. °°

Ebner, Michael H. *Creating Chicago's North Shore: A Suburban History.* Chicago: University of Chicago Press, 1988.

————. "Re-reading Suburban America: Urban Population Deconcentration, 1810–1980." *American Quarterly* 37:3 (1985): 368–81. Bibliographical essay.

Findlay, John M. *Magic Lands: Western Cityscapes and American Cultures after 1940.* Berkeley: University of California Press, 1992.

Fogelson, Robert M. *America's Amories: Architecture, Society, and Public Order.* Cambridge: Harvard University Press, 1989.

————. *The Fragmented Metropolis: Los Angeles, 1850–1930.* Berkeley: University of California Press, 1967.

Garner, John S., ed. *The Company Town: Architecture and Society in the Early Industrial Age.* New York: Oxford University Press, 1992.

Groth, Paul. "Parking Gardens." In *The Meaning of Gardens,* ed. Mark Francis and Randolph T. Hester, Jr., 130–37. Cambridge: MIT Press, 1990. The importance of parking spaces.

————. "Streetgrids as Frameworks for Urban Variety." *Harvard Architecture Review* 2 (1981), 68–75. °°

————. "Vernacular Parks." In *Denatured Visions: Landscape and Culture in the Twentieth Century,* ed. Stuart Wrede and William Howard Adams, 135–37. New York: Museum of Modern Art, 1991.

Hales, Peter Bacon. *Silver Cities: The Photography of American Urbanization, 1839–1915.* Philadelphia: Temple University Press, 1984.

Hall, Millicent. "The Park at the End of the Trolley." *Landscape* 22:1 (Autumn 1977): 11–18.

Horowitz, Helen Lefkowitz. *Culture and the City: Cultural Philanthropy in Chicago from the 1880s to 1917.* Chicago: University of Chicago Press, 1976.

Jackson, John Brinckerhoff. "The Discovery of the Street." In *The Necessity for Ruins,* 57–66. °°° S

————. "Other-Directed Houses," *Landscape* 6:2 (Winter 1956–57): 29–35. Reprinted in *Landscapes* and *Landscape in Sight.* On the commercial highway strip. °°

————. "The Past and Future Park." In *A Sense of Place, a Sense of Time,* 107–16.

————. "The Public Landscape." In *Landscapes* (see Jackson [books]), 153–60. °°

————. "The Stranger's Path." *Landscape* 7:1 (Autumn 1957): 11–15. Reprinted in *Landscapes* and *Landscape in Sight.* °°° S

————. "The Sunbelt City: The Modern City, the Strip, and the Civic Center." In *The Southern Landscape Tradition in Texas,* 25–35.

————. "To Pity the Plumage but Forget the Dying Bird." *Landscape* 17:1 (Autumn 1967): 1–3. Reprinted in *Landscapes.* °°

————. "Truck City." In *A Sense of Place, a Sense of Time,* 171–84. Reprinted in *Landscape in Sight.* °°

————. "Urban Circumstances." *Design Quarterly* 128 (1985): 1–32.

Jackson, Kenneth T. *Crabgrass Frontier: The Suburbanization of the United States.* New York: Oxford University Press, 1985. °°°

Johnson, Paul E. *A Shopkeeper's Millennium: Society and Revivals in Rochester, New York, 1815–1837.* New York: Hill and Wang, 1978. °°

Kulik, Gary, et al. *The New England Mill Village, 1790–1860.* Cambridge: MIT Press, 1982. S

Lai, David Chuenyan. *Chinatowns: Towns within Cities in Canada.* Vancouver: University of British Columbia Press, 1988. S

Ley, David, and Roman Cybriwsky. "Urban Graffiti as Territorial Markers." *Annals of the Association of American Geographers* 64 (1974): 491–505. S

Lewis, Peirce. *New Orleans: The Making of an Urban Landscape.* Cambridge, Mass.: Ballinger, 1976. (Also available in John Adams, ed., *Contemporary Metropolitan America,* 4 vols.) °°° S

————. "Small Town in Pennsylvania." In *Regions of the United States,* ed. John Fraser Hart, 323–51. S

Liebs, Chester H. *Main Street to Miracle Mile: American Roadside Architecture.* Boston: Little, Brown, 1985. °°

Malcher, Fritz. "A Traffic Planner Imagines a City." *American City* (March 1931): 134–35. S

Marsh, Margaret. *Suburban Lives.* New Brunswick, N.J.: Rutgers University Press, 1990.

Mayer, Harold, and Richard Wade. *Chicago: Growth of a Metropolis.* Chicago: University of Chicago Press, 1969. °° S

McShane, Clay. "Transforming the Use of Urban Space: A Look at the Revolution in Street Pavements, 1880–1924," *Journal of Urban History* 5:3 (1979): 279–307. °°

Muller, Edward K. "The Americanization of the City." In *The Making of the American Landscape,* 269–92 (see Conzen, Michael P., ed.).

Nelson, Daniel. *Managers and Workers: Origins of the New Factory System in the United States,* 1880–1920. Madison: University of Wisconsin Press, 1975. Excellent chapter on factory environments.

Olson, Sherry H. "Baltimore Imitates the Spider." *Annals of the Association of American Geographers,* 69:4 (1979): 557–74. °°

Owens, Bill. *Suburbia.* San Francisco: Straight Arrow, 1973. S

Paar, Albert Eide. "The Child in the City: Urbanity and the Urban Scene." *Landscape* 16:3 (Spring 1967): 3–5.

Reps, John W. *The Making of Urban America: A History of City Planning in the United States.* Princeton: Princeton University Press, 1965.

Relph, Edward. *The Modern Urban Landscape.* Baltimore: Johns Hopkins University Press, 1987.

Richardson, Dorothy. *The Long Day: The Story of a New York Working Girl* (first published in 1905). In *Women at Work,* ed. William O'Neill, 1–270. Chicago: Quadrangle Books, 1972.

Riis, Jacob. *How the Other Half Lives: Studies among the Tenements of New York.* New York: Dover, 1971; first published in 1890.

Rosenzweig, Roy. *Eight Hours for What We Will: Workers and Leisure in an Industrial City, 1870–1920.* New York: Cambridge University Press, 1983.

————. "Middle-Class Parks and Working-Class Play: The Struggle over Recreational Space in Worchester, Massachusetts, 1870–1910." *Radical History Review* 21 (Fall 1979): 31–46.

Rosenzweig, Roy, and Elizabeth Blackmar. *The Park and the People: A History of Central Park.* Ithaca: Cornell University Press, 1992.

Rubin, Barbara. "Aesthetic Ideology and Urban Design." *Annals of the Association of American Geographers* 69:3 (1979): 339–61. Compares exposition midways and highway strips. °°

Upton, Dell. "The City as Material Culture." In *The Art and Mystery of Historical Archaeology: Essays in Honor of James Deetz,* ed. Anne Elizabeth Yentsch and Mary C. Beaudry, 51–74. Boca Raton, Fl.: CRC Press, 1992.

Vance, James E., Jr. *The Continuing City: Urban Morphology in Western Civilization*. Baltimore: Johns Hopkins University Press, 1990. °° S

Walker, Richard. "A Theory of Suburbanization: Capitalism and the Construction of Urban Space in the United States." In *Urbanization and Urban Planning in Capitalist Society,* ed. Michael Dear and Allen Scott, 383–410. New York: Methuen, 1981. °°

Warner, Sam Bass, Jr. *The Urban Wilderness: A History of the American City*. New York: Harper and Row, 1972. S

———. *Streetcar Suburbs: The Process of Growth in Boston, 1870–1900*. Cambridge: Harvard University Press, 1962.

Weightman, Barbara. "Gay Bars as Private Places." *Landscape* 24:1 (1980): 9–16.

Weiss, Marc. *The Rise of the Community Builders: The American Real Estate Industry and Urban Land Planning*. New York: Columbia University Press, 1987. On 1920s zoning and large-scale suburban development.

Wolfe, Albert Benedict. *The Lodging House Problem in Boston*. Boston: Houghton Mifflin, 1906. S

Yip, Christopher Lee. "San Francisco's Chinatown: An Architectural and Urban History." Ph.D. diss., University of California, Berkeley, 1985.

Zube, Erwin H., ed. *Landscapes: Collected Writings of John Brinckerhoff Jackson*. Amherst: University of Massachusetts Press, 1975. °°°

Zunz, Olivier. *The Changing Face of Inequality: Urbanization, Industrial Development, and Immigrants in Detroit, 1880–1920*. Chicago: University of Chicago Press, 1982.

Zunz, Olivier. "Inside the Skyscraper." In *Making America Corporate, 1870–1920*, 103–12. Chicago: University of Chicago Press, 1990.

Contributors

JAY APPLETON is a geographer and an advocate of landscape appreciation. He has campaigned for an interdisciplinary approach to the subject through many channels, including the Landscape Research Group, which he chaired from 1976 to 1978 and again from 1981 to 1984. His books on landscapes include *The Experience of Landscape* (1975), which introduced his well-known prospect-refuge theory; *The Poetry of Habitat* (1978); an edited collection, *The Aesthetics of Landscape* (1980); and *The Symbolism of Habitat: An Interpretation of Landscape in the Arts* (1990). He has also written about transportation and historical geography. He is an emeritus professor of geography at the University of Hull, where he worked for thirty-five years until his retirement in 1985.

JAMES BORCHERT, professor of history at Cleveland State University, is a social historian whose research focuses on the social lives and landscapes of urban and suburban communities. He wrote *Alley Life in Washington: Family, Community, Religion, and Folklife in the City, 1850–1970* (1980) and is the coauthor of *Lakewood: The First Hundred Years, 1889–1989* (1989). His articles have appeared in *Landscape, Studies in Visual Communication, Society, Journal of Interdisciplinary History, Journal of Urban History*, and *Historical Methods*.

TODD W. BRESSI is an editor, writer, and teacher in New York City. He is executive editor of the environmental design journal *Places* and editor of *Planning and Zoning New York City* (1993). He has taught urban design at Hunter College, New York University, and Pratt Institute. His articles on design and the environment have appeared in many newspapers and magazines.

DENIS COSGROVE is a cultural geographer who has written extensively on theoretical relations between society and landscape, often using the sixteenth-century Venetian landscape as an exemplar. He has published *Social Formation and Symbolic Landscape* (1984), edited with S. J. Daniels; *The Iconography of Landscape: Essays on the Symbolic Representation, Design, and Use of Past Environments* (1988); and *Water, Engi-*

neering, and Landscape (1990), with G. Petts. His latest book, *The Palladian Landscape* (1993), summarizes his Venetian work. He is currently editor of *Ecumene*, a cross-disciplinary journal of environment, culture, and meaning, and professor of human geography at Royal Holloway College, University of London.

PAUL GROTH is a cultural landscape historian. He has published interpretations of urban street grids, parking lots, vernacular parks, and the parallels between American factory space and residential space. His book *Living Downtown: The History of Residential Hotels in the United States* was published by the University of California Press in 1994. He is past president of the Vernacular Architecture Forum and associate professor of architecture and geography at the University of California, Berkeley, where he teaches the history of U.S. cultural landscapes.

DOLORES HAYDEN is professor of architecture, urbanism, and American studies at Yale University. She is the author of *Seven American Utopias* (1976), *The Grand Domestic Revolution* (1981), and *Redesigning the American Dream: The Future of Housing, Work, and Family Life* (1984). "Urban Landscape History: The Sense of Place and the Politics of Space" is drawn from her book *The Power of Place: Urban Landscapes as Public History* (1995).

DERYCK W. HOLDSWORTH is a geographer whose research interests include housing form and social identity, the long-term dynamics of office districts, proto-industrial landscapes, and the historical geography of Pennsylvania in the nineteenth century. His articles have appeared in *Urban History Review,* the *Public Historian,* and the *American Review of Canadian Studies*, in addition to numerous geography journals. He has written *The Parking Authority of Toronto, 1952–1987* (1987), edited *Reviving Main Street* (1985), and is the coeditor (with D. Kerr) of volume 3 of *Historical Atlas of Canada: Addressing the Twentieth Century, 1891–1961* (1990). He has taught at the University of Toronto and the University of British Columbia, and is currently professor of geography at Pennsylvania State University.

CATHERINE M. HOWETT is a landscape architect, historian, and critic in the School of Environmental Design at the University of Georgia. She brings a historical outlook to her research and writing on nineteenth- and twentieth-century American landscape design. She has curated and written catalogue essays for a number of exhibitions of environmental art and landscape design, and has contributed to such journals as *Places, Landscape,* and *Landscape Journal.* She is currently a senior fellow in the Studies in Landscape Architecture program of Dumbarton Oaks, Washington, D.C.

JOHN BRINCKERHOFF JACKSON, a writer and philosopher whose work dominates American cultural landscape studies, died in 1996. He was known best for his learned and speculative essays about the meaning of American human environments and their European antecedents. He studied history and literature at Harvard and in 1951 founded *Landscape* magazine, which he published and edited for seventeen years. He published six collections of essays and established courses in the history of American cultural landscapes at the University of California, Berkeley, and Harvard.

ANTHONY D. KING combines in his work backgrounds in history, architecture, cultural studies, and sociology. Recent books include *Global Cities: Post-Imperialism and the Internationalization of London* (1990), *Urbanism, Colonialism, and the World-Economy: Cultural and Spatial Foundations of the World Urban System* (1990), and two edited collections: *Culture, Globalization, and the World-System* (1990) and *Re-presenting the City: Ethnicity, Capital, and Culture in the Twenty-first-Century Metropolis* (1996).

Since 1988 he has been professor of art history and sociology in the Department of Art History at the State University of New York, Binghamton.

DAVID CHUENYAN LAI studied geography at the University of Hong Kong and the London School of Economics. He is professor of geography at the University of Victoria, British Columbia, where he has taught since 1968. He has published six books, most recently *Land of Genghis Khan: The Rise and Fall of Nation-States in China's Northern Frontiers* (1995). His interests in Chinatowns and Chinese communities in North America have led him to active roles in community service, historic preservation, and urban design.

DAVID LOWENTHAL, formerly secretary of the American Geographical Society, is emeritus professor of geography at University College, London, and visiting professor of heritage studies at St. Mary's University College, Strawberry Hill, Twickenham, England. He taught landscape architecture at Harvard University (1966–68), chaired the Landscape Research Group in Britain (1984–89), and coedited *Landscape Meanings and Values* (1981). Among his books are *George Perkins Marsh* (1958; rev. ed. 1997), *West Indian Societies* (1972), *The Past Is a Foreign Country* (1985), and *Possessed by the Past: The Heritage Crusade and the Spoils of History* (1996).

REUBEN M. RAINEY is professor of landscape architecture at the University of Virginia, where he teaches the history and theory of landscape architecture. Prior to his professional education as a landscape architect, he taught comparative religion and psychology of religion at Columbia University and Middlebury College. His publications include studies of nineteenth-century American parks and monuments, as well as critical investigations of the work of major American landscape architects of the twentieth century.

ROBERT B. RILEY is professor of landscape architecture and architecture at the University of Illinois, Urbana-Champaign. From 1970 to 1985 he was head of the university's Department of Landscape Architecture. His major professional interests are the development and perception of the human landscape, cultural aspects of design, and theory in landscape design. His articles have appeared in *Landscape, Landscape Journal,* and *Places.* He is a past president of the Council of Educators in Landscape Architecture of the Environmental Design Research Association and is active in the American Institute of Architects. He has practiced architecture in New Mexico and Maryland. From 1966 to 1970 he was associate editor of *Landscape* magazine, and from 1988 to 1995 editor of *Landscape Journal.*

RINA SWENTZELL is a native of Santa Clara Pueblo in New Mexico. She holds a master's degree in architectural design and a Ph.D. in American studies from the University of New Mexico. She has taught at her alma mater, the College of Santa Fe, and the Institute of American Indian Arts. She works as a consultant to organizations, institutions, and private firms involved in Native American architectural and educational projects. Her scholarly work centers on the philosophical and cultural basis of the Pueblo world and its educational, artistic, and architectural expressions. She lives in Santa Clara Pueblo and Santa Fe. She is the author of *Children of Clay* (1991) and coauthor of *To Touch the Past* (1996).

DELL UPTON is associate professor of architectural history at the University of California, Berkeley, where he has taught since 1983. His research and writing have established him as a leader in the fields of vernacular architecture, material culture, and American studies. He is also a founder of the Vernacular Architecture Forum and was for ten years the editor of its newsletter. He is the author of *Holy Things and Profane: Anglican Parish Churches in Colonial Virginia* (1986) and *Madaline: Love and Survival in Antebellum New Orleans* (1996), and editor of *America's Architectural Roots: Ethnic Groups that Built America* (1986) and (with John Michael Vlach) *Common Places: Readings in American Vernacular Architecture* (1985).

RICHARD WALKER is professor of geography at the University of California, Berkeley, where he has taught since 1975. He has written on suburban development, urban history, environmental policy, agribusiness, philosophy, industrial location, and California. He is coauthor, with Michael Storper, of *The Capitalist Imperative: Territory, Technology and Industrial Growth* (1989) and, with Andrew Sayer, of *The New Social Economy: Reworking the Division of Labor* (1992). He is a long-time activist in public affairs with such groups as the Coalition to Stop the Peripheral Canal and the Faculty for Human Rights in El Salvador and Central America.

WILBUR ZELINSKY is a geographer and professor emeritus at Pennsylvania State University, where he began teaching in 1963. His first article was a historical geography of the Negro population of Latin America, published in 1949 in the *Journal of Negro History*. His research interests have continued to include the full diversity of social and historical geography of North America, geography and social policy, demography, and cultural geography. His books include *The Cultural Geography of the United States* (1973; rpt. 1992) and *Nation into State: The Shifting Symbolic Foundations of American Nationalism* (1988). He is coauthor of *A Basic Geographical Library* (1966; rpt. 1985), *This Remarkable Continent: An Atlas of North American Society and Cultures* (1982), and *The Atlas of Pennsylvania* (1989). He has received a Guggenheim Fellowship and major research grants from the National Science Foundation and the U.S. Department of Health, Education, and Welfare Center for Population Research.

Index